D0930499

Northwestern University Publications
in Analytical Philosophy

Reflections

ON

Frege's

Philosophy

Reinhardt Grossmann

Northwestern University Press

EVANSTON · 1969

*Reinhardt Grossmann is Professor of Philosophy
at Indiana University.*

Contents

Editorial Foreword	vii
Preface	ix
Note	xv

CHAPTER I · *Begriffsschrift*: Three Confusions	3
Act and Content	5
Subject and Predicate	13
Identity and Description	19
Function and Argument	23

CHAPTER II · *Grundlagen*: Two Distinctions	28
Ideas	29
Concepts	50
Objects	83
Reduction	108

CHAPTER III · *Sinn und Bedeutung*: A Solution	153
Identity	154
Truth	181

Contents

CHAPTER IV · Later Papers: Second Thoughts   224

About Sense and Reference   226

About Definitions   248

Index   255

Editorial Foreword

THE PUBLICATION of Professor Grossmann's study of Frege, together with the recent appearance of E. D. Klemke's study, *The Epistemology of G. E. Moore*, mark the inception of a publishing project which is meant to redress a possible imbalance in contemporary analytical philosophy. There are already, of course, a number of series in which current work in analytic philosophy is ably represented; but such series are not infrequently characterized by a certain narrowness of scope which obscures our vision of the continuity of philosophical problems. These series tend to ignore or underplay the genuine relevance of analytically oriented historical studies to contemporary problems. What has happened is that such publishing programs implement only one philosophical program or publish work guided by only one method of analytical philosophy. One result of this is that pernicious division common today between mere history on the one hand and philosophy proper on the other, where "philosophy proper" is usually identified with the current fashion in philosophical analysis. While nobody — save, perhaps, Croce — would equate historical claims with philosophical claims, the concentration on one current method or body of doctrine gives rise to something which is far more dangerous to the health of philosophy because it works in a subtler way. Philosophy then tends to be conceived as the enterprise which is coterminous with what our contempo-

vii

raries are saying about the problems, while claims about what philosophers in the past have said are relegated to the limbo of philology or, worse yet, to that bastard child of philosophy and philology, the history of ideas. The Northwestern University Publications in Analytical Philosophy program is meant to show that what separates contemporary from traditional philosophy is not the problems but at most the methods for solving them; hence studies of philosophical problems that are historical in character will appear in this program because they are relevant to the problems that philosophers are working on today.

But this is not only an attempt to take history seriously. An attempt will be made, within the context of the program, to broaden the scope of what is called analytical philosophy. There is a place not only for historical manuscripts but also for an assessment of the basic presuppositions of various programs of philosophical analysis. There are, to be sure, many detailed assessments of particular positions in philosophy. But these are mainly assessments of moves in a game whose presiding rules are not questioned. There has been a tendency in contemporary analytical philosophy to assume that most kinds of avowedly ontological analysis are simply not viable; hence what was a kind of ontological analysis in the work of earlier analysts has been replaced by analysis of language, and whatever could not be accommodated to these new theories was jettisoned. Yet it is not at all obvious that the one method of analytical philosophy is necessarily more viable or fruitful than the other which it was intended to replace. The absence of comparative discussions of these methods constitutes a gap in analytic philosophy publication today. Our program will undertake to fill that gap.

MOLTKE S. GRAM

Preface

I CHOSE THE TITLE "Reflections on Frege's Philosophy" rather than, say, "An Outline of Frege's Philosophy" because I wanted to indicate that this book is not a systematic treatise on all or even most of Frege's views. I did not set out to write an exposition of Frege's philosophy, nor did I intend to provide a detailed commentary on his most important works.[1] My goal was rather modest in regard to Frege. I hoped to be able to discuss a few selected ontological problems within a very narrow setting. Frege's philosophy, as I found out, most conveniently provides such a setting. Not only does it center around the very questions which I wanted to take up, but it also deals with them in a manner which I find most congenial. Even though the ontological problems were foremost in my mind, however, I would be very pleased if my efforts contribute to a better understanding of Frege's philosophy as a whole.

In philosophy, it is the fashion today to practice some kind of method. For a number of reasons, contemporary philosophers have invented and

---

1. There are now several books on Frege: R. V. Birjukov, *Two Soviet Studies on Frege*, trans. and ed. Ignacio Angelelli (Dordrecht, 1964); Jeremy D. B. Walker, *A Study of Frege* (Oxford, 1965); Christian Thiel, *Sinn und Bedeutung in der Logik Gottlob Freges* (Meisenheim, 1965); and R. Sternfeld, *Frege's Logical Theory* (Carbondale, 1966). When I prepared the manuscript of this book for publication, I was only acquainted with Walker's exposition of Frege's philosophy.

pursued a whole range of new ways of philosophizing. The members of a school are no longer united by a common doctrine but by a common method. Phenomenologists practice the phenomenological method, while so-called ordinary-language philosophers are supposed to take their methodological cues from what we ordinarily say. There are now very few philosophers who acknowledge openly that they are metaphysicians. In some circles metaphysics is rejected as unscientific, and is thought of as sort of poetry. Others consider as a matter of established fact that there is no such thing as a metaphysical problem.

Every new method, of course, promises to solve or dissolve the accumulated stock of metaphysical problems. That, no doubt, explains the great attraction of method philosophizing. Moreover, it is much easier to learn the method — and the jargon that usually goes with it — than to study the issues in their complicated historical contexts. By the time that a philosopher has finally become convinced that his method is not half so effective as he had been led to believe by his teacher and that it may be necessary for him to read at least some of the maligned metaphysicians, another method has, unfortunately, appeared on the scene. The members of the new school make fun of the older method, but they maintain, just as confidently as their precursors, that their method will at long last provide all the answers. In our century, phenomenology was supplanted by the study of the logical syntax of the language of science. Then there emerged a whole spectrum of methods, the so-called ordinary-language school, going all the way from a more or less explicit belief that a philosopher is a kind of psychoanalyst to a conception of philosophy as the prolegomenon to any future science of linguistics. More recently we have been told that the knowledge of transformational grammar is the key to success in philosophy. Judging from the past, we can expect a varied array of methods in the future.

Frege, by contrast, did not espouse any particular philosophical methods. He was an undisguised metaphysician. That is why I find his style of philosophizing so congenial. He discussed the existence and nature of objects and concepts, numbers and functions, ideas and what he called thoughts. As a result, he fashioned an ontology more complete and accurate than any that had ever been proposed before. In the process, it is true, he probed into the meaning of such phrases as "All mammals have red blood" and "Whoever discovered the elliptic form of the planetary orbits died in misery." He even invented a whole new symbolism, but he also firmly believed that ordinary discourse may occasionally mislead an ontologist.

And he discussed the nature of numbers, for example, without using a single symbol, much less a whole calculus. Nor did he ever agonize over the question of what philosophy is; instead, he pondered the traditional problems: What are the ontological categories of the world? How do these categories hang together? To what category do certain kinds of entities such as numbers belong? These and similar issues form the very center of Frege's investigations. Most of his answers are by now familiar: Every entity is either an object or a function, and every entity is either objective or subjective; numbers are a subcategory of objects — they are extensions of concepts — and they are objective rather than subjective entities; and so on.

But it is not only Frege's conception of philosophy with which I find myself in agreement; I also accept some of his most important views. Consider the realism-idealism controversy. Until rather recently, various versions of phenomenalism dominated the scene. Chairs and tables were somehow constructed out of sense-impressions. Then, most likely as a reaction to all that attention being given to sense-impressions, mental entities began to be treated with suspicion and hostility. Some ordinary-language philosophers now go so far as to ask for a proof that there are such things as sense-impressions and mental acts. Others identify mental entities with dispositions to behave. And there are even a growing number of materialists who identify mental entities with processes in the brain. Frege, by contrast, does not believe that the moon, for example, is in any sense of the term a "construct" out of sense-impressions, nor does he go to the other extreme and hold that sense-impressions and mental acts are the invention of zealous metaphysicians. Since I agree with him in both respects, I have been able to take much for granted in discussing some of his views about the privacy of mental entities.

Or take the realism-nominalism issue. Nominalism, in one form or another, has been the favorite alternative for almost a thousand years. Nowadays some philosophers decide the issue simply by refusing to quantify property variables. Others decree that the so-called ideal language may mention a part-whole relation but may not have either exemplification or class-membership. In either case, the success of the method is measured in terms of how much of what we ordinarily wish to say can be shown to be isomorphic to the ideal language. Never mind that the two languages do not even deal with the same facts. If one group of entities proves to be isomorphic to another, then some modern reductionists seem to conclude that the one group is the other. Why else, if this is not the way they reason, should they think that their calculi have anything to do with the traditional realism-nominalism issue? Frege, of course, is not a nominalist. He insists that there are concepts (properties) as well as objects. He even believes that there are extensions (classes). Since I agree with Frege's ontological position, I can concentrate on the alleged predicative nature of concepts and saturatedness of objects.

Or consider the contemporary consensus on the nature of logic. It is generally agreed, I submit, that such logical words as 'all,' 'and,' 'some,' and 'or' are syncategorematic — that is, they do not represent anything. According to this prevailing view, logic is in some sense a matter of convention, it depends, somehow, on the way in which we use language. Needless to say, Frege attacked any form of conventionalism in logic. He points out that logical laws are as objective as the laws of science. According to him, logical words are not just empty signs; they represent definite concepts and relations. Since I agree with him on this point as well, I have taken some highly controversial matters for granted and concentrated instead on a few selected problems of the philosophy of logic.

Frege's views on such matters as the realism-idealism issue, the realism-nominalism controversy, and the realism-conventionalism problem as it arises with regard to arithmetic and logic provide the background for my investigations.

But I realize, too, that neither Frege's approach nor his particular solutions are very popular today. At the same time he is widely read and highly praised. I am inclined to think that many of my contemporaries pick whatever they like out of Frege's writings and neglect the rest. Some admire his achievements in pure logic, but they disregard the ontology on which that logic is built. Others are fascinated by his ingenious attempt at reducing arithmetic to logic, but do not pay attention to his views on the ontological status of numbers. Still others praise his distinction between sense and reference, but do not acknowledge the ontological root of that distinction. This list could easily be continued. I hope that the present book may help to dispel some of these misinterpretations or misrepresentations of Frege's intentions.

It was clear to me from the beginning that Frege's views would have to be discussed with an eye on their gradual development. There are several definite stages in Frege's advancement, I believe, and his later views grow out of earlier ones. This conviction explains the structure of the present book. The first chapter is about the *Begriffsschrift.* I try to uncover the origins of the main themes of Frege's philosophy. These themes have their roots, I think, in three basic confusions: subjective and objective entities are not sharply distinguished; objects are not clearly separated from concepts; and identity is conceived of at times as a relation between signs, and at other times as a relation between entities. In the second chapter, the emphasis is on two cornerstones of Frege's mature philosophy, namely, his distinction between objective and subjective entities, and his notion of the difference between objects and concepts. But his attempt to reduce arithmetic to logic raises the unsolved problem of identity. These topics are discussed against the background of the *Grundlagen*. Frege's philosophical development reaches a second peak with the three classical papers published in 1891 and 1892. These articles, especially "Über Sinn und Bedeutung," explain Frege's views on identity and truth. Both of these views rest on his distinction between sense and reference. The third chapter is about that distinction and its consequences. Frege's later published and unpublished manuscripts contain modifications, qualifications, and second thoughts about his earlier solutions. In Chapter Four I deal with some of these later ideas but this is rather an epilogue; the real drama occurs in the second and third chapters.

I would like to thank Professor Hermes and Dr. Schwering for their assistance during my visit at Münster in 1965. I would also like to express my gratitude to the National Science Foundation for a grant which allowed me to study Frege's work during the summers of 1965 and 1966.

Bloomington 1967 R. G.

Note

The following abbreviations have been used in the footnotes:

WORKS OF GOTTLOB FREGE

B   *Begriffsschrift, eine der arithmetischen nachgebildete Formelsprache des reinen Denkens* (Halle, 1879).

BG   "Über Begriff und Gegenstand," *Vierteljahrsschrift für wissenschaftliche Philosophie*, XVI (1892), 192–205, translated as "On Concept and Object" in *T*, pp. 42–55.

F   *The Foundations of Arithmetic*, German text and English translation of *GL* by J. L. Austin, 2d rev. ed. (Evanston, Ill., 1968).

FB   *Function und Begriff* (Jena, 1891), translated as "Function and Concept" in *T*, pp. 21–41.

FN   Frege Nachlass (manuscripts at the University of Münster).

G   "Der Gedanke, eine logische Untersuchung," *Beiträge zur Philosophie des deutschen Idealismus*, I (1918), 58–77, translated by A. M. and Marcelle Quinton as "The Thought," *Mind*, LXV (1956), 289–311.

GG   *Grundgesetze der Arithmetik, begriffsschriftlich abgeleitet*, 2 vols. (Jena, 1893, 1903). Part of this book has been translated and edited by M. Furth, *The Basic Laws of Arithmetic* (Berkeley and Los Angeles, 1964).

GL   *Die Grundlagen der Arithmetik, eine logisch mathematische Untersuchung über den Begriff der Zahl* (Breslau, 1884).

SB   "Über Sinn und Bedeutung," *Zeitschrift für Philosophie und philosophische Kritik*, C (1892), 25–50, translated as "On Sense and Reference" in *T*, pp. 56–78.

T   *Translations from the Philosophical Writings of Gottlob Frege*, edited by Peter Geach and Max Black (Oxford, 1952), containing translations of *BG*, *FB*, and *SB*, parts of *B* and *GL*, and other writings of Frege.

OTHER WORKS

EO   E. B. Allaire, *et al.*, *Essays in Ontology* (The Hague, 1963).

LR   Gustav Bergmann, *Logic and Reality* (Madison, 1964).

ME   ——, *Meaning and Existence* (Madison, 1960).

PM   Alfred North Whitehead and Bertrand Russell, *Principia Mathematica*, 3 vols. (Cambridge, 1910, 1912, 1913).

SM   Reinhardt Grossmann, *The Structure of Mind* (Madison and Milwaukee, 1965).

Reflections
on Frege's Philosophy

Begriffsschrift:
Three Confusions

T HE FIRST COMPREHENSIVE SYSTEM of logic is contained in Frege's *Begriffsschrift*. It is undoubtedly one of the most important books on the subject,[1] but it also contains a number of philosophical mistakes; or perhaps I should rather say that it contains a number of confusions, for we find several incompatible views side by side. However, I am not suggesting that we compare Frege's logic with his philosophy. I do not think that the two can be separated. Rather, I wish to call attention to a curious gap between Frege's new logic and the traditional way in which he looks at it. It is as if he had discovered some important truths without fully realizing any of their consequences. As a result, we find new ideas and old notions side by side. The tension between the old way and the new way is eventually resolved in Frege's later works, but in the *Begriffsschrift* it appears in the form of four unsolved problems.

There is, first of all, the problem of the nature of logic. Most of the time, Frege talks like an idealist of the Kantian variety, but there are passages in which he clearly departs from the Kantian custom of talking about logic in psychological terms. Second, there is the problem of the analysis of the

---

1. For Frege's place in the history of logic, see the excellent account by William and Martha Kneale, *The Development of Logic* (Oxford, 1962).

basic kinds of propositions. Frege's new system demands an analysis quite different from the Aristotelian one, yet the *Begriffsschrift* has many of the traditional features. In particular, there is no clear distinction between individual things on the one hand and properties and relations on the other. Third, although Frege talks briefly about identity, he does not recognize the problem which this notion raises — namely, how identity statements can be informative. He holds that identity is a relation between expressions, but believes at the same time that certain identity statements acquire their importance because one and the same entity can be presented in different ways. Finally, there is the fourth problem, that of truth: What makes a proposition true? Frege seems to say that truth resides in an act of affirmation; however, he also seems to say, in other places, that truth is a property of propositions. We shall see that he never gave a satisfactory answer to this question.

Frege's philosophical development may, I think, be viewed as a series of attempts to solve these four problems. In the *Grundlagen*, he proposes solutions for the first two. He distinguishes sharply between mental and nonmental entities, and he breaks with the Aristotelian ontology by distinguishing between objects and concepts. But the problems of identity and truth remain unsolved. The problem of identity now becomes the central problem of Frege's philosophy, for Frege's very idea of a reduction of arithmetic to logic rests, as it were, on the notion of informative identity statements. In the famous paper "Über Sinn und Bedeutung" Frege later proposes a radical solution to the problem of identity. This solution is generalized by Frege so as to yield, in addition, a solution to the problem of truth. At the time of the *Grundgesetze*, Frege's philosophical system is essentially complete. In later years, however, Frege changes some of his views and modifies others. These second thoughts about the four problems are expressed in several unpublished manuscripts and in his last three published papers.[2]

The four problems — their form in the *Begriffsschrift* and their eventual solutions at successive stages of Frege's philosophical development — will provide us with guideposts through Frege's complicated system.

2. *G*; "Die Verneinung, Eine logische Untersuchung," *Beiträge zur Philosophie des deutschen Idealismus*, I (1919), 143–57, trans. as "Negation" in *T*, pp. 117–36; and "Logische Untersuchungen, Dritter Teil: Gedankengefüge," *Beiträge zur Philosophie des deutschen Idealismus*, III (1923), 36–51, trans. R. H. Stoothoff, *Mind*, LXXII (1963), 1–17.

ACT AND CONTENT

IN THE SECOND PARAGRAPH of the *Begriffsschrift*, Frege distinguishes between three entities which he represents by '*A*,' '——*A*,' '⊢*A*.' What is the philosophical point of this distinction? It seems to me that we reflect Frege's intentions most accurately if we assume that: (a) '*A*' represents a complex idea (*Vorstellungsverbindung*); (b) '——*A*' represents the mental act of having the idea *A*, of considering or thinking the idea *A*; and (c) '⊢*A*' represents the mental act of judging that *A* is true, of affirming *A*.[3]

According to this interpretation, one important point of the second paragraph consists in the separation of mental acts from their objects. Frege distinguishes between *mental acts* such as considering and judging on the one hand, and the *contents* of considerations or judgments on the other. One and the same content can occur as the content of different kinds of acts. For example, one may either merely consider the content *A* or judge it to be true (that is, affirm it).

Since Frege speaks of contents rather than objects, I must point out in passing that the traditional terminology is somewhat confused. What some philosophers call contents of mental acts are what others call objects of such acts. In order to avoid misunderstandings, I used the term 'intention' (of a mental act) in a recently published book.[4] The confusion is compounded by the further fact that some philosophers distinguish between the content and the object of a mental act.[5] A content, in their sense of the word, is not intended by a mental act, but is a part (property) of the act that intends an object. It is quite clear from the context, I think, that Frege uses 'content' as others use 'object' and I used 'intention.' He does not think of contents as parts of mental acts. This is why I paraphrased Frege by saying that he distinguishes between acts and objects.

According to this interpretation, Frege distinguishes further between at least two kinds of mental acts, namely, acts of thinking (assuming, presenting) on the one hand and acts of affirming (judging) on the other. Here, too, there is a terminological difficulty. The case is clear for judg-

---

3. Whenever I think that it may be important, I shall add the German term or phrase in parentheses or the German text in a footnote.

4. *SM*.

5. Compare, for example, K. Twardowski, *Zur Lehre vom Inhalt und Gegenstand der Vorstellungen* (Vienna, 1894); A. Meinong, *Über Annahmen*, 2d ed. (Leipzig, 1910); E. Husserl, *Logische Untersuchungen*, 2d ed. (Halle, 1913).

ments; the German *Urteil* translates straightforwardly into 'judgment.' But there is no similar unproblematic translation of the German verb *vorstellen*. I shall translate the noun *Vorstellung* as 'idea'; we have then a word for the *object* of a certain kind of mental act. But I can only talk appropriately about the corresponding act by using different expressions in different contexts; for example, I shall sometimes speak of having an idea, at other times of thinking a thought, and, at still different times, of being presented with an idea.

Finally, if this interpretation is correct, Frege holds in the *Begriffsschrift* that the objects of thoughts and judgments are complex ideas.

As I said before, this reading of the second paragraph appears to reflect Frege's thought most accurately. It seems to me that he wanted to separate contents from acts and thoughts from judgments, and that he conceived of contents as complex ideas. However, a number of remarks in the second paragraph and elsewhere do not agree with my interpretation. The most important of these disagreements concerns the meaning of '——*A*.' Frege says, for instance: "If we *omit* the little vertical stroke at the left end of the horizontal stroke, then the judgment is to be transformed into *a mere complex of ideas*."[6] This may be taken to mean that '——*A*' and not, as I claimed, '*A*' represents a complex idea. I think, though, that Frege did not express his true meaning by his choice of words, for the main point of the paragraph is the distinction between thought and judgment, between mere assumption and affirmation. Nor does this pronouncement by Frege agree with his explicit statement that '⊢' is put in front of the sign for a content or idea.[7]

I shall therefore maintain my original interpretation. But it should also be emphasized that one may attach a certain significance to the fact that Frege so easily and repeatedly confused *A* and ——*A* in his own mind, although he had just made a distinction between them. For certain purposes, it may be necessary to distinguish between mental acts and their objects and hence between an idea and the having of an idea. But the main topic of the *Begriffsschrift* does not depend on this distinction. After Frege has pointed out, once and for all, that the mere having of an idea must be distinguished from a judgment or affirmation, he could have used '*A*' to

6. "Wenn man den kleinen senkrechten Strich am linken Ende des wagerechten fortlässt, so soll dies das Urteil in eine blosse *Vorstellungsverbindung* verwandeln."

7. "Not every content can be turned into a judgment by prefixing ⊢ to a symbol for the content."

stand indifferently for both the idea and the having of the idea. For logical purposes the objects or contents of mental acts matter, but not the acts themselves. Indeed, in Frege's later philosophy the so-called content stroke plays a completely different role than in the *Begriffsschrift*. It no longer represents a mental act but, rather, a certain truth-function.[8] That the same does not hold for the so-called judgment stroke is due to a peculiarity of Frege's philosophy which I shall point out presently.

□

To repeat, then, '*A*' and '——*A*' represent an idea and the having of an idea, respectively. In order to discover some of the consequences of this interpretation, let us compare it with a completely different one which was recently proposed by Gustav Bergmann.[9] Bergmann relies heavily on the passage cited earlier in which Frege seems to be saying that '——*A*' represents a complex idea rather than the having of such an idea. In order to explain his analysis in greater detail, I must introduce a few of Bergmann's own distinctions.

First, following philosophers like Meinong and Husserl, Bergmann distinguishes between mental acts and their objects or intentions. Considering a mental act of, say, thinking that the earth is round, he separates the mental act of thinking from its intention, which in this case consists of the state of affairs represented by the sentence 'The earth is round.' Second, according to Bergmann and again following Meinong and Husserl, every mental act has a certain content. This so-called content is a property of the mental act; it is that characteristic feature of a given mental act which determines its direction toward a particular object or intention. Now, according to Bergmann, Frege's '*A*' represents the intention of a mental act, '——*A*' represents the content of a mental act, and '⊢*A*' represents the mental act as a whole. This interpretation of the second paragraph differs from mine in the following important respects:

(1) While Bergmann thinks that Frege does not commit himself as to whether *A* is complex or simple, it follows from my account that Frege conceives of *A* as a complex idea whenever *A* is judgmental in character.

(2) Bergmann believes that '——*A*' represents a complex idea. His belief, as I noted, rests on the passage quoted above. He makes three further

8. Compare *FB*; *I*, pp. 21–41.
9. "Ontological Alternatives," in *LR*.

claims: (a) ——*A*, he thinks, is a mental entity. I agree, for '——*A*' represents, on my interpretation, a mental act and, hence, a mental entity. (b) He concludes also that Frege has not yet hypostasized thoughts (propositions) into objective entities which appear as intentions of mental acts. On my interpretation, however, it is not ——*A* that is turned into an objective entity in Frege's later philosophy, but rather *A*. (It is true, though, that the content stroke acquires an objective function later, representing a truth-function. But this is obviously not the change that Bergmann has in mind.) It is, in our terminology, the content and not the thinking of the content which is later split up into thought and truth-value.[10] (c) Bergmann also concludes that Frege thought of contents as being complex.[11] No similar conclusion follows from my interpretation. What follows is merely that Frege thought of certain intentions, namely, the intentions of judgments, as being complex.

(3) Bergmann holds that ——*A* is a content, that is, a property which can be common to both judgment and mere assumption or thought. If I am correct, it is *A* and not ——*A* which is common to different kinds of mental acts. But *A* is not a property of a judgment or assumption, as a content would be; it is an intention. Two mental acts may thus have the same intention, that is, concern the same complex idea.

(4) There is a place where Frege says that the content stroke serves to combine the signs following it into a whole. Bergmann thinks that the only way of making sense out of this remark is to read it as an assertion of the "unity of thought" in the idealistic tradition.[12] I do not think that anything in the *Begriffsschrift* even hints at such an assertion. But I shall return to this passage presently.

(5) Bergmann contends that Frege does not tell us what else ⊢*A* contains in addition to ——*A*. At this point, according to Bergmann, Frege leaves "a blank that eventually becomes a blur." I agree that ——*A* is not the whole of ⊢*A*; first comes the presentation (*Vorstellung*) of *A*; then, built upon this presentation, occurs affirmation or judgment. Every mental act, as Brentano used to put it, is founded upon presentation. But the blank does not occur at this place in Frege's philosophy; it exists elsewhere.

10. Compare *GG*, I, x.

11. I use 'content' here not as Frege uses it, but as Bergmann does — that is, for a certain property of the mental act, not for its intention or object.

12. Bergmann claims to follow here Egidi's interpretation. See R. Egidi, "La Consistenza filosofica della Logica di Frege," *Giornale critico della filosofia italiana*, XVI (1962), 194–208; and "Matematica, logica e filosofia nell' opera di Gottlob Frege," *Physis*, IV (1962), 5–32.

(6) Finally, Bergmann asserts that A and $——A$ are two different entities and that there is no indication that A is somehow a part of $——A$. Hence he concludes that Frege espouses a realistic view (as opposed to an idealistic one), or one that is at least compatible with realism. A and $——A$ are indeed two different entities. If we further agree that A is the intention of a mental act, while $——A$ is the mental act which intends A, then the question of whether or not Frege is a realist turns on what kind of entity A is. If it is (always) in some sense mental, then Frege must be said to hold an idealistic position. Since A is not a part of $——A$, I agree with Bergmann that Frege's view is indeed compatible with realism. However, the *Begriffsschrift* contains several idealistic features. Most important, there is the fact that A, the intention of a thought or judgment, is called a complex idea; and, ideas are commonly held to be mental rather than nonmental entities. In fact, when Frege later distinguishes sharply between subjective and objective entities, he uses the term 'idea' (*Vorstellung*) for the subjective side.

■

This concludes the exposition of my interpretation. Let us turn to what I consider to be the most interesting aspect of the second paragraph. About the expression '$——A$' Frege says: "In this case we *qualify* the expression with the words '*the circumstance that*' or '*the proposition that*.'" [13] This sentence again raises the question: Does Frege really mean to talk about $——A$ or, rather, about A? Once more I shall assume the latter. On my interpretation, if anything can be called *the circumstance that* or *the proposition that*, it is A rather than $——A$. Taking this point for granted, we would expect Frege to say that A can be read *the idea that A* rather than *the circumstance that A*; for A is said to be a complex idea. We must insist on a distinction between an idea and a circumstance. An idea is a mental entity, while a circumstance need not be mental. Frege blurs this distinction by speaking of the idea A as well as of the circumstance A. He does not distinguish sharply between the objective and the subjective, and because of this blur it is impossible to classify him either as a realist or as an idealist. Someone who nevertheless puts Frege into either one of these two groups will have to stress either his talk about complex ideas or his talk about circumstances, one at the expense of the other.

13. "Wir umschreiben in diesem Falle durch die Worte 'der Umstand, dass' oder 'der Satz, dass.' "

9

The best interpretation, it seems to me, acknowledges the blur rather than tries to hide it.

The second paragraph, then, contains a confusion between mental and nonmental entities. This fact should not surprise anyone who has studied the idealistic influence on philosophy during the last five centuries. Frege merely repeats the Berkeleyan confusion between an idea and what the idea is of, between a *Vorstellung* as a mental entity and as the nonmental object of such an entity. At this point the whole Kantian terminology is suspect. A tree, for example, is called a *Vorstellung*. This could mean that the tree is thought of as the *object* of a certain kind of mental act. If so, no idealistic commitment need be involved in the use of this term. But *Vorstellung* is also used to refer to a mental act. As a result, one confuses act and object, a mental entity with what need not be mental at all — namely, the object. And this is not all. Sometimes *Vorstellung* is used to refer to some sort of mental picture or image; it then plays the same role as the word 'idea' in the empiricistic British tradition. One can then speak about, say, the association of ideas. Hence one may confuse once more a mental with a nonmental entity, a mental image or picture with the object of a mental act. Moreover, one further confuses images or mental pictures with mental acts, one kind of mental entity with an entirely different kind. Small wonder that the Kantians, as Frege so bitterly complains, confuse logic with psychology.[14] Nor is the idealistic muddle confined to the philosophies of Kant and his followers; one need only read certain passages in Berkeley to recognize the same confusion between mental act, object of act, and mental picture.

Idealism can only be averted if one distinguishes between these three different kinds of entities. Bolzano, the great critic of Kant, distinguished therefore between a *Vorstellung* as a mental entity, subject to the laws of psychology, and a so-called *Vorstellung an sich* as its objective counterpart.[15] Frege follows in Bolzano's footsteps in his later works, but he has a more elegant terminology and uses *Vorstellung* only for mental pictures.[16]

However, at the time of the *Begriffsschrift* Frege did not distinguish sharply between the mental and the nonmental, between the subjective and the objective. This is shown by the fact that he calls the intentions of

14. Compare Frege's criticism of B. Erdmann's *Logik* in *GG*, pp. xix–xxvi. See also Frege's remarks on Kant's use of *Vorstellung* in *GL*, p. 37n.

15. See B. Bolzano, *Wissenschaftslehre*, new ed. (Leipzig, 1929).

16. Compare *F*, pp. xxii, 37.

mental acts sometimes complex ideas and sometimes circumstances (or sentences). It is also shown in another way. Frege explains at first that '⊢ *A*' represents a judgment or affirmation of *A*. A little later, however, he says that '⊢ *A*' means that *A* is a fact.[17] If one distinguishes between the mental and the nonmental, these two explanations are incompatible. The judgment that '*A*' is true, or the affirmation of *A*, must be distinguished from the fact — if fact it be — that *A* is a fact, or that '*A*' is true. To say that *A* has been affirmed or has been judged to be true is obviously not to say that *A* is true. In the double role which Frege assigns to the judgment stroke, we find the same confusion between the mental and nonmental that we pointed out in connection with the intention *A*.

According to Frege, the content stroke has three further functions: (1) "As a constituent of the sign ⊢ *the horizontal stroke combines the symbols following it into a whole; assertion, which is expressed by the vertical stroke at the left end of the horizontal one, relates to the whole thus formed.*" (2) "The content stroke is also to serve the purpose of relating any sign whatsoever to the whole formed by the symbols following the stroke." (3) *What follows the content stroke must always be a possible content of judgment.*" [18]

What Frege has in mind seems to be the following: (1) The content stroke tells that the whole of what follows is (to be) affirmed. Affirmation, in other words, applies always to a judgmental content and never just to a part of such a content. (2) The content stroke takes over the function of parentheses in certain contexts. (3) One obtains a well-formed expression if an expression for a judgmental content is added to the content stroke, but not otherwise.

This last function of the content stroke raises an important problem: What is there in or about certain contents that differentiates them from others which are not judgmental in character? For example, what is there that makes the complex content expressed by 'This is a house' judgmental

---

17. Compare the end of paragraph 3 of the *Begriffsschrift*.

18. "Der Wagerechte Strich, aus dem das Zeichen ⊢ gebildet ist, *verbindet die darauf folgenden Zeichen zu einem Ganzen, und auf dieses Ganze bezieht sich die Bejahung, welche durch den senkrechten Strich am linken Ende des wagerechten ausgedrückt wird.*" "Der Inhaltsstrich diene auch sonst dazu, irgendwelche Zeichen zu dem Ganzen der darauf folgenden Zeichen in Beziehung zu setzen." "*Was auf den Inhaltsstrich folgt, muss immer einen beurtheilbaren Inhalt haben.*"

and that is absent from the complex content expressed by 'green house'?
That there is a sharp distinction between these two kinds of contents is
Frege's explicit view. He divides all contents into those that are *beurtheil-
bar* and those that are not, but he never discusses the difference between
them. As a matter of fact, he even blurs his theoretical distinction in practice by calling judgmental contents complex ideas. When one thinks of
them as circumstances, as Frege also does, then it appears evident that
there is a difference between judgmental and other contents; for the circumstance *that* this is a house clearly differs from the complex idea
expressed by 'green house.' In order to bring out the nature of this difference, one would have to discuss the structure of circumstances (or
states of affairs). That Frege does not see this problem is due, I believe, to
his thinking of judgmental contents more often than not as complex
ideas. If one conceives of them in this way, then they do not seem to differ
internally from other complex ideas.

When Frege thinks of judgmental contents sometimes as complex ideas
and at other times as circumstances, he blurs the distinction between complex concepts (properties) and states of affairs as well as the distinction
between mental and nonmental entities. The former confusion no less
than the latter is a trademark of the Kantian tradition. According to that
tradition, the content of a judgment is a complex idea. Judgment is characterized as a kind of presentation (*Vorstellung*).[19] Hence what is
presented in acts of presentation proper and in judgments is of the same
kind; it is always a presentation. The difference between complex concepts (properties) and states of affairs does not lie in the content but, according to the Kantian tradition, in the acts; in judgment one adds
affirmation (or denial) to the basic act of presentation.

But the very fact that there are these two blurs in Frege's *Begriffsschrift*
means that he was dimly aware of the shortcomings of the Kantian approach. That he calls judgmental contents circumstances after having
called them complex ideas just a paragraph earlier shows that he had
taken the first step on the road to realism. That he thought of judgmental
contents — and only such contents — as circumstances shows that he had
caught a first glimpse of the internal structure of states of affairs.

To sum up, I have offered an interpretation of certain passages of the

---

19. Compare, for example, the following explanation from Kant's *Logik*: "Ein Urtheil ist
die Vorstellung der Einheit des Bewusstseins verschiedener Vorstellungen oder die Vorstellung
des Verhältnisses derselben, sofern sie einen Begriff ausmachen."

second paragraph. I admitted that this interpretation does not agree with several sentences in which Frege seems to speak about —— A when he should be speaking, according to my interpretation, about A. To explain my view further, I contrasted it with a different interpretation which was recently proposed by Bergmann. Then I made two points; I asserted (a) that Frege, in the *Begriffsschrift*, did not sharply distinguish between mental and nonmental entities, and (b) that he did not sharply distinguish between complex concepts (properties) and states of affairs. Finally, I noted that while these two confusions have a distinctly Kantian flavor, they also show that Frege was ready to break out of the idealistic tradition.

SUBJECT AND PREDICATE

IN THE THIRD PARAGRAPH, Frege says that a distinction between subject and predicate has no place in his way of representing judgments. He holds that only so-called conceptual contents (*begriffliche Inhalte*) of judgments are of any significance for the purposes of his symbolic language. What is a conceptual content? And in what form does Frege reject the subject-predicate distinction?

Frege draws a distinction between the content and the conceptual content of a judgment. Two judgments with different contents may yet have the same conceptual content. In this connection, Frege also uses the term 'sense' (*Sinn*) for content. He mentions two sentences which, according to him, have slightly different senses but agree in their conceptual content. In order to exclude possible misunderstandings and to separate Frege's earlier from his later view, I shall only use 'content' and 'conceptual content' in my explanation of Frege's position as developed in the *Begriffsschrift*.

Frege's explication of the notion of a conceptual content is straightforward: two judgments have the same conceptual content if and only if all inferences that can be drawn from the first judgment when combined with certain other judgments can also be drawn from the second judgment when combined with the same further judgments. In other words, two judgments have the same conceptual content if and only if they are *logically equivalent*.

But Frege's explanation of the notion of conceptual content is somewhat at odds with the example which he gives as an illustration. He says

13

that the two sentences (a) "The Greeks defeated the Persians at Plataea" and (b) "The Persians were defeated by the Greeks at Plataea" differ in sense but have the same conceptual content. From this example, one might get the impression that Frege had a stronger condition than logical equivalence in mind when he introduced the notion of conceptual content. The only difference between the two sentences (a) and (b) is the change from the active to the passive form, and that kind of difference may well be considered as merely linguistic. To put it differently, one who holds that two logically equivalent sentences may yet represent different thoughts could still hold that the two sentences (a) and (b) express the same thought. He may therefore think that Frege did not just have logical equivalence in mind but also some stronger condition, say, intentional equivalence.[20] It must be emphasized that this is not the case.

It follows that a conceptual content is not the same as what Frege later calls the sense of a sentence, for, two logically equivalent sentences do not necessarily express the same sense, according to his later view.[21] That a conceptual content is not what he later calls the reference of a sentence is obvious. Thus neither the notion of a sense nor that of a reference coincides with his notion of a conceptual content. The development in his view is due to a shift in emphasis. For the purposes of a logical system such as the *Begriffsschrift*, it is indeed only necessary to distinguish between sentences which are not logically equivalent. Later in his philosophical development, however, problems of identity, definition, and intentionality attract his attention. In order to solve these problems, Frege introduces the notions of sense and reference.

Let us grant, then, that different sentences may have the same conceptual content, that is, that they may be logically equivalent. Let us grant further that for Frege's purposes one needs to distinguish only between sentences with different conceptual contents. How does all this show that the subject-predicate distinction is superfluous? How does Frege argue for this latter contention?

Consider his example. In sentence (a) the subject is 'the Greeks,' while in (b) it is 'the Persians,' yet these two sentences have the same concep-

20. Compare *SM*, pp. 123–38.
21. Compare, for instance, *FB*.

tual content. Frege points out that one and the same conceptual content can be expressed in two sentences in which the word order differs. Hence the word order, the *grammatical* distinction between subject and predicate, does not matter for his system of logic.

Now Frege is certainly right when he claims that the subject-predicate distinction *in this form* is purely a linguistic matter, a matter of communication, and that it can therefore be neglected for the purposes of logic. Whether we write '*a* is green' or 'green (*a*)' is unimportant. But for that very reason one would expect him to say that the two sentences (a) and (b) do not merely have the same conceptual content but have the same content as well. For if we take it that contents are not linguistic entities, and if we assume further that (a) and (b) differ only in the manner in which '*a* is green' differs from 'green (*a*),' then it seems to follow that (a) and (b) must represent the same content and not just the same conceptual content. This consideration shows how unclear Frege's notion of a content is. If one thinks of contents as nonlinguistic entities, one must conclude that the subject-predicate distinction, though it may be irrelevant for logical purposes, is not completely a matter of arbitrary linguistic conventions, because it affects the contents of judgments. Otherwise, one may conclude that Frege's example shows that contents must be linguistic entities.[22] Be that as it may, it seems to me that there is a deeper reason for his rejection of the subject-predicate distinction.

One could look at the two sentences (c) '*a* is green' and (d) 'green (*a*)' and consider that '*a*' is the subject of the first sentence but the predicate of the second, while 'green' is the predicate of the first but the subject of the second sentence. The distinction between subject and predicate would then ultimately rest on nothing more than the order in which certain signs are written down. On the other hand, one could insist that (c) mentions (at least) two kinds of entities or, rather, two entities of different kinds, namely, an individual thing and a property. Of course, 'green (*a*)' mentions the same two entities, only it mentions them in a different order. Further, one may stipulate that sentences are to be written in only

---

22. In an unpublished manuscript, Frege explains that two sentences which express the same thought (in his technical sense of 'thought') may yet differ in the psychological effects which they produce. Perhaps it is this kind of psychological response which he has in mind when he says that (a) and (b) have different contents. If so, then a content is neither a linguistic nor an objective (nonmental) entity. Rather, it consists of the sum total of psychological responses which an average listener or speaker may make. (The manuscript is "Fragmentarischer Entwurf zu einer Einleitung in die Logik," *FN*, no. 8.)

one way — for example, mentioning the individual thing first. After this proposal is adopted, one can then distinguish between an individual-place and a property-place in every (singular) sentence. In a sense, even this distinction is arbitrary; one could have proposed and adopted a different way of writing the sentence. Yet in another sense it is not arbitrary, for the individual-place can only be filled with the name of an individual thing, while the property-place can only be filled with the sign for a property; and whether an entity is an individual thing or a property is not, in any sense, an arbitrary linguistic matter. It depends not on our way of talking about it but on the entity itself.

Let us assume that Frege had adopted just one way of writing down (singular) sentences. Would he have distinguished between an individual-place and a property-place? Did he think of a conceptual content (or content) as being made up of entities of (at least) two kinds? I do not believe that he did. Frege rejects not only the grammatical or linguistic subject-predicate distinction but also the ontological distinction between two kinds of entities, whatever these two kinds may be called — particulars and universals, objects and concepts, or individual things and properties. A conceptual content consists, according to him, of only one kind of entity, namely, of concepts. Put differently, a conceptual content is merely a complex concept, that is, a complex idea. At this stage of his philosophical development, even *the number 20* is said to be a concept.[23] Of course, this analysis agrees with what I said earlier about Frege's confusion between complex ideas and circumstances. Most of the time he thinks of judgmental contents as complex ideas (or complex concepts); his talk about them as circumstances, we might say, has the character of a "realistic slip." [24]

But notice that Frege does not argue for his ontological position; he gives an explicit argument only for neglecting the grammatical subject-predicate distinction; nor does he argue that all ingredients of conceptual contents are concepts; I think he simply took that for granted. But even though one can separate the two distinctions, the grammatical and the on-

23. Compare *T*, p. 14.

24. Note also that the confusion between mental and nonmental entities may be said to appear in the use of the two terms 'idea' and 'concept' for the same entity. Ideas, of course, are mental; concepts, as conceived of by some philosophers, need not be. Later, Frege uses the two terms in just this fashion.

tological, they are closely connected — how closely, we shall see when we discuss Frege's later distinction between objects and concepts.

It is in the light of these considerations that Frege's remarks concerning the peculiar predicate 'is a fact' show their importance. The whole point of these remarks is that a conceptual content is nothing but a complex concept. Frege argues that Archimedes is not a different kind of entity from the conceptual content represented by 'Archimedes perished at the capture of Syracuse.' Archimedes is a concept and so is the content of this sentence. That this complex concept is not usually mentioned by a subject term is merely a peculiarity of our language. This peculiarity, moreover, is eliminated from Frege's symbolic language. According to Frege, the sign '⊢' is the common predicate of all the sentences of his clarified language.

Frege's implicit rejection of the ontological subject-predicate distinction has a further corollary. It tends to blur the distinction between such entities as individual things and properties on the one hand and states of affairs on the other. In Frege's case it amounts to a rejection of states of affairs in favor of complex properties. We can now understand why Frege is unable to explain the difference between judgmental and other contents in terms of their inner structure. No ontology that acknowledges just one category of entities can give such an explanation. As I remarked earlier, the difference between the two kinds of contents is therefore shifted from the contents themselves to mental acts. But states of affairs cannot forever be suppressed. In Frege's *Begriffsschrift*, they reappear in connection with the peculiar predicate 'is a fact' (or 'is true'). The distinction between concepts and states of affairs is somehow contained in the function of the judgment stroke. Granted that the content *A* is a concept, the sentence '*A* is a fact' could hardly also name a concept. Frege did not recognize this clearly in the *Begriffsschrift*. He did not see that even though a whole sentence may be viewed as the subject term of a sentence, predication reappears in the form of the judgment stroke. No doubt, the ambiguity of using the judgment stroke to represent both a judgment or affirmation on the one hand and the property *is a fact* on the other may have clouded the issue for Frege and dimmed his perception. But he later recognized clearly the peculiar function of the judgment stroke, as is shown by the following remark: "The assertion sign cannot be used to construct a function expression; for it does not serve, in conjunction with other signs, to designate an object. '⊢2+3=5' does not designate anything; it asserts something." [25]

'⊢2+3=5' is just an expression, and expressions do not assert or affirm anything. It is we who assert or affirm; and it is in judgments, through mental acts, that we affirm. Hence there seems to be only one plausible interpretation of Frege's statement; he must mean that the quoted expression represents a judgment. The quoted expression must represent the same as what the sentence '2+3=5 is affirmed (or judged to be true)' represents. Yet this cannot be the correct interpretation of Frege's remark, for he explicitly denies that the expression represents anything. Hence it could not possibly represent the circumstance that a certain arithmetical equation is affirmed. But if this is not what Frege means, what does he have in mind? I do not think that there is an obvious answer to the question. I am confident, however, that the following kind of consideration may be relevant. When Frege asserts that the expression '⊢2+3=5' does not represent anything, we might take this to mean that it does not refer to the "usual" kind of entity, namely, a truth-value. Nor does the expression refer to some other kind of entity which occurs in Frege's ontology. If Frege had pursued the matter positively rather than merely denying that the sentence refers to some kind of entity, he would have been forced to hold that it represents an entity entirely different from anything explicitly listed in his ontology, namely, a state of affairs. The mysterious function of the judgment stroke signifies the gap in Frege's system that needs to be filled with states of affairs. Frege himself calls attention to the gap, but he never explains how it should be filled with the proper ontological building stone.

We may also look at the matter from a different point of view. Traditionally, the distinction between states of affairs and all other kinds of entities is closely related to the distinction between expressions that are not names and expressions that are. Only entities which are not states of affairs can be named. States of affairs must not be represented by names but in some other way. Now recall also that, according to Frege's later philosophy, all expressions — even sentences — are names. Or rather, there is only one expression in his whole system which is not a name, and that is the peculiar sign '⊢.' Russell's and Wittgenstein's insistence that sen-

25. *T*, p. 34n.

tences are not names is, ultimately, a defense of states of affairs as an irreducible ontological kind. Frege acknowledges this kind only insofar as
he admits that '⊢' is not a name.

We have seen that Frege's notion of a conceptual content is unambigu-
ous. We noted further that his rejection of the grammatical subject-predicate distinction is based on the fact that for logical purposes one needs to
distinguish only between sentences with different conceptual contents. But
the grammatical distinction between subject and predicate must not be
confused with the ontological distinction between individual thing and
property, between object and concept. In the *Begriffsschrift* Frege does
not argue explicitly against this ontological distinction. He seems to take
for granted that a conceptual content consists of nothing but concepts.

IDENTITY AND DESCRIPTION

In the eighth paragraph, Frege introduces a sign for the equality of
content (*Inhaltsgleichheit*). He explains that equality of content — or, as I
shall say, identity of content — relates to names and not to contents:
"Names appear *in propria persona* so soon as they are joined together by
the symbol for equality of content; for this signifies the circumstance of
two names' having the same content."

In order to show the importance of the notion of identity, Frege gives
an example from geometry: One and the same point is labeled '*A*' and is
also described as the point *B* which corresponds to the straight line's being
perpendicular to the diameter. He says that one and the same point is
here determined in two different ways: (1) it is directly given in experience (*unmittelbar durch die Anschauung gegeben*), and (2) it is given as
the point determined by the description. "To each of these two ways of
determining it [*Bestimmungsweisen*], there answers a separate name. The
need of a symbol for identity of content thus rests on the following fact:
The same content can be fully determined in different ways."

Frege thus attributes the importance of identity to the fact that the same
content can be given in acquaintance and through description. Of course,
it may also be given through two different descriptions. Ultimately, it is
the existence of descriptions which makes the notion of identity interesting. But notice that Frege does not distinguish between mere labels and
descriptions; he calls both '*A*' and the description names. Thus while he

acknowledges a rather fundamental distinction between two ways in which a content can be determined — acquaintance and description — he does not acknowledge a corresponding distinction between the two kinds of expressions — labels and descriptions.

Frege further claims that identity statements are synthetic if they involve different ways in which the same conceptual content is determined. Thus all interesting identity statements are synthetic, and, hence, identity is not a superfluous notion.

This account of the nature and importance of identity raises a number of problems. Indeed, we shall see that the most pressing of these problems are not resolved to Frege's own satisfaction until he later writes about sense and reference.

Note that Frege speaks generally about identity of *content*, except when he introduces a sign for identity in the last sentence of the paragraph. We saw that the notion of a content is not the same as that of a conceptual content; sentences which express different contents may yet represent the same conceptual content. What, then, does Frege really have in mind? I think that he means to talk about conceptual contents rather than contents. But since the distinction between the two is rather vague, he often uses both terms as if they were interchangeable.

Note also that Frege's example of identity of conceptual content concerns a nonjudgmental content, while he generally talks about judgmental conceptual contents. It is customary to distinguish between identity and equivalence. Briefly, identity is said to hold between such entities as individual things, properties, relations, etc., while equivalence holds between states of affairs. Frege does not make this distinction. The omission is not surprising in the light of our previous discussion of the nature of conceptual contents. Recall that I claimed that judgmental as well as nonjudgmental contents are nothing but complex concepts (complex ideas). Since there is therefore no distinction between concepts and states of affairs, there is also no distinction between identity and equivalence. I shall adopt Frege's point of view for the time being and talk about identity of judgmental as well as nonjudgmental contents, but I shall distinguish in the usual manner between identity and equivalence whenever the point under discussion requires it.

◻

Keeping these considerations in mind, how does Frege's account of identity agree with his explanation of the notion of a conceptual content?

Two conceptual contents, we recall, are the same if and only if they are logically equivalent. Hence the concept A and the concept B are the same if and only if the statement '$A = B$' is a logical truth. However, according to Frege's analysis of identity, all interesting cases of identity are synthetic rather than analytic. This means that two sentences p and q may represent the same conceptual content even though the inferences that can be drawn from p when combined with certain other sentences cannot also be drawn from q when combined with the same further sentences. And this contradicts Frege's previous explication of a conceptual content.

But we cannot conclude from this that Frege must have meant to speak about contents rather than conceptual contents. Whatever the conditions for sameness of content may be, it is clear that they must be even stronger than those for identity of conceptual content, for sentences which represent the same conceptual content may express different contents, while sentences with the same content have automatically the same conceptual content. Hence the condition for identity of content must be even stronger than logical identity, and, therefore, could not possibly be synthetic identity.

As I remarked earlier, I think that Frege meant to talk about the identity of conceptual contents rather than the identity of contents, because only the former is important for his logical system. Therefore, there remains the blatant contradiction I have pointed out. How does it arise? What are its roots in Frege's system?

We may take our clue from an obvious point which we have so far neglected. A conceptual content consists of concepts. In fact, it is nothing but a complex concept. But when Frege explains the importance of identity, he does not talk about a concept at all; instead, he talks about an object or individual thing. Of course, Frege does not as yet distinguish between objects and concepts. This distinction appears only later in the *Grundlagen*. The point A can be nothing but a concept within the framework of the *Begriffsschrift*; but since it is in fact not a concept but an object, Frege is faced with the contradiction mentioned earlier.

Consider two sentences P and Q which agree in all respects except that P contains the description D, while Q contains the description E. Assume that D contains the concept word 'F,' while E contains the concept word 'G.' When Frege thinks about the conceptual content of the two sentences, he thinks, I believe, of the concepts mentioned in the two sentences. For example, the concept F would be part of the conceptual content of P, while the concept G would be part of Q. If so, then it is clear that P and Q would not have the same conceptual content. This way of looking at the conceptual content agrees with the condition in terms of logical identity (equivalence). For even if we assume that D and E describe in fact the same thing, the conceptual content of P would be different from the conceptual content of Q, because the first contains the concept F, while the second contains the concept G. And, of course, P is not logically equivalent to Q. On the other hand, if we have two sentences which are logically equivalent, then they cannot contain different descriptions (in terms of different concepts) of the same individual thing.

However, when Frege discusses the notion of identity, he does not think primarily of whole sentences or judgmental contents, but rather of names and descriptions or nonjudgmental contents. He realizes that the significance of the notion of identity derives from the occurrence of descriptions. Moreover, he thinks quite naturally that a description like 'the point B corresponding to the straight line's being perpendicular to the diameter' represents a certain point A. But in doing so, he overlooks his previous commitment to the view that the description represents a complex concept consisting, in part, of such concepts as that of a line and of a diameter. Since he thinks of 'A' and the description as two names of a point, he concludes that some identity statements are synthetic. Had he thought of the description not as a name of the point A but as a name of a certain complex concept, then he could not even have held, as he does, that the identity statement is true. For whatever 'A' may represent, it does not represent a complex concept consisting in part of the concepts of a line and of a diameter.

The source of the contradiction is now apparent. Frege holds, on the one hand, that all expressions represent concepts. If so, then it is natural to think that a description represents a complex concept, rather than the object uniquely specified by the description. On the other hand, when he talks about identity, he starts out with the common-sense knowledge that one and the same individual thing can be both labeled and described, or described in different ways. And this leads him to think of descriptions not as representing complex concepts but as names of objects.

If we take it that the "meaning" of a description is the entity described, then different descriptions have the same "meaning," as long as they describe the same thing. On the other hand, if we assume that the "meaning" of a description involves the properties (or concepts) mentioned by the description, then descriptions of the same thing may have different "meanings." It is tempting at this point to build a few verbal bridges. Instead of speaking of the "meaning" of a description in the second sense, we could talk about the manner in which an object is determined. The manner in which an object is determined then depends on the concepts mentioned by the description. Indeed, that manner may be identified with the complex concept that is the "meaning" of the description. Recall now that Frege speaks of different ways in which the same point is determined (*Bestimmungsweisen*). He does not see that these different ways are really nothing else but conceptual contents (of descriptions). Instead, he distinguishes, at least implicitly, between conceptual contents and the ways in which these are determined. The point A is a conceptual content, and that content is determined in two different ways.

To repeat, Frege does not see that certain conceptual contents (or complex concepts) are nothing but the different determinations he mentions elsewhere. And this, as we shall see, is a fundamental oversight which is never corrected and which ultimately leads to his ontology of senses. When he distinguishes later between objects and concepts, he still does not identify concepts and determinations. As a result, his ontology quite explicitly contains, for a while, concepts and objects, and also, though only in the shadow, so to speak, ways of determination. In the end, these ways of determination are recognized as independent entities and called senses. Hence Frege's ontology contains, in the end, not only objects and concepts but also a third and strange kind of entity, senses.

FUNCTION AND ARGUMENT

IN PARAGRAPH NINE Frege introduces the notion of a *function*. The expressions which make up a sentence (or any other complex sign) can be divided into function and argument. Two things should be emphasized. First, function and argument are called expressions, not what expressions represent.[26] Second, there is no corresponding distinction between the referents of parts of sentences.

Consider, for example, the sentence '$R(a, b)$.' Now imagine 'a' replaceable by another expression. The expression 'a' is then thought of as an

---

26. W. Pabst therefore accuses Frege of having confused expression with reference. See his "Gottlob Frege als Philosoph," Dissertation (Berlin, 1932), p. 17.

argument, while the rest of the sentence is thought of as a function. The sentence 'red(a)' thus yields the following three functions: (1) '$f(a)$,' that is, a's falling under something; (2) 'red(x),' that is, something's falling under red; and (3) '$f(x)$,' that is, something's falling under something. This shows clearly that the division of expressions into functions and arguments does not depend on an ontological distinction between two kinds of entities. An expression is not a function, because it represents a certain kind of entity. Nor could it depend on any ontological distinction between two kinds of referents; we already saw that a sentence represents, according to Frege, a complex concept — that is, an entity which consists of nothing but concepts. Frege himself makes it clear that the distinction between function and argument does not concern the conceptual content: "This distinction has nothing to do with the conceptual content; it concerns only our way of looking at it." [27]

Thus the argument no less than the function in 'green(a)' represents a concept. But if we follow Frege and assume that 'a' represents a concept, we cannot exclude the possibility that something may fall under a. In other words, Frege's account does not bring out the fact that while the concept *green* is predicative, the alleged concept a is not. For this reason, we should reformulate our descriptions of the three functions attainable from 'green(a).' To leave no doubt that Frege's analysis does not involve a distinction between, say, object and concept or between individual thing and property, we have to rephrase the functions so as to avoid the asymmetry connected with the expression 'falls under.' It would be more in the spirit of the *Begriffsschrift* if we would read '$f(a)$' as 'a's being *connected* with a concept'; 'red(x)' as 'red's being *connected* with a concept'; and '$f(x)$' *as* 'a concept's being *connected* with a concept.'

But even though Frege conceives of proper names and descriptions as well as predicates as names of concepts, he also claims that there is a difference between the description 'the number 20' and the expression 'every positive integer.' He says that they do not represent concepts of the same rank (*Begriffe gleichen Ranges*).[28] What does he have in mind?

27. It follows from his view in *B* that functions are not divisible into concepts and functions proper as in his later writings, for functions are linguistic entities while concepts are not. See, however, note 28 below.

28. Frege says that the *expressions* 'the number 20' and 'every positive integer' are not

He remarks that (a) what is asserted of the number 20 cannot be asserted in the same sense of the concept *every positive integer*; and (b) the expression 'every positive integer' by itself, unlike the expression 'the number 20,' gives no independent idea (*selbständige Vorstellung*).[29] It gets a sense (*Sinn*) only through the context of the sentence (*Zusammenhang des Satzes*).

One may be tempted to regard these rather cryptic remarks as an anticipation of one of his later views. Frege may have (1) intended to bring out the difference between concepts of first and second level; (2) had in mind some vague distinction between predicative and nonpredicative entities, that is, between concepts and objects; or, finally, (3) thought to separate dependent from independent entities.

What Frege says in (b) seems to speak for the third interpretation. Yet, his particular example is then inappropriate. Frege claims, in effect, that the concept *for all x, if x is a positive integer* is not independent; he does not give such an obvious example as the concept *(is) a positive integer*. His example of a dependent idea is not what he later calls an unsaturated concept. But even if we assume that he could or should have selected a better example, that is, something of the form '(is) a *F*,' his distinction between dependent and independent ideas remains obscure. Granted that the expression 'every positive integer' gets a sense only through the context of a sentence because it is a dependent expression, does not the same hold for the expression 'the number 20'? Both expressions represent concepts; there is no difference in this respect. Hence if an expression has a sense, if it represents a concept, then both expressions have a sense as they stand, by themselves. On the other hand, neither expression represents a judgmental content; neither expression is as yet a sentence. Thus if an expression is thought to have a sense if and only if it represents a judgmental content, then neither expression could possibly represent a sense. From this point of view, 'the number 20' would be as dependent an expression as 'every positive integer.' But if these two interpretations do not work, what plausible alternatives are left? It seems to me that Frege's occasional talk about dependent and independent entities, whether it occurs in the *Begriffsschrift* or in later works, remains obscure.

---

concepts of the same rank. I take him to mean that what they represent are not concepts of the same rank.

29. In *T*, Geach translates *selbständige Vorstellung* as '*complete* idea'; it should, I think, be '*independent* idea.'

However, we could assume that this distinction coincides with what he later describes as the distinction between saturated and unsaturated entities. Then we must consider the second interpretation, for the unsaturatedness of concepts consists in their predicative nature. From this point of view, Frege's talk about dependent, independent, unsaturated, and saturated entities rests ultimately on his distinction between predicative concepts and nonpredicative objects. The latter distinction is relatively clear; unfortunately, it does not appear in the *Begriffsschrift* at all. Whatever difference there may be between the two concepts *the number 20* and *every positive integer* can only be a difference between concepts, not between objects and concepts. Nor, for that matter, does Frege's example lend itself readily to the second interpretation. The concept *every positive integer*, if it looks like anything, looks more like a subject than a predicative entity. It is, at the very least, a poor example of a predicative entity.

This leaves us with the first interpretation, namely, that the passage anticipates his later distinction between first and second level concepts. This interpretation derives some plausibility from the particular example chosen, keeping in mind that *the number 20* is thought to be a concept at this point just like, say, *green*. It also agrees with Frege's remark that what is asserted of *the number 20* cannot be asserted in the same sense of the concept *every positive integer*. But it does not help to illuminate Frege's further remarks about independence and sense; concepts of first and second level seem to be equally dependent and are equally predicative.

For these various reasons, it seems to me that Frege probably did have the distinction between first and second level entities in mind, though rather vaguely. What he wishes to call to our attention, above all, is that any analysis is wrong which treats 'the number 20' and 'every positive integer' as equal subjects of the function 'can be represented as the sum of four squares.' In effect, he is preparing the ground for his analysis of universal sentences. He is saying that although it is correct to think of the sentence 'The number 20 can be represented as the sum of four squares' as being analyzable into the subject 'the number 20' and a function, it would be a mistake to think that a similar analysis is appropriate for the sentence 'Every positive integer can be represented as the sum of four squares.' The expression 'every positive integer,' even though it represents a concept, represents something that requires further analysis. Ordinary language at this point hides the real structure of certain judgmental contents. If this is a correct description of Frege's thoughts, his remarks aim primarily at the notion of generality. And insofar as his analysis of this notion involves the universal quantifier, we may see in his remarks in paragraph nine an anticipation of the distinction between first and second level concepts.

I have now discussed some philosophical views of the *Begriffsschrift*. In doing so, I stressed several points. For example, I emphasized that conceptual contents are sometimes identified with complex ideas and other times with objective circumstances. Moreover, Frege confuses the objective fact that a certain content is a fact with the subjective act of affirmation of the content. And he does not account for the internal difference between judgmental and nonjudgmental contents. The relation of identity is said to hold between signs rather than what they represent. And it remains obscure whether identity indirectly concerns concepts or the entities which fall under concepts. Whatever problems there are as a consequence of these and other confusions and inconsistencies, I believe, can be traced back to three basic shortcomings. First, Frege makes no sharp distinction between the mental and the nonmental, between the objective and the subjective realm. Second, he does not recognize the ontological difference between predicative and nonpredicative entities, between concepts and objects. Hence he cannot account for the difference between judgmental contents and mere complex concepts or ideas. Third, he does not realize that there is a problem in holding simultaneously that identity concerns signs and that identity statements are often informative — informative not about language but about the world. More generally, even though he does see that identity statements are not superfluous because of the existence of descriptions, he does not see a number of problems which arise in the wake of this insight.

These shortcomings of the *Begriffsschrift* are soon recognized by Frege. In the *Grundlagen*, he avoids the first two. In "Über Sinn und Bedeutung" he solves to his own satisfaction the problem of identity. Later publications can be viewed as attempts to fortify and defend his newly acquired positions. This, in short, is the way in which Frege's philosophy developed from the ideas of the *Begriffsschrift*. In the following chapters, I shall trace this development in greater detail.

I I

Grundlagen:
Two Distinctions

FREGE EXPLAINS, in the *Grundlagen*, two of the most important distinctions of his whole philosophy, namely, the distinction
between subjective and objective entities and the distinction between objects and concepts. In addition, there is also a rather vague doctrine to the
effect that words have meaning only in the contexts of sentences. In the
introduction to the *Grundlagen*, Frege makes these three points by an-
nouncing that he has followed three fundamental principles:

> always to separate sharply the psychological from the logical,
> the subjective from the objective;
> never to ask for the meaning of a word in isolation, but only
> in the context of a proposition;
> never to lose sight of the distinction between concept and object.[1]

In the following sections, we shall take a closer look at Frege's principles.

---

1. "Als Grundsätze habe ich in dieser Untersuchung folgende festgehalten
es ist das Psychologische von dem Logischen, das Subjective von
dem Objectiven scharf zu trennen;
nach der Bedeutung der Wörter muss im Satzzusammenhange, nicht
in ihrer Vereinzelung gefragt werden;
der Unterschied zwischen Begriff und Gegenstand ist im
Auge zu behalten" (*GL*, p. x; *F*, p. x).

IDEAS

FREGE SPEAKS of the contents of judgments or assumptions as complex ideas (*Vorstellungsverbindungen*) in the *Begriffsschrift*. I have argued that all conceptual contents consist, according to Frege, of concepts. But traditionally one distinguishes, first, between ideas (*Vorstellungen*) and judgments (*Urteile*) and, second, between two kinds of ideas, namely, intuitions (*Anschauungen*) and concepts (*Begriffe*). According to this Kantian schema, a complex idea could contain an intuition as well as a concept. Frege, though, thinks of contents as consisting of nothing but concepts, although we noted that there is at least one passage where he implicitly contrasts intuitions with concepts. There he holds that the same point can be given directly in intuition and also through a description. He seems to imply that the point as a content is an intuition. Be that as it may, how does Frege use the crucial term 'idea' in the *Grundlagen*?

Frege is fully aware of the dangerous idealistic implications of the philosophical use of the term 'idea' in the Kantian tradition. He remarks that Kant's view assumed a very subjective and idealistic complexion, because Kant associated both a subjective and an objective meaning with the term 'idea.' [2] Frege himself proposes to distinguish between subjective and objective ideas.[3] In order to mark this distinction, he uses the term 'idea' only with the subjective meaning. Such ideas, according to Frege, have three characteristics: First, they are the proper objects of the psychological laws of association. Second, they are of a sensible, pictorial nature. And, third, they are numerically different in different people. To put it differently, Frege holds that ideas are (a) mental, (b) either sense-impressions or images, and (c) numerically different from person to person. Notice that ideas resemble what other philosophers call intuitions in that they have a pictorial character.

Objective ideas, in contrast to ideas, belong to the realm of logic. They are essentially non-sensible, and they are the same for all people. Objective ideas are of two kinds: they are either concepts or objects.

---

2. *F*, p. 37n.

3. He follows the example of Bolzano, who thought it necessary to distinguish between individual ideas (*subjective Einzelvorstellungen*), general ideas (*subjective Allgemeinvorstellungen*), and thoughts (gedachte Sätze) on the one hand, and individual concepts (*objective Einzelvorstellungen*), general concepts (*objective Allgemeinvorstellungen*), and propositions (*Sätze an sich*) on the other. Compare his *Wissenschaftslehre*, 4 vols., new ed. (Leipzig, 1929). For a detailed discussion of Bolzano's realistic views, see J. Berg, *Bolzano's Logic* (Stockholm, 1962).

Now, depending on our point of view, we can stress either of two aspects of Frege's improvement on the Kantian ontology. First, we could assume that his main distinction is that between subjective and objective entities. Then we might say that Frege simply keeps the Kantian distinction between intuitions and concepts in the form of the distinction between objects and concepts, but that he adds a new realm to this realm of objective entities in the form of subjective ideas.[4] He takes for granted, in other words, that there is a distinction between intuitions and concepts and that both are objective. To insure that this point is never lost sight of, he adds the subjective side. The distinction between objects and concepts is conceived of as logical or ontological. This distinction is attributed to Kant in the form of the distinction between intuitions and concepts; but Kant did not clearly distinguish between mental and nonmental entities. Notice, in this connection, that Frege calls attention to the fact that Kant in his *Logik* equates the distinction between intuitions and concepts with the distinction between singular ideas and general ideas. Sensibility appears only as an essential characteristic of intuitions in the transcendental aesthetic.[5] Frege, one might say, adopts the distinction of Kant's *Logik*, changes the term 'intuition' to 'object,' and adds a realm of subjective entities in the form of sense-impressions and images.

Second, we could take the following point of view. We emphasize first that intuition (*Anschauung*) is primarily an epistemological notion. As such, it does not differ from the notion of sensibility. Knowledge, according to a familiar pattern, results from the combined vision of two different "eyes" — the eye of the senses and the eye of reason. Intuition is the eye of the senses. I do not have to stress how well this pattern agrees with much of Kant's philosophy. But if intuitions primarily yield the sensory raw material for reason, there must be some other ground for holding that they are always singular. This ground is quite obvious; space and time, we are told, are the forms of intuition. Hence all intuitions are localized in space and/or time, and therefore they must be singular or individual.[6] Only if there could be intuition or sensibility without the forms of space and time could there be general intuition or, perhaps better, intuition of the general. From this point of view we get the

4. Ideas, I believe, are not the only mental entities of Frege's ontology; according to him, there are also mental acts.

5. *F*, p. 19.

6. On sensory intuition and the doctrine that all intuitions must be localized, compare *SM*. See also my "Sensory Intuition and the Dogma of Localization," in *EO*.

following picture of Frege's strategy. Intuitions, he realizes, are all inner pictures; they are sense-impressions or images. Frege, however, changes the term 'intuition' to 'idea.' Concepts, on the other hand, belong to the objective realm; they constitute the eye of reason. He leaves concepts untouched. His great innovation consists in the addition of objects. Objects, we must recall, are essentially non-sensible. They are therefore quite different from Kant's intuitions. Neither do they resemble Kantian concepts. From this point of view, Frege accepts the distinction between sensible and non-sensible entities, calls the former 'ideas' rather than 'intuitions,' and adds a third, new kind of entity in the form of objects.

It is not important that we argue for one or the other of these two ways of viewing Frege's break with the Kantian tradition. Nor is it, I think, really possible to decide between them. The Kantian system itself contains two aspects: an ontological distinction between universals and particulars, and an epistemological distinction between sensations and concepts. The terms 'intuition' and 'concept' have to do double duty: the first means a singular entity as well as a subjective mental entity, while the second signifies a general entity as well as an objective entity of reason. Small wonder that the Kantian tradition is beset by all the well-known ambiguities and confusions. Nor is it surprising that such great ontologists as Bolzano and Frege had to break with the Kantian terminology in order to express their realistic views.

Even though Frege avoids some of the idealistic pitfalls by drawing a distinction between subjective mental and objective nonmental entities, this success is marred by one serious mistake in his philosophy of mind.

To go to the heart of the matter, let us consider what Frege has to say about colors. Is the color blue, for example, an idea, a concept, or an object? Frege distinguishes between blue as an objective concept and blue as a sense-impression. The blue color, the objective concept, belongs to a surface quite independently of us. It consists of a power to reflect certain light rays.[7] When we see such a blue surface we also have a peculiar sense-impression. We recognize this sense-impression when we are in the presence of another blue surface.[8]

What, then, is the meaning or reference of the word 'blue' — the objec-

7. *F*, p. 29.
8. *Ibid.*, p. 31.

tive concept or the subjective sense-impression? From certain passages, one may get the impression that Frege holds that 'blue' can be used to speak about the sense-impression as well as the objective concept. But there is also ample evidence for the view that he wishes to hold that the color word always refers to the concept and never to the sense-impression.

According to what I shall call the first view, Frege holds that some words represent subjective mental entities. Consider, for example, the following statement: "The word 'white' ordinarily makes us think of a certain sensation, which is, of course, entirely subjective; but even in ordinary everyday speech, it often bears, I think, an objective sense." [9] A little later in the same paragraph he concludes: "Often, therefore, a color word does not signify our subjective sensation, which we cannot know to agree with anyone else's (for obviously our calling things by the same name does not guarantee as much) but rather an objective quality." Notice that Frege says 'often' rather than 'always,' implying that sometimes, at least, a word like 'white' may have a subjective sense or reference.

On the other hand, there are many more passages which indicate that he holds a different view, namely, that all words purporting to represent subjective entities represent, in reality, objective entities. This second view is not only expressed in occasional remarks but is an essential premise of one of Frege's crucial arguments against idealism. But before I describe the second view in greater detail, let me briefly mention one other possible interpretation.

One could hold that Frege distinguishes implicitly between two connections: the word 'white,' for example, *corresponds* to a certain sense-impression which is subjective and hence private, but it *means* a certain property which is objective and hence public. This distinction, one may hold, appears quite clearly when we contrast the following two statements by Frege. "When we see a blue surface, we have an impression of a unique sort, which corresponds (*entspricht*) to the word 'blue'; this impression we recognize again, when we catch sight of another blue surface." [10] However, when Frege speaks of objective concepts, he says that they are the *meanings* of words: "We can therefore still say that this word means for them something objective, provided only that by this meaning (*Bedeutung*) we do not understand any of the peculiarities of their respective intuitions." [11] According to this reading of Frege, ordinary discourse al-

---

9. *Ibid.*, p. 36.   10. *Ibid.*, p. 31.   11. *Ibid.*, p. 36.

ways represents objective entities. All expressions of ordinary discourse, insofar as they represent anything at all, *mean* objective entitites. But to such words, there also *correspond* certain subjective entities. We recognize the objective entity white — which is the meaning of the word 'white' — by a peculiar sense-impression which corresponds to the word 'white.' What Frege meant to say was that, even though we may have a certain sense-impression in mind when we use a word like 'blue,' the referent of the word, when it is used to communicate, is not this sense-impression but an objective concept.

The second view is implied by certain brief passages in the *Grundlagen*, but it also occurs as a premise in what we may call "Frege's refutation of idealism." First, an example from the *Grundlagen*. At one point, Frege claims that the objective world is expressible in words, while the purely intuitable is not communicable.[12] The sense-impression blue, since it is only intuitable, cannot be communicated. And from this fact it seems to follow that it cannot be the meaning of the word 'blue' as we ordinarily use it. Hence it must be the concept blue which is represented by the word 'blue.'

Frege's argument against idealism recurs time and again in his writings. It can be extracted from the *Grundlagen*, it is outlined in the *Grundgesetze*, and it occurs in detail in the paper "Der Gedanke." Compare, for example, the following passage from the *Grundgesetze*:

If everyone designated something different by the name 'moon,' namely one of his ideas, much as he expresses his pain by the expression 'Ouch,' then of course the psychological point of view would be justified; but an argument about the properties of the moon would be pointless: One person could perfectly well assert of his moon the opposite of what the other person, with equal right, said of his. If we could not grasp anything but what is within ourselves, then a conflict of opinions, a mutual understanding, would be impossible, because a common ground would be lacking, and no idea in the psychological sense can provide such a ground.[13]

12. Compare *GL*, p. 35: "Objectiv ist darin das Gesetzmässige, Begriffliche, Beurtheilbare, was sich in Worten ausdrücken lässt. Das rein Anschauliche ist nicht mittheilbar."

13. *GG*, p. xix. Notice that Frege here compares an expression for an idea with a natural exclamation. It seems to me that many of Frege's remarks on the privacy of mental entities and on the problems which this privacy poses are further elaborated in Wittgenstein's *Philosophical Investigations* (Oxford, 1953). This section on Frege's philosophy of mind may therefore be of some interest to the student of recent philosophical schools.

The same basic argument occurs in the paper "Der Gedanke": (1) If thoughts, in Frege's special sense of the term, are ideas and hence belong to individual minds, then they could not be recognized by other people. (2) Since there would then be no common thought, but only my thought as a content of my consciousness and your thought as a content of your consciousness, there would be no common subject for the predicate 'true.' (3) But this means (a) that truth would be restricted to my consciousness, so that it would remain doubtful whether or not something comparable occurs in the consciousness of others; it means (b) that there would be no science common to man; and it means (c) that it would be completely idle to dispute about truth. (4) But, of course, truth is not restricted to my consciousness alone, there is a common science, and it is not futile to dispute about truth. (5) Hence thoughts cannot be subjective ideas, but must be objective entities.

Frege's argument assumes that one cannot communicate about mental entities. Hence it presupposes that one cannot really communicate about, say, pains and sense-impressions. His argument, if sound, would not only establish that there are objective entities but it would also imply that these objective entities are the only ones about which mutual understanding and genuine dispute is possible. Nor is this all. The following argument runs parallel to Frege's refutation of idealism: (1) If all those words which seem to represent subjective ideas actually represented such ideas, then we could not possibly communicate by means of them. A conflict of opinions or a mutual understanding about such feelings as pains would be impossible. (2) But we do in fact communicate by means of such words as 'pain.' (3) Hence such words cannot possibly represent subjective ideas, but must represent objective entities. Frege's argument, we see, may also lead to the conclusion that all words which purport to represent mental entities do not in fact do so.

However, his line of reasoning is far from convincing. Quite to the contrary, one might reasonably claim that one of the premises of the argument must be false, since the argument is valid but its conclusion false. Since it is undeniable that some words represent mental entities, and since it is also undeniable that we communicate by means of them, it must be false that one cannot communicate by means of words which represent subjective ideas. Why should anyone, particularly Frege, be inclined to think otherwise?

Whenever Frege argues that we cannot communicate about subjective ideas, he claims that we cannot compare our ideas with the ideas of other people because we cannot lay the two sets of ideas side by side, as it were.[14] He claims that therefore we can never know that our ideas agree with the ideas of other people. He repeatedly insists that ideas are "private" in the sense that no two people have the same ideas. It is this privacy of ideas which leads him to say that we cannot communicate about them. He seems to reason as follows: (1) Ideas are private in the sense that no two people share the same ideas. (2) Since they are private, one cannot compare one's own ideas with the ideas of other people. (3) Since one cannot compare one's own ideas with the ideas of other people, one cannot know whether these ideas agree with each other. (4) Since one can never know that another person's ideas agree with his own, it is impossible to communicate about them. This argument furnishes the crucial premise for Frege's argument against idealism.

Is it true that ideas are private? Is it true, in other words, that no two people have the same ideas? I think so. Frege is right: I cannot have your sense-impressions and I cannot feel your pain.[15] If we make the further assumption that I can only compare my ideas with yours if I actually have your ideas, then it follows that I cannot compare my ideas with yours. But we do in fact often compare our ideas with the ideas of another person. For example, I may find out that you are color-blind by comparing my visual sense-impressions of a certain colored surface with yours. If it is possible to compare our ideas in this fashion, then it is also possible to know whether or not they agree with each other. This seems to contradict Frege's assertion that I can never know that my ideas agree with the ideas of another person.

However, there is really no contradiction. The issue is more complicated than I have so far indicated. When we administer a standard test for color-blindness, we take for granted that we can compare one person's visual sense-impressions with the sense-impressions of other people. But what would happen, for example, if the tested person uses color words in a systematically misleading fashion? Could we discover that a certain person sees an inverted spectrum? Clearly, it is this kind of consideration that

14. Compare *F*, pp. 35–36; and the example of the color-blind man in *G*.

15. I think that this is a matter not of logic or linguistic convention but of fact. I do not say that it is a conceptual truth, because I am not sure what is meant by a conceptual truth. But I am sure that the assertions that I do or do not feel your pains and the assertions that I can or cannot read your mind make perfect sense.

leads Frege to say that we can never know that another person's ideas agree with our own.[16] Frege is claiming that we could not possibly discover the man with the inverted spectrum, because we cannot compare his sense-impressions with our own by having both sets of them. There are only two ways in which we could discover the man with the inverted spectrum. First, we may watch his behavior, including his verbal behavior, that is, the things he says. Or, second, we may try to compare his sense-impressions directly with ours. Obviously, we cannot do the latter, since we cannot have his sense-impressions. This leaves only the first possibility. But his behavior is of no use to us as long as we assume that he may be behaving in a systematically misleading manner. Hence there is really no way of finding out that the person under investigation has different sense-impressions from ours. Frege, no doubt, has this type of situation in mind when he claims that we can never know that our ideas agree with the ideas of other people. I think there can be no doubt that his reasoning is sound up to this point.

So far I have explained what Frege and any other reasonable person may mean by saying that ideas are private, that one cannot compare ideas with those of other people, and that one therefore cannot know that another person has the same ideas. But does it follow from this explication that one cannot communicate about ideas, as Frege holds?

Shall we say that two people are communicating with each other about their ideas if they use the same words but use them for different ideas? If we do, then the privacy of ideas is certainly no barrier to communication. But surely this is not what is meant by communication in the present context. It is not enough for two people merely to utter the same sounds and to have the *illusion* that they are talking about the same things. In order to communicate, they must not only be under the impression that they are talking about the same things but they must actually be doing so. Even if we add this further condition, there is still no reason why the privacy of ideas should prevent us from being able to communicate about them. Two persons may not just think that they are talking about the same things, they may actually do so; and yet they may be in no position to *know for certain* that they are successful. It just so happens, as it were,

16. Compare the example of the color-blind man in *G*.

that they use the same noises and signs for the same things, even though they have no absolutely sure way of checking each other's procedure. We see that the privacy of ideas does not prevent us from communicating about them. It merely prevents us from *"knowing for sure"* whether or not we are successful.

Now earlier I claimed that we do, in fact, successfully communicate about our ideas. How can I possibly know that we are successful? How can I be sure that all of us use the word 'pain' for the same kind of feeling? If I know that other people do not behave in a systematically misleading manner, then I know also that we are talking about the same thing when we use the word 'pain.' On the other hand, if I know that other people behave in a systematically misleading way then I also know that we do not talk about the same thing when we use the word 'pain.' Ordinarily, we take for granted that the behavior of most people is not systematically misleading. Our firm conviction that we successfully communicate about private ideas rests on this belief. Whatever is evidence for this belief is also evidence for our contention that we successfully communicate about ideas. And whatever is evidence against this belief is also evidence against our contention. We can only be as certain that we are communicating about our ideas as we are that other people do not behave in a systematically misleading fashion.

Let us recall the argument for the conclusion that all terms which represent anything represent objective entities: (1) We know that we successfully communicate by means of such words as 'pain.' (2) If these words really represented ideas, as they seem to, then we could not possibly know that we successfully communicate by means of them. (3) Hence words like 'pain' do not really represent ideas. Rather, they represent objective concepts. We see now where the argument breaks down. The very same assertion which is adduced to back the second premise contradicts the first. This is the assertion that we cannot know that we are communicating about ideas, because the behavior of other people may be systematically misleading. Now if this assertion is true, then it follows not only that we cannot know that we are communicating, as long as the word 'pain' is supposed to represent an idea, but also that we cannot be sure that we are communicating at all by means of this word. If the behavior of other people may be systematically misleading, then it might not be the case, after all, that we successfully communicate by means of such ordinary words as 'pain.' The more seriously we take the suggestion of systematically misleading behavior, the less we can put our trust in the first premise. On the other hand, if we assume that other people do not behave in a systematically misleading fashion, then we can be quite sure not only that we communicate by means of mental terms but also that we talk about ideas by means of such terms.

This is not all. If we take seriously the possibility of systematically misleading behavior, we must conclude not only that we cannot know for sure that we are communicating about ideas but also that we cannot know for sure that we are communicating about objective entities. Take the word 'chair'; it is supposed to represent an objective concept rather than a subjective idea. But how can we be sure that other people use this word for the same property as we do, so long as we assume that they may behave in a systematically misleading fashion? After all, as little as we can feel another person's pain, just so little can we read his mind; and if we cannot read his mind, how then are we to know what property he means by the word 'chair'? The assumption of the possibility of systematically misleading behavior leads not only to skepticism with regard to mental terms but also to skepticism with regard to all communication.

Frege makes at least two mistakes. First, he believes that the possibility of systematically misleading behavior somehow shows that one cannot communicate about subjective ideas. Second, he does not see that the possibility of systematically misleading behavior also shows, if it shows anything, that one cannot communicate about objective entities as well. In his refutation of idealism he argues that not all words represent ideas, because otherwise there would be no communication; yet such communication is a fact. Ultimately, as we saw, this refutation rests on the possibility of systematically misleading behavior. But this possibility, as we also saw, affects Frege's premise that successful communication is a fact.

Why, we may ask, does Frege think that successful communication exists, even though people may be behaving in a misleading manner? Put differently, why does he believe that the possibility of misleading behavior does not affect the possibility of communicating about *objective* entities, but does affect the possibility of communicating about *subjective* entities? I know of only one place where Frege may be said to give a direct answer.[17]

17. *F*, pp. 35–36.

In this passage, Frege discusses the objective entities which constitute space. He holds that there are spatial intuitions which are, of course, subjective and hence not communicable. But space consists also of objective entities, and whenever we talk with each other about spatial matters we are talking about these objective entities, not about our subjective intuitions. Now, if my criticism of Frege's argument against idealism is correct, he is not entitled to conclude that agreement in verbal behavior about spatial matters suffices to guarantee that people are talking about the same objective entities. Such agreement in behavior cannot *prove* that people are talking about the same things, be they subjective or objective, because of the alleged possibility of systematically misleading behavior. Yet, Frege tries to show that a verbal agreement about spatial matters proves the existence of objective spatial entities. He assumes that there are two people who agree about all the axioms and theorems of geometry; however, they connect different ideas with the spatial terms in these axioms and theorems. For example, one person connects with the word 'point' the subjective idea of a point, while the other connects with this word the subjective idea of a plane. On the other hand, while the first person connects with the word 'plane' the subjective idea of a plane, the second connects with it the idea of a point, and so on. Frege assumes not only that the two people do not know whether they connect the same ideas with the same words but that they actually connect different ideas with the same words. Still, he contends that they are talking about the same objective spatial entities:

In these circumstances they could understand one another quite well and would never realize the difference between their intuitions, since in projective geometry every proposition has its dual counterpart; any disagreements about points of aesthetic appreciation would not be conclusive evidence. Over all geometrical theorems they would be in complete agreement, only interpreting the words differently in terms of their respective intuitions. With the word 'point,' for example, one would connect one intuition and the other another. We can therefore still say that this word has for them an objective meaning, provided only that by this meaning we do not understand any of the peculiarities of their respective intuitions.

Assume that we replace all descriptive spatial terms in the axioms and theorems of geometry with mere letters of the alphabet. We leave only the so-called logical words like 'all,' 'some,' 'is,' and so on. Assume further that we tell someone who does not know in what manner we replaced English words with letters that the proper interpretation of the letters will turn all expressions into true sentences. Does he now know what the letters *mean*? Have we given him an *interpretation* of the letters? Have we given him a *definition* of the spatial entities involved? Obviously, the answer to all three questions is No. By telling him that the proper interpretation turns all expressions into true sentences, we have merely limited the number of acceptable interpretations. We have merely told him to look for a certain *kind* of interpretation, namely, one that turns all expressions into true sentences. To tell him this much is not to give him the actual interpretation; it is not even to give him that interpretation *implicitly*.

Let us now consider Frege's example. If we assume that the two persons do not think of different interpretations but simply agree to search for an interpretation which makes all expressions come out true, then it is quite clear that they cannot as yet be talking about the same objective entities. As long as the letters remain uninterpreted, they cannot be said to have any reference, either objective or subjective.[18]

However, Frege's example is actually quite different. We do not have one uninterpreted system and two prospective interpreters who agree that an acceptable interpretation must yield true sentences; rather, we already have two interpretations. There is no room for any further interpretation and, hence, no room for an "objective" one. Each person has already interpreted the spatial terms. When the one person utters the sound 'point,' he is talking about a point, while the other person means by the same sound not a point but a plane. The sound 'point,' of course, does not mean anything by itself; it is merely a sound. But we can use such sounds in order to talk about things. The first being uses the sound 'point' in order to talk about a point, while the second person uses it to talk about a plane. But neither person uses it in order to talk about some third kind of entity — the alleged objective reference of the word. Nor, of course, do these two persons just make funny noises. Since neither person uses the word in

18. Frege, it must be pointed out, never again claimed that terms may be "implicitly defined." To the contrary, he repeatedly criticized the notion of an implicit definition in his later works. Compare especially "Über die Grundlagen der Geometrie," *Jahresberichte der deutschen Mathematiker-Vereinigung*, XII (1903), 319–24, 368–75; XV (1906), 293–309, 377–403, 423–30 (see the translation in *Philosophical Review*, LXIX [1960], 3–17). For a recent defense of the notion of implicit definition, see W. V. Quine, "Implicit Definitions Sustained," *Journal of Philosophy*, LIX (1964), 71–74; for a criticism of this article, see F. Wilson, "Implicit Definitions Once Again," *ibid.*, LXII (1965), 364–74.

order to represent some objective entity, then the word simply does not represent such an objective entity, contrary to Frege's contention.

I have assumed that the two persons agree in their interpretation of the so-called logical words. But we can, of course, raise a problem in regard to logical words. Just as we cannot conclude that the two persons must be talking about the same objective spatial entities simply because they behave similarly, so we cannot necessarily conclude that they must be talking about the same logical entities. Indeed, we cannot even be sure that they mean the same thing when they both agree that all the expressions under discussion are *true*, so long as we allow for the possibility of systematically misleading behavior.

We must conclude, therefore, that Frege has failed to explain how communication about objective entities is possible when different people represent different ideas by the same words. If we are convinced that the possibility of systematically misleading behavior is to be taken seriously, then we can never infer that we are communicating about something from the fact that we behave similarly. Assume now that someone is haunted by this possibility. Assume also that he pursues the matter along Fregean lines. Is there another way out?

I submit that one may argue as follows. The skeptical challenge, it appears from our considerations, cannot be met as long as we assume that words acquire their reference by being used to mean certain things. If it may be the case that we behave in systematically misleading ways, then it may be the case that we mean different things, although we utter the same noises. But why should we assume that words get their meaning from being meant to represent certain things? If we hold instead that they get their meaning through their use — 'use' properly understood — then skepticism can no longer triumph, for the use of words, so understood, is as open to public inspection as the very behavior of people. Indeed, the use of words, in this sense of the term, consists of nothing but observable behavior of people. We can determine whether or not two people utter the same sounds with the same facial expressions and the same gestures in similar situations, regardless of whether or not their behavior is systematically misleading.

At last we see the whole problem in the proper perspective. Skepticism in regard to communication does not arise just because there are words which seem to represent subjective mental entities. The real issue is not at all the existence or nonexistence of mental entities and whether or not we can communicate about them. The problem has a completely different source. Skepticism, as we can now see clearly, arises from the assumption that communication depends on what people *mean* by the words they utter and the marks they write, for what people mean (intend, think of, have in mind) — and this is the crux of the matter — is not open to direct inspection. What a person means by the word 'chair,' for example, is as hidden from the outside observer as what he means by the word 'pain.' In short, the crucial assumptions are that a word represents something because a person or group of persons means that something by the word, and that what a person or group of persons means to talk about is not open to inspection as their behavior is.

We may put the matter in this way. Even if we could feel another person's pain, we still could not be sure that we are talking about the same thing when we use the word 'pain' as long as we assume (a) that his behavior may be systematically misleading, and (b) that we have no direct access to his *thoughts*. We cannot be sure that communication is successful under these circumstances because we cannot trust his behavior, and we cannot find out what he means by the word 'pain' since we cannot read his thoughts. It is not the privacy of sense-impressions, feelings, and the like that invites skepticism in regard to communication; rather, it is the assumption that certain mental acts — acts which we may call acts of meaning and understanding — are private. Neither the so-called reference theory of meaning nor the so-called privacy of our sensations is at stake. There can be no serious question as to whether or not we *refer* to things by means of words; of course we do. Nor can there be any serious question as to whether or not our sensations are *private*; of course they are. Any attempt to answer the skeptic by denying these obvious facts must end in failure. From this point of view it may appear that the skeptic can only be refuted if one makes the rather drastic assumption that there are no mental acts of "meaning something" and "understanding something" by a word.

However, notice once more what is not at issue and you will see why even this heroic defense against the skeptic is doomed. There is no question of whether there are such *irreducible* mental acts as meaning something by a word and understanding a word. We may assume that there are no such acts. The skeptical challenge still remains. It is undeniable that people *think*, that *thoughts* are private, and that what people mean by their words or understand by the words of others depends on what they *think* of when they utter them or hear them. The skeptical challenge arises because we cannot read the *thoughts* of other people.

I mentioned above one possible interpretation of the slogan "meaning is use." According to this interpretation, words get their meaning not through private mental acts such as thoughts but through the observable behavior of people. If this were a true account of the situation, then it would silence the skeptic. Or, rather, it would constitute a first step toward his eventual defeat, for one would have to explain in detail, without mentioning any thoughts, how words get their meaning through use. It might be said that this notion of use has to be explained in terms of the further notion of a rule. If so, then it is clear that the notion of a rule must not in turn involve such mental acts as thoughts. Otherwise, the skeptical issue merely shifts to another place, centering now around the question: How can one ever know that another person understands a certain rule or means a certain rule by his words if his behavior may be misleading and his thoughts are inaccessible? Moreover, if one tries to refute the skeptic along these lines, one has to argue either that there are no such mental acts as thoughts or else that, even though they exist, they have nothing to do with communication. I do not think that one can succeed, for I believe that there are thoughts and that without them words can have no reference.

If we reject even this reply, how else can we answer the skeptic? Recall that the skeptical argument contains two essential premises. One has to do with the privacy of thoughts, and the other maintains that we may be behaving in systematically misleading ways. It is the latter, I think, which must be scrutinized. I believe that it is as probable that we are not actually communicating, contrary to all appearance, as it is that we are all behaving in systematically misleading ways. In the end, the thoughtful skeptic claims only that the assertion that we are not behaving misleadingly, if true, is neither a truth of logic, nor of mathematics, nor of linguistic conventions, but is on a par with other very general empirical statements. If this is what the skeptic means, then there can be no refutation of his position, for he is surely right.

□

Frege, we saw, thinks that one cannot communicate about mental entities. The words which we use successfully must therefore represent objective entities. This view has the strange consequence that words like 'pain' cannot really represent subjective feelings. But this is not the only strange feature of Frege's philosophy of mind. There is another one.

Consider again what Frege says about colors. He contrasts, first, our subjective sensation with the objective quality. But the latter is not the objective color as we all understand it; it is instead a property to reflect certain light rays, a property which a blind man can recognize.[19] Now, of course, there is such a physical property; but there is also, we must insist, the objective color which we can see and which a blind man cannot see. This color is not subjective; it belongs to a surface independently of any choice of ours, and our way of regarding it cannot make the slightest difference to it.[20] What holds for colors holds *ipso facto* for all other perceptual properties of things; they are all as objective as Frege's so-called objective entities. Whether something is or is not a chair does not depend on us.

How could Frege have overlooked the existence of the objective color which is neither a sense-impression nor a wave length? More generally, how could he have neglected the perceptual world in favor of intuitions on the one hand and physical entities on the other? There are, most likely, many reasons for this oversight, mistake, or whatever one wants to call it. The most important of these, I think, is the following: Recall that Frege distinguishes between objects and concepts in the objective realm, but that there is no corresponding explicit distinction for the subjective part of the world. This, too, is a most surprising omission. Is it not perfectly clear that a subjective entity is no less an object which falls under certain concepts than is an objective entity? An idea, for example, is just as much an object in the ontological sense of the term as is a chair or the number 2. The distinction between objects and concepts thus applies equally well whether we consider subjective objects and the concepts under which they fall or whether we consider objective objects and their concepts. Mental entities no less than nonmental ones divide into objects and concepts; yet we know that Frege distinguishes explicitly only between objects and concepts for the objective part of the world.

As a consequence of this mistake, he can no longer distinguish between a green sense-impression and a green perceptual object. Or, rather, he thinks of green as a sense-impression. Being a sense-impression, (the per-

19. *F*, p. 36.
20. *Ibid.*, p. 29.

ceptual color) green would obviously be subjective. But if the color green is thus a subjective sense-impression, it cannot exist objectively in the world. What exists in the objective world is not the color, but a certain wave length. Hence there are only two entities: the subjective sense-impression green and the objective wave length. There is no perceptual property green.

This identification of the color green with a sense-impression is only possible if one does not sharply distinguish between object and concept for sense-impressions. A sense-impression is an object, while the color green is a concept. Hence the sense-impression cannot possibly be the same as the color, and it is false to think of the color as a sense-impression. Rather, one should say that there is a sense-impression which is, among other things, green — in other words, which falls under the concept green. Now just because a certain sense-impression falls under this concept, we must not conclude that something else may not also fall under the same concept. For example, a table — which is another object — may be green, that is, it may fall under the same concept as the sense-impression we considered. This does not mean that there are two concepts *green*, one exemplified by sense-impressions and the other by perceptual objects, just as it does not follow that there are two concepts *green* because there are two green tables. There is only one such concept, but under this one concept different objects may fall. Under this concept falls both a subjective object, namely, a sense-impression, and an objective object, namely, a table. The concept itself is therefore neither subjective nor objective; it is neither mental nor nonmental. But it can be exemplified by both mental and nonmental objects. Of course, all this can be said clearly only if one quite explicitly applies the distinction between objects and concepts also to subjective entities. If one does not and follows Frege, then one may easily be misled into thinking of the color green as a subjective entity. And if one thinks of the color green as a subjective entity, there is no structural reason left why one should not also think of all other perceptual properties as subjective. And if one does this, then nothing remains of the perceptual world. According to Frege, we do not see the real world with our eyes but contemplate it through the eye of reason alone.[21]

Frege is not the only great philosopher of the recent past who failed to

21. Compare, for example, the following statement: "In the outside world, the totality of what is spatial, there are no concepts, no properties of concepts, no numbers" (*ibid.*, p. 99).

realize that sense-impressions are objects (individual things). Consider the following passage from G. E. Moore:

> I will begin by describing *part* of what happened to me. I saw a patch of a particular whitish color, having a certain size, and a certain shape, a shape with rather sharp angles or corners and bounded by fairly straight lines. These things: this patch of a whitish color, and its size and shape I did actually see. And I propose to call these things, the color and size and shape, *sense-data*, things *given* or presented by the senses — given, in this case, by my sense of sight.[22]

Moore here calls the three properties or concepts — a certain color, a certain size, and a certain shape — sense-data. But in a footnote, added later, he realizes his mistake and remarks: "I should now make, and have for many years made, a sharp distinction between what I have called the 'patch,' on the one hand, and the color, size, and shape, *of* which it is, on the other; and should call, and have called, *only* the patch, *not* its color, size, or shape, a 'sense-datum.'" Anyone who has read Moore's second lecture — and many other papers of that period as well — can see how close he comes to falling into the same trap as Frege. Since he has identified perceptual properties with subjective sense-impressions, he cannot find a good argument against the idealistic view that perceptual objects are bundles of sense-impressions. He does not really embrace this view, it is true, but only his good sense, not any particular argument, prevents him from doing so. Frege, as we saw, was not that fortunate; or perhaps we should say that he was more consistent.[23] He did not confuse perceptual objects with sense-impressions, as Moore was inclined to do, but he confused perceptual objects with physical ones, colors with light rays.

Before we turn to Frege's distinction between objects and concepts, there is one last question which must be raised: Assuming that there are objective entities, how are these presented to the mind? A discussion of this question will afford us an opportunity to shed some light on what may otherwise remain a rather obscure principle in Frege, namely, his

22. *Some Main Problems of Philosophy* (New York, Collier Book Edition, 1962), p 48; see also pp. 52, 54, 67.

23. I do not wish to claim, of course, that one can defend a realistic view of perception by merely distinguishing between objects and concepts for sense-impressions; further arguments are obviously needed. Compare *SM*.

claim that one must never ask for the meaning of a word in isolation, but only in the context of a sentence.[24] It will be best if, for this purpose, we contrast Frege's view on number with his view on color.

Frege holds that color is something sensible but that number is not.[25] Of course, he does not mean that the objective concept, say, blue, is something sensible in the sense that it is a sense-impression. But it may be said to be sensible in that there corresponds to this objective concept a certain peculiar sense-impression. Under normal conditions, we recognize that we are in the presence of a blue surface by having that peculiar sense-impression. In the case of number, there is no corresponding idea. While we have sense-impressions of objective colors, we do not have such impressions of objective numbers.

If this is true, how are numbers given to us? When we look at a triangle, we have some sort of impression which corresponds to the word 'triangle,' but we do not have an impression which corresponds to the word 'three.' The three in the triangle we do not literally see. What we do see is "something upon which can fasten an intellectual activity of ours leading to a judgment in which the number 3 occurs." [26]

In another place, Frege explains that objective entities are independent of sensation, intuition, and imagination, but not of reason: "For what are things independent of the reason? To answer that would be as much as to judge without judging, or to wash the fur without wetting it." [27] Though Frege expresses his thought here rather badly, it is clear enough that he wants to say that objective entities are not presented through sensation, intuition, or imagination but through a faculty called reason. What he does not wish to say, though it may appear that he does, is that objective

24. M. Dummett, in his article "Nominalism" (*Philosophical Review*, LXV [1956], 491–505), claims that this may be the most important philosophical statement which Frege ever made. I strongly disagree. Perhaps his judgment was influenced by the fact that similar statements occur in Wittgenstein's *Tractatus Logico-Philosophicus* (German text with English translation by D. F. Pears and B. F. McGuiness [London, 1961], § 3.3), and in the *Philosophical Investigations*, § 49. Dummett interprets Frege's statement in this way "Frege's statement can be expressed thus: When I know the sense of all the sentences in which a word is used, then I know the sense of that word; what is then lacking to me if I am to determine its reference is not linguistic knowledge" (p. 492). Aside from the fact that I doubt this interpretation, I do not see that the view itself makes much sense. It seems clear to me that unless I know the meaning of a word I cannot find out the meaning of a sentence in which it occurs. Frege, too, holds that the sense of a sentence is a function of the senses of its parts.

25. *F*, pp. 31–32.
26. *Ibid.*, p. 32.
27. *Ibid.*, p. 36.

entities depend for their existence or nature on reason. He emphasizes time and again that objective entities do not in any way depend on our knowledge of them. For example, he stresses that an objective entity "is not a creature of thought, the product of a psychological process, but is only recognized or apprehended by thought."[28]

It is clear, then, that all objective entities, according to Frege, are presented to us through the faculty of reason. More specifically, it is through judgments that we get acquainted with them.[29] Thus, in addition to sensibility, there is judgment. Strictly speaking, sensibility presents us only with ideas. Since some of these ideas are connected with objective entities, and since they correspond to objective entities, one can say that sensibility acquaints us indirectly with certain objective entities. But this kind of indirect acquaintance must be distingushed from the proper way in which objective entities are presented — namely, through judgments. It must be distinguished from knowledge, which is only possible through judgments. Furthermore, there are certain objective entities which are not even indirectly given through ideas, for example, numbers. But even though we have no corresponding ideas of numbers, we can still make judgments about them.

Now if judgment is the eye of reason, it follows that objective entities are always given within a context expressed by a sentence; for judgment, as ordinarily conceived, is expressed by a sentence and not by a word or a nonpredicative expression. But this means that we shall not find the meaning or referent of an objective expression if we look for it outside of the contexts expressed by sentences. We now understand the full significance of Frege's principle that words have a meaning only in the context of a sentence.[30] He does not mean to say that "meaning is use." Rather, he is insisting that though one can distinguish between the different objective parts of a context expressed by a sentence, these parts are never *given* separated from the context. The only place where one can find the referent of

28. *Ibid.*, p. 35. Compare also p. 115, where Frege says that we do not come to know the objects of arithmetic through the medium of the senses but, rather, directly through the faculty of reason, to which these objects are utterly transparent, because they are so closely related.

29. We might wish to add assumptions to judgments as another channel of reason. Meinong, for example, holds that assumptions play a major part in acquaintance.

30. Since Frege talks about words and meaning in general, one could take this passage in the introduction of the *Grundlagen* as further evidence that he holds that all expressions represent objective entities.

a word is a context, because the only way in which one can get acquainted with such a referent is through judgment.

Frege holds that the meaning of a word appears only within the context of a sentence, because he believes that objective entities are presented only through judgments. Why does he subscribe to this view? We have two clues. The first is where Frege says that if one does not hold this view, "one is almost forced to take as the meanings of words mental pictures or acts of the individual mind." [31] The second is where he claims that only by adhering to this view can one "avoid a physical view of number without slipping into a psychological view of it." [32] Let us try to fill in the gaps.

In the background lurks once more a piece of Kantian doctrine, according to which the mind has two eyes, namely, the presentation of ideas (*Vorstellungen*) and the making of judgments (*Urteile*). Moreover, judgments are based or built on ideas as their foundation. Now recall Frege's revision of this dichotomy. He identifies ideas with subjective mental entities. The first mental eye thus "sees" nothing but subjective mental things. Since he does not add another kind of nonpropositional mental act, only judgment is left to account for our acquaintance with anything that is not subjective. To put it differently, Frege thinks that if one does not hold that objective meanings are presented through judgments — and hence always within a context — there is only one alternative left, namely, that they must be presented through acts of presentation.[33] This means that they must be "mental pictures or acts of the individual mind." [34]

I think this explains the first of the two quotations. In order to see the thought behind the second, we must again turn to the Kantian background. Ideas, according to Kant, divide into intuitions and concepts. Intuitions, whatever else they may be, are thought of as singular entities, while concepts are conceived of as general entities. In this respect, intuitions and concepts agree with Frege's objects and concepts. Now Frege insists, for reasons which we shall discuss later, that numbers are objects rather than concepts. This means that they are singular entities rather than general ones, and, in Kantian terminology, that they are intuitions rather than concepts. A Kantian could therefore argue as follows: If num-

31. *F*, p. xxii.
32. *Ibid.*, p. 116.
33. I have to use the phrase 'act of presentation' because there is no verb connected with the term 'idea' as there is with its German translation '*Vorstellung*.' I mean by this expression the mental act which presents us with ideas.
34. *F*, p. xxii.

bers are intuitions rather than concepts, they must be either "outer" or "inner" intuitions; that is, they must be either perceptual objects or mental pictures.[35] Now Frege declares, and tries to prove, that numbers are not perceptual objects; if he is right, then numbers must be subjective mental pictures. It is this conclusion which Frege tries to avoid. He argues in effect that numbers, although they are singular entities, are not given as intuitions at all; they are not presented either as "independent" outside objects or as "independent" inner pictures. Rather, they only occur dependently in certain complexes which are presented to judgments. Thus he avoids the physical as well as the psychological view of number.

Throughout our discussion of Frege's distinction between objective and subjective entities, I have assumed the existence of the other important dichotomy which first occurs in the *Grundlagen*, that between objects and concepts. This will be taken up in the next two sections.

CONCEPTS

OBJECTIVE ENTITIES, according to Frege, can be divided into objects and concepts.[36] This division yields mutually exclusive classes: a concept is never an object, and vice versa.[37] To this ontological distinction there is a corresponding grammatical one between proper names and concept words. The former represent objects; the latter, concepts. How does one recognize that a certain linguistic expression is a proper name rather than a concept word, or that it is a concept word rather than a proper name? Some expressions are quite obviously proper names: for instance, names of people, names of mountains, names of rivers. But there are also expressions which are formed from concept words and yet are proper names. These expressions, according to Frege, can be recognized as proper names by the fact that they contain either the definite article or a demonstrative pronoun. The two expressions 'the number 2' and 'this horse' are exam-

35. It is not clear, of course, whether perceptual objects are really supposed to be "outer" intuitions, according to the Kantian system, but I think that some Kantians do sometimes think of them in this manner. At other times, these same philosophers might not, for the muddle that is the Kantian system invites this kind of confusion. Compare *ibid.*, p. 101.

36. Frege's choice of the word 'concept' is rather unfortunate, for concepts are often thought of as mental entities. The word 'property' would have been more appropriate. Indeed, Frege says at one point that the term 'property' can be used instead of his 'concept' (*BG*, p. 201; *T*, p. 51).

37. Compare *F*, p. x: "It is a mere illusion to suppose that a concept can be made an object without altering it."

ples of these two kinds of proper names.[38] On the other hand, it is a sure sign, according to Frege, that we have before us a concept word if we can form a plural for it.[39] For example, we can form a plural for 'horse' and speak of horses or of five horses, but we cannot form a plural for 'the number 2'; there are not several numbers 2 but only one.[40]

One important consequence of Frege's distinction between proper names and concept words is that there are in his view no common names.[41] He insists that concept words represent concepts and not, as the common-name doctrine would have it, objects.[42] For example, the concept word 'horse' represents the concept *horse* and does not name "commonly" or "indifferently" all the individual horses in the world.[43]

This is a good point at which to introduce some terminological conventions. By proper names and concept words, I shall always mean expressions which represent objects and concepts, respectively. Let us introduce a further distinction between proper names and names: While a proper name represents an object, a name is any expression which represents one and only one entity be it an object or a concept; it is to be contrasted with a so-called common name, which is supposed to represent more than one entity. Thus, both proper names and concept words are names because they are not thought of as common names. According to Frege, therefore, all (descriptive) expressions are names — that is, either names of objects or names of concepts (functions).[44] At a later stage I shall make a further distinction between names which are labels and names which are descriptions.

The most important ontological principle governing objects and concepts is, according to Frege, that objects can fall under concepts but nothing can fall under objects. He expresses this fundamental distinction in these words: "With a concept the question is always whether anything, and if so what,

38. *Ibid.*, p. 63. Of course, not every expression that starts with 'the' is a definite description and hence a proper name referring to an object. Logic books make this point by citing the sentence 'The whale is a mammal.' I shall take this as understood.

39. *Ibid.*, p. 64.

40. *Ibid.*, p. 49.

41. Compare, for example, *ibid.*, pp. 63–64. (One should here replace Frege's word 'thing' by 'object,' in order to avoid misunderstandings). See also Frege's review of Husserl's *Philosophie der Arithmetik* in the *Zeitschrift für Philosophie und philosophische Kritik*, CIII (1894), 313–32.

42. Compare my paper "Common Names" in *EO*.

43. Compare, however, our discussion below of 'the concept horse.'

44. There is one exception, though: the assertion sign. Frege uses the expression 'name' in this way most explicitly in *GG*.

falls under it. With a proper name such questions make no sense."[45] Let us characterize this asymmetry by saying that concepts are *predicative*, while objects are not.

□

Frege thus insists on at least two points with which I fully agree. First, he insists that proper names and concept words are both names, rather than common names. Second, he holds that concepts are different from objects in that they are predicative. But Frege errs in his characterization of proper names and concept words; he mistakenly asserts that any expression which begins with the definite article or a demonstrative pronoun represents an object. This leads him to hold that an expression like 'the concept horse' does not represent a concept but refers to an object. The same mistaken conclusion follows from an application of Frege's criterion of forming a plural; presumably we cannot form a plural for the expression 'the concept horse,' and this shows that it must represent an object rather than a concept. What has gone wrong?[46] Two things seem to be at odds with each other. There is an ontological distinction between predicative and nonpredicative entities, and there is a linguistic distinction between two kinds of expressions. Frege coordinates these two distinctions in such a way that concepts cannot be represented by expressions which start with the definite article. Yet we do in fact often represent concepts in this manner. Where he has gone wrong, if I may put it so, is not in the two distinctions themselves but in the coordination of them.

'The concept horse' names a concept which is also represented by 'horse.' There can be no doubt about this point. If we continue to use 'proper name' for an expression which represents an object, then we must deny that 'the concept horse' is a proper name. Instead, we should say, using Frege's meaning of the term, that 'the concept horse' is a concept word. On the other hand, if we agree with Frege to call 'the concept horse' a proper name, then we must reject his rule that proper names represent objects. What shall we do? We must introduce a further distinction. We must distinguish between labels on the one hand and descrip-

45. *F*, p. 64. Frege speaks here of proper names, but it is clear that he must mean objects instead.

46. Fisk thinks that Frege's view leads to a paradox in his semantics. I do not think so. I agree with Sternfeld that Fisk's argument contains premises which Frege would reject. See M. Fisk, "A Paradox in Frege's Semantics," *Philosophical Studies*, XV, (1963), 56–62; and R. Sternfeld, "Note on 'A Paradox in Frege's Semantics,'" *ibid.*, XVI (1965), 12–14.

tions on the other.[47] For example, we shall agree with Frege that there is a difference between 'horse' and 'the concept horse'; the former is a mere label while the latter is a description. But we can at the same time disagree with Frege and insist that these two expressions represent the same entity, namely, a certain concept. 'Horse' is a label for this concept, while 'the concept horse' describes the concept. Using 'proper name' as before, neither 'horse' nor 'the concept horse' is a proper name; both are concept words. But we can also express Frege's grammatical distinction in terms of the definite article by saying that 'horse' is a label, while 'the concept horse' is a description.

Even though we can take for granted that 'horse' and 'the concept horse' represent the same entity, there is the undeniable fact that the two expressions look quite different. Nor can we deny that the two expressions behave differently from a grammatical point of view. For example, 'This is a horse' is a grammatical sentence, but 'This is the concept horse' can be ungrammatical or false. It is ungrammatical if we take the 'is' to signify predication rather than identity. It is false if we take the 'is' to represent identity but assume that the 'this' is a horse rather than being the concept horse. On the other hand, 'The concept horse is formed by abstraction' is a grammatical sentence, while 'Horse is formed by abstraction' may be regarded as puzzling. According to our view, however, these differences are merely grammatical or stylistic. They do not have any ontological significance.[48] We have here a case where grammar does not faithfully mirror the world. It may mislead us. Frege was misled.[49]

So-called proper names of persons, rivers, mountains, and so forth are labels of objects.[50] Simple concept words, such as 'green,' 'round,' and 'tiger,' are labels of concepts. There are also definite descriptions of objects and concepts, which are always formed from certain labels and the definite article. For example, 'the horse in front of our house' is a description of a

47. This distinction between labels and descriptions is not the same as Russell's distinction between so-called logical proper names and descriptions. Compare the further remarks about labels and descriptions below, pp. 157–60.

48. They would therefore not appear in a so-called ideal or clarified language like that of B.

49. Geach, too, was misled when he argued: " 'The property of being a man' does not stand for the property of being a man, because we cannot say 'Socrates is the property of being a man.' " I would remind him of his own remark a little while later: ". . . but English grammar is here no safe guide." See P. Geach, "Subject and Predicate," *Mind*, LIX (1950), 473, 481.

50. I assume for the moment that there are no abbreviations of descriptions.

certain horse and thus a description of an object. But 'the concept horse' is a description of a certain concept. Just as there are labels of concepts as well as labels of objects, so there are descriptions of concepts as well as descriptions of objects. Just as we cannot tell from a label per se whether it represents an object or a concept, so we cannot tell from the occurrence of the definite article alone whether a description represents an object or a concept. We can, of course, tell whether an expression is a mere label or a description, for a description contains the definite article while a label does not. In the sentence 'That, over there, is a horse,' the expression 'horse' is a label of the concept *horse*. In the sentence 'The concept horse can be abstracted,' the expression 'horse' occurs as part of the description 'the concept horse' which describes the concept *horse*. Finally, in the sentence 'The horse in front of my house is brown,' 'horse' is again part of a description, but the description 'the horse in front of my house' describes an object and not a concept.

Why did Frege insist that all descriptions must represent objects, when it is so obvious that there are descriptions of concepts? Why did he fail to see that concepts, just like anything else, can be either labeled or described? How could he possibly have overlooked the fact that, in regard to descriptions, grammar is no safe guide? Frege, we must recall, understood the nature of descriptions very well; yet he made what appears to be a rather elementary mistake when he insisted that they always refer to objects and never to concepts.

In the *Grundlagen*, as in all of Frege's later work on arithmetic, the formalists loom large as enemies of his philosophical approach. According to Frege, one of their basic mistakes is clearly exhibited by their theory of fractions and of negative and complex numbers.[51] Frege describes this mistake in the following way:

It is made a postulate that the familiar rules of calculation shall still hold, where possible, for the newly-introduced numbers, and from this their general properties and relations are deduced. If no contradiction is anywhere encountered, the introduction of the new number is held to be justified, as though it were impossible for a contradiction still to be lurking somewhere nevertheless, and as though freedom from contradiction amounted straight away to existence.[52]

51. *F*, pp. 104–9.
52. *Ibid.*, p. 108.

The source of the formalists' mistake, according to Frege, is the confusion of object and concept. For example, nothing prevents us from using the expression 'square root of −1.' But we are not entitled, without further ado, to add the definite article to this concept word. Just because the expression 'square root of −1' represents something, it does not follow that there is the square root of −1.

Frege claims that a concept word has a sense or meaning even if nothing falls under it. It can be used even if we do not know whether something falls under it. But when we form a definite description by means of such a concept word, the resulting expression has a meaning only if there is exactly one thing represented by the expression.[53] Even though a concept word has a referent, and even if nothing falls under the corresponding concept, this does not mean that a description formed from the concept word must have a referent.

So far, I think, there can be no quarrel with Frege's analysis. We cannot assume, as Frege correctly points out, that every description represents something. He is wrong, though, when he asserts that concepts exist even if nothing falls under them. However, I shall not insist on this point for the moment. Let us consider the really important question: Why does Frege think that the admittedly illegal step from a concept word to the corresponding description involves a confusion between objects and concepts?

Consider the two expressions 'horse in front of my house' and 'the horse in front of my house.' The first refers to a concept under which objects may fall; the second represents, if it represents anything, an object. If one does not see this clearly, if one mistakenly thinks that the second expression also represents a concept, then one may believe that he is justified in using the second expression in the same manner as the first, that is, without first having made sure that it has a referent. This is Frege's point. He reasons that a formalist can only proceed as he does because he does not

---

53. Compare *ibid.*, pp. 87–88n.: "On the other hand, the concept *fraction smaller than 1 and such that no fraction smaller than 1 exceeds it in magnitude* is quite unexceptional: in order, indeed, to prove that there exists no such fraction, we must make use of just this concept, despite its containing a contradiction. If, however, we wished to use this concept for defining an object falling under it, it would, of course, be necessary first to show two distinct things:

1. that some object falls under this concept;
2. that only one object falls under it.

Now since the first of these propositions, not to mention the second, is false, it follows that the expression 'the largest proper fraction' is senseless."

clearly distinguish between objects and concepts, for only thus will he step from a legitimate concept word to a description of an object, assuming that the existence of the concept guarantees referents for both expressions.

Frege's point is well taken. A description like 'the horse in front of my house' does indeed represent an object and not a concept. Perhaps Frege was particularly sensitive to any confusion between object and concept, since he himself had earlier held that 'the number 20' represents a concept.[54] Be that as it may, how do these considerations show that 'the concept horse' must represent an object rather than a concept? The definite description of an object is formed by means of a concept word; hence there is some danger of confusing object and concept. However, the expression 'the concept horse' is not the description of an object but of a concept, and, because of this, it is quite different from the expression 'the horse in front of my house.' Frege's view that all descriptions represent objects may rest on, among other things, a mistaken generalization. He first makes a point about descriptions of objects and then generalizes this point to cover all descriptions, not realizing that the step from a predicate to a description yields in some cases descriptions of objects and in others descriptions of concepts. He correctly sees that one gets a description of an object if one adds the definite article to a certain predicate. In such a case it is true that the predicate and the description represent different ontological kinds. But then Frege may have jumped to the conclusion that this is always the case; he thinks that one always gets a description of an object if one adds the definite article to a concept word. Consequently, he lays down the rule that the occurrence of the definite article indicates in all cases that we are talking about an object rather than a concept.

One might try to defend Frege's view in the following way. Even when we form a description from a concept word, there remains a fundamental difference between concept word and description — a concept word has a referent even if nothing falls under it, while a description has no referent if it does not describe something. In particular, a description will not describe anything if the relevant concept mentioned in the description has nothing that falls under it. From this it follows, one might argue, that the concept word and the description cannot possibly have the same referent; what 'the concept horse' represents cannot possibly be the same as what 'horse' represents. Hence 'the concept horse' cannot possibly represent a concept if we assume that 'horse' represents this concept.

54. *B*, p. 17; *T*, p. 14.

However, this argument is not sound. The fact that a concept word always has a referent — though I do not think that this is a fact — ought to lead one to conclude that the corresponding description of the concept always has a referent, and not that the description cannot have the same referent as the concept word. The argument appears plausible only if one has already confused descriptions of objects with descriptions of concepts. It may be plausible that the referent of 'mermaid' cannot be the same as the referent of 'the mermaid in my pond,' assuming that the concept *mermaid* exists, while there is no mermaid in my pond; however, it is not plausible to claim a similar case for the two expressions 'mermaid' and 'the concept mermaid.' Of course, one may also quite reasonably doubt that a concept word has a referent when there is nothing that falls under the concept, and hence one may doubt, with excellent reason, that there is such an entity as the concept *mermaid*. If one does, then the argument just outlined breaks down for still another reason, which I shall discuss later.

I conclude that Frege's characterization of all descriptions as proper names is false. Not every description is a proper name. Nor is this the only flaw in his ontology of objects and concepts. In order to bring out Frege's second fundamental mistake, I shall simply follow his line of thought in defense of his distinction between objects and concepts against Kerry.[55]

In "Über Begriff und Gegenstand" Frege points out that his disagreement with Kerry is partially a terminological matter. In order to see what is involved, let us distinguish for a moment between Individuals and Properties on the one hand and Objects and Concepts on the other. We shall assume that every entity is either an Individual or a Property but not both. On the other hand, 'Object' and 'Concept' are assumed to be relative terms. Whenever we have an assertion to the effect that some entity falls under another entity, then the former is called an Object relative to the entity under which it falls, while the latter is called a Concept relative to the entity which falls under it. Finally, let us assume that nothing can ever fall under an Individual, while Properties can have something that falls under them and can also fall under other Properties. It follows that

55. B. Kerry's articles appeared in a number of volumes of the *Vierteljahrsschrift für wissenschaftliche Philosophie* from 1885 to 1891 under the title "Über Anschauung und ihre wissenschaftliche Verarbeitung." Frege's defense is *BG*.

Individuals can never occur as Concepts and, further, that Properties can appear both as Objects and as Concepts. For example, the Property green is a Concept relative to the Individuals which fall under it, but it is also an Object relative to the Property of being a color.

It is clear that Frege's distinction between objects and concepts is like the distinction between Individuals and Properties in that it is absolute rather than relative. Kerry's distinction, however, is relative, like the distinction between Objects and Concepts.[56] Quite often he does not talk about the kind of distinction which Frege wishes to make and, consequently, most of his objections miss their mark. Nevertheless, we can raise an interesting question which is suggested by Kerry's criticism. The possibility that a Property can be both Object and Concept rests on the ontological fact that it may be the Property of something and may itself have Properties. We may express this by saying that a Property can occur both predicatively and nonpredicatively.[57] Do Fregean concepts resemble Properties in this respect? Frege's answer may appear to be contradictory. He seems to say that concepts always occur predicatively, and yet he also insists that concepts can fall under higher concepts. Whether this apparent contradiction is genuine is the main question of our present inquiry.

After his remarks about matters of terminology, Frege points out that concepts are predicative while objects are not. In other words, he asserts that there is an absolute distinction between these two kinds of entities. In this connection, Frege also points out quite correctly that the nexus of falling under, unlike identity, is not symmetrical. He observes that the distinction between entities which can occur only as Objects and all other entities does not as yet touch Kerry's claim that some entities can occur both as Object and as Concept. He turns to this view next.

Frege states once more his criterion for proper names, in terms of the singular definite article, in order to show that the expression 'the concept horse' must represent an object rather than a concept. If so, Frege continues, then the sentence 'The concept horse is a concept easily attained' cannot be about a concept but must be about an object. This sentence does not express that a certain concept falls under another concept, but rather that a certain object falls under a concept. I have already discussed this

---

56. Kerry's notion of a concept resembles the notion of the content of a mental act. This explains in part his insistence that a concept can be an object of another concept.

57. In order to avoid cumbersome locutions, I shall speak of both concepts and concept words as being predicative.

part of Frege's theory, but let me just add a few words about one of Frege's moves, by means of which he tries to make the implausible more plausible.

When we talk or, rather, try to talk about a concept, we cannot do so, according to Frege, by means of expressions of the form 'the concept *F*.' How, then, can we talk about concepts? Frege answers that we can only do so after we have converted the concept into an object, "or, speaking more precisely, *represented* [the concept] by an object." [58] How can one possibly represent one ontological kind by another? What could Frege reasonably mean by 'represent' in this context? What kind of a connection is there between a given concept and "its" representing object? That there must be some kind of special connection is obvious, for not every object can represent a given concept. What features must an object have in order to represent a certain concept and no other? Frege does not answer these questions. Nor is his silence surprising, if our criticism of his criterion for proper names is just. There simply are no reasonable answers to these questions.

Frege mentions a certain justification in connection with this condition for proper names. He argues that a definite description must represent an object because it can never occur predicatively. He turns to a certain grammatical feature of our language to show that, in the sentence 'Bucephalus is a horse,' for example, we cannot substitute for 'horse' the phrase 'the concept horse.' For the sake of grammar we have to rephrase the whole sentence and say 'Bucephalus falls under the concept horse.' We have to use some such expression as 'falls under' whenever we substitute 'the concept *F*' for '*F*.' But why, we may ask, should this fact mean that the expression 'the concept horse' cannot represent a concept? As I said earlier, a grammatical fact is just that — a grammatical and not an ontological fact. The very fact that we can rephrase the sentence 'Bucephalus is a horse' in such a way that we express the same thought in the sentence 'Bucephalus falls under the concept horse' shows quite clearly that Frege is wrong. Frege, of course, would disagree. But he can do so only after having made still another claim. He maintains that in the sentence 'Bucephalus falls under the concept horse,' the expression 'the concept horse' is not the predicate but only part of the predicate. If it were the predicate, he seems to reason, then our argument would be vindicated; 'the concept horse' would then occur predicatively and hence would represent a

58. *BG*, p. 197; *T*, p. 46.

concept.[59] Why does he think that 'the concept horse' is only part of the whole predicate?

'The concept horse' does not mention the nexus of falling under. But why should it have to mention this nexus in order to be used predicatively? The word 'horse' does not mention the nexus represented by 'is,' and yet we do not hesitate to say that it is used predicatively in 'Bucephalus is a horse.' Moreover, the nexus of falling under is not symmetrical. The position in the nexus determines the predicative entity. If so, then there can be no doubt whatsoever that 'the concept horse' is used predicatively in 'Bucephalus falls under the concept horse.' On the other hand, if one insists, as Frege does, that the predicate is 'something falling under the concept horse,' rather than just 'the concept horse,' then one may well hold that the latter expression is only part of the whole predicate. In this case, it is obvious that the so-called predicate mentions two clearly distinguishable entities, namely, the nexus of falling under and the concept. To say that 'the concept horse' cannot occur predicatively amounts, then, to saying that this expression does not mention the nexus.[60] Such expressions as 'horse' and 'a horse' do not mention the nexus either; nonetheless, they are said to be predicative. No matter how we look at it, there seems to be no genuine difference, other than a grammatical one, between the two expressions 'horse' and 'the concept horse.' Hence there is no difference which can justify Frege's claim that the first expression can occur predicatively while the second cannot.

Frege's view that concepts always occur predicatively forces him to argue not only that 'the concept horse' does not occur predicatively but also that genuine concept words occur predicatively even when they do not appear to do so. This is his next task. Before we go on, let us note

59. Frege makes the same point when he defends his view that numbers are objects rather than concepts. He claims that the word 'o' is only an element of the expression 'the number o belongs to.' See, for example, *F*, pp. 68–69. Compare our discussion below of this point.

60. Marshall has argued that 'is a man' is logically different from 'the concept man.' They cannot refer to the same kind of entity. Hence, if 'is a man' refers to a concept, then 'the concept man' cannot refer to a concept (W. Marshall, "Sense and Reference, A Reply," *Philosophical Review*, LXV [1956], 342–61). I think that there are several things wrong with this line of reasoning. Most importantly, though, the example is already biased. One ought to compare either the two expressions 'a man' and 'the concept man,' or the two expressions 'is a man' and 'falls under the concept man.' Of course, 'is a man' is "logically" different from 'the concept man,' because the former mentions the nexus of predication, while the latter does not.

once and for all that the predicative nature of concepts, as Frege explains in a footnote, is just a special case of the need for supplementation — the unsaturatedness which he mentions as the essential characteristic of functions in another article.[61] Hence to say that concepts are always predicative is to say that they are unsaturated.[62]

Frege considers first the sentence 'All mammals have red blood.' It would seem that the concept word 'mammal' is not used predicatively. Frege argues that this first impression is deceptive. If we express the same Thought in the sentence 'If anything is a mammal, then it has red blood,' we see clearly that the concept *mammal* is predicated of something.[63] The concept word occurs in the predicate place of a complex expression; the corresponding subject place is occupied by a variable. Thus, even though grammar may hide the fact, the concept word 'mammal' does nevertheless occur predicatively in 'All mammals have red blood.' Notice that in this instance Frege does not rely on grammar for his guide to ontological difference. Rather, he argues that a certain Thought is more accurately expressed in a less common sentence, that a certain word occurs predicatively in the less common sentence, and that, therefore, the referent of the word really occurs predicatively and is a concept. Notice also that a concept word is said to occur predicatively, not only in connection with a proper name but also in connection with a variable. We may now explicate Frege's assertion that concepts are unsaturated as the claim that they always occur as predicated of definite entities or of kinds of entities — that is, concept words always occur in the proper connection with either names or variables.

Now we are again confronted with the difficulty noted earlier. Since Frege holds that concepts fall under higher concepts, and since, in such a case, only the higher concept seems to occur predicatively, it seems to be false to say that concepts always occur predicatively. Frege is aware of this difficulty. He tries to get around it by holding that the lower concept, as

---

61. *BG*, p. 197; *T*, p. 47.

62. Quite a number of articles have been written about the possible significance of Frege's distinction between saturated and unsaturated entities. Compare, for example, the following: M. Black, "Frege on Functions," in *Problems of Analysis* (Ithaca, 1954); H. Khatchadourian, "Frege on Concepts," *Theoria*, XXII (1956), 85–100; W. Marshall, "Frege's Theory of Functions and Objects," *Philosophical Review*, LXII (1953), 374–90; and Gustav Bergmann, "Frege's Hidden Nominalism," *Philosophical Review*, LXVII (1958), 561–70.

63. I shall distinguish between Thoughts and thoughts. By a Thought I mean a Fregean, objective entity as explicated in *SB*.

well as the higher one, occurs predicatively whenever we assert that the lower concept falls under the higher one. "What has been shown here in one example holds good generally; the behavior of the concept is essentially predicative, even where something is being asserted about it; consequently it can be replaced there only by another concept, never by an object."[64]

Frege's example is the sentence 'There is at least one square root of 4.' He claims that we have here an assertion about the concept *square root of 4*, namely, that this concept is not empty, that something falls under it. Although the sentence does not present the concept *square root of 4* as the subject, it can nevertheless be said to express that this concept falls under a higher concept. This way of regarding it, according to Frege, finds its adequate expression in the reformulation 'There is at least one object which is a square root of 4.' This reformulation shows clearly that 'square root of 4' occurs predicatively. Not only is a certain concept predicated of the concept *square root of 4*, but the latter is also predicated of something — the concept word occurs in connection with a variable. To make his point, Frege has to rephrase the original sentence, as he did when he considered the sentence 'All mammals have red blood.' In both cases there is the implicit claim that certain expressions show more clearly than others how things stand. In both cases I think Frege is right. The structure of the thought (or state of affairs) commonly expressed by 'All mammals have red blood' is more adequately expressed by 'If anything is a mammal, then it has red blood.'[65] And the structure of the thought (or state of affairs) commonly expressed by 'There is at least one square root of 4' is more adequately expressed by the sentence 'There is at least one object which is a square root of 4.' Frege is therefore right when he claims that the respective concepts occur predicatively in these two cases. Has he thus shown that concepts are unsaturated? Has he shown that a concept word never occurs without being predicated of something? Before we try to answer this question, let us briefly look at some further difficulties.

Frege seems to defeat his own purpose by claiming that 'There is at least one square root of 4' is an assertion about a concept to the effect that it is not empty. If this is so, then we should also be able to express this Thought in the sentence 'The concept *square root of 4* is not empty.' But

---

64. *BG*, p. 201; *T*, p. 50.

65. This does not exclude the possibility that the same thought may be even more adequately expressed by, say, 'All objects are such that if any object is a mammal, then it has red blood.'

if we can express it adequately in this manner, then it appears that 'square root of 4' is not predicated of anything. All we say then is that a certain concept falls under the concept of being realized. Frege holds that the following two sentences express the very same Thought: (1) 'There is at least one square root of 4'; and (2) 'The concept *square root of 4* is not empty.' However, he also holds that the first six words of (2) name an object, and that, therefore, (2) asserts something about an object while (1) asserts something about a concept. But this makes no sense if we assume, with Frege, that (1) and (2) express the very same Thought. We should conclude from this and from the superficial difference between (1) and (2) that grammar is no reliable guide to the structure of a Thought. Of course, this conclusion agrees with our general criticism of Frege's distinction between objects and concepts up to this point. We may agree with Frege that (1) is a more adequate expression of the Thought than (2), and since we can also agree that the same Thought would be even better expressed by 'There is at least one object which is a square root of 4,' we can also agree that the concept *square root of 4* occurs predicatively in *this Thought*. But by the very same token, we must also insist that the expression 'the square root of 4' represents a concept, and not, as Frege maintains, an object. Since (2) represents the same Thought as (1), and since (1) presumably represents a Thought in which there occur two concepts (each used predicatively) but no particular object, it follows that (2) cannot possibly mention a particular object. Put differently, either a Thought — which is not a linguistic entity — contains an object or it does not. Hence we must either conclude that (1) and (2) do not express the same Thought, since the latter mentions an object while the former does not, or else we must conclude that (2) does not mention an object, since it expresses the same Thought as (1) and (1) does not mention an object. We cannot have it both ways; we cannot hold, as Frege does, that (1) and (2) express the same Thought and also that (2) mentions an object while (1) does not.

Frege tries to find a way out of this dilemma by considering different analyses of the same Thought. A Thought, he holds, can be split up in many ways, "so that now one thing, now another, appears as subject or predicate. The Thought itself does not yet determine what is to be regarded as the subject." [66] A few sentences later he concludes: "It need not then surprise us that the same sentence may be conceived as an assertion

66. *BG*, p. 199; *T*, p. 49.

about a concept and also as an assertion about an object; only we must observe that what is asserted is different." I do not think that these considerations resolve the dilemma. A Thought as an objective entity is what it is, independently of our way of looking at it. It cannot be split up in different ways into subject and predicate for at least two reasons. First, 'subject' and 'predicate,' as we have used them are grammatical terms and therefore applicable only to sentences, not to Thoughts. Second, unless we hold that the entities of which Thoughts are composed are "relative entities," there is only one way of splitting up a Thought into its elements. We simply have no choice. We can, of course, *express* a Thought in many different ways: We can stress any one part of a Thought by making it the grammatical subject of the sentence. Assuming that we can express the same Thought either by (3) 'Bucephalus is a horse' or by (4) 'The concept *horse* is fulfilled by Bucephalus,' in (3) the object Bucephalus occurs as the subject, while in (4) the concept *horse* occurs as the subject. Only in this sense can it be maintained, first, that in (3) an object is the subject while in (4) a concept is the subject, and, second, that the Thought itself does not as yet determine what is to be regarded as a subject. What does not follow and what cannot be maintained is that the Thought does not as yet determine what entities it contains, so that it may contain — depending on how we look at it — an object in addition to Bucephalus in (4) or just the object Bucephalus in (3).

Frege concludes not only that the concept *square root of 4* occurs predicatively in 'There is at least one square root of 4' but also that what is asserted about this concept can never be asserted about an object, "for a proper name can never be a predicative expression, though it can be part of one." [67] Now, it is true, as I conceded earlier, that individual things cannot occur predicatively. But does this suffice to prove that whatever can be asserted of a concept cannot be asserted of an object? It suffices only if what is asserted can only be truly asserted of a predicative entity. Or, rather, it suffices only if what is asserted makes sense only when asserted of a predicative entity. Frege states: "I do not want to say that it is false to assert about an object what is asserted here about a concept; I want to say it is impossible, senseless, to do so. The sentence 'There is Julius Caesar' is

67. *BG*, p. 200; *T*, p. 50.

neither true nor false but senseless." [68] Now, there is a great temptation to formulate the crucial question in this way: Is Frege correct in saying that existence can only be meaningfully asserted of concepts, that is, of predicative entities? To do so, however, would be a grave mistake, for if we are convinced of the soundness of Frege's reasoning, we would have to conclude, in terms of the question, that it makes no sense to assert the existence of individual things. Russell, I believe, reached that conclusion:

> But if you could get hold of the actual person who did actually write those poems (supposing there was such a person), to say of him that he existed would be uttering nonsense, not a falsehood but nonsense, because it is only of persons described that it can be significantly said that they exist. [69]

He concludes with these words: "So the individuals that there are in the world do not exist, or rather it is nonsense to say that they exist and nonsense to say that they do not exist."

Surely Russell must be wrong. It is not only perfectly meaningful to say that the individual things in the world exist but it is also true. It is not nonsense to say that the pen on my desk exists or that Julius Caesar exists. As a matter of fact, existence is a property of everything except things which we merely imagine or invent. But since it is a property of everything, it is a queer property indeed. It forms a category of its own and hence should not be treated as a property at all. At any rate, since existence belongs to everything, it cannot be nonsense to say that a certain entity exists.

It may be objected that we have misinterpreted Russell. The fact that he talks of persons *described* should have given us a clue to his true meaning. Russell, we may be told according to this interpretation of his view, completely agrees with our position that the sentence 'Julius Caesar exists' makes sense. He agrees that it is not nonsense, because he holds that 'Julius Caesar' is an abbreviation of a description and not a mere label. What the sentence really says, according to Russell, is something like this: 'There is a man called Julius Caesar.' Russell claims only that it is nonsense to say '*a* exists' as long as '*a*' is merely a label. [70]

68. *Ibid.*

69. B. Russell, "The Philosophy of Logical Atomism," in *Logic and Knowledge*, ed. R. Marsh (London, 1956), p. 252.

70. Compare: "You see, therefore, that this proposition 'Romulus existed' or 'Romulus did not exist' does introduce a propositional function, because the name 'Romulus' is not really

According to this interpretation, it is nonsense to say that things which are labeled exist; we can only talk sensibly about them in some other way. I do not deny that this view played an important role in Russell's thoughts. But I think, first, that it is false, and, second, that it is not the only view that influenced him. Why should it be nonsense to say that *a* exists, where '*a*' is a label, when it makes perfect sense to say that the thing called '*a*' exists? After all, we are talking about the same thing in both cases, and we are saying the same thing about it. What, then, is Russell's argument for this extraordinary view? As far as I can see, there is only one, summarized in the following statement: "If it were really a name, the question of existence could not arise, because a name has got to name something, or it is not a name." [71] If I know that a certain mark or sound is a label of something, then I also know that what it represents exists. Hence I need not be told that its referent exists; and if I am told this, then I have learned nothing new. In short, the question of existence does not arise for the referents of labels as long as we know that all labels represent something. But this does not mean that it is nonsense to say that *a* exists. What is implicitly understood cannot be nonsense, otherwise it could not be understood. Russell is therefore mistaken when he holds that it is nonsense to say that a thing which is labeled exists.

It seems to me, however, that another view also plays a role in Russell's thinking. This second view, I believe, is the same as that held by Frege, who, we recall, claims that it is nonsense to say 'There is Julius Caesar.' His reason has nothing to do with a distinction between labels and descriptions; rather, it is the conviction that what we assert of a concept *F* when we say 'there is an *F*' cannot be asserted of an object. Let us assume for the moment that this is true. Now we need only one more step to arrive at the mistaken view that existence cannot be asserted of individual things — the identification of 'There is an *F*' with '*F* exists.' This assumes that 'There is (an),' as it occurs in 'There is an *F*,' expresses the notion of existence. I am fairly sure that Russell sometimes took this second step, but I am less sure that Frege did. Be that as it may, let us take a closer look at the two steps just mentioned.

Frege holds that (1) 'There is at least one square root of 4' expresses the

---

a name but a sort of truncated description. It stands for a person who did such-and-such things, who killed Remus, and founded Rome, and so on. It is short for that description; if you like, it is short for 'the person who was called "Romulus" ' " (*ibid.*, p. 243).

71. *Ibid.*

same Thought as (2) 'The concept *square root of 4* is not empty.'[72] Instead of (2), I think, we could say (3) 'Something falls under the concept *square root of 4*.' If so, then sentence (4) 'There is Julius Caesar' would be short for (5) 'Something falls under Julius Caesar.' But (5), one might agree, is not simply false but meaningless, for Julius Caesar, being an object, is the kind of entity under which nothing can possibly fall. Up to this point the argument is sound. But now someone may reason as follows. 'There is Julius Caesar' is merely an ungrammatical version of 'Julius Caesar exists.' Hence 'Julius Caesar exists' means the same as 'Something falls under Julius Caesar.' Since this latter expression makes no sense, the former is nonsense, too. Hence one cannot meaningfully assert that an individual thing exists.

If we hold that 'There is Julius Caesar' is merely an ungrammatical version of 'Julius Caesar exists,' then we cannot also hold that the former is short for (5). Conversely, if we hold that (4) is short for (5), we cannot then also assert that it is a mere version of 'Julius Caesar exists.' It does not matter too much from which assumption we start. I am inclined to say that 'There is Julius Caesar' is short for (5), since it is constructed solely in analogy to 'There is a square root of 4.' If so, then we have two sentences, namely, (5) and 'Julius Caesar exists.' It seems obvious to me that they could not possibly say the same thing. While 'Julius Caesar exists' is a perfectly clear statement, (5) is not. As I would prefer to put it, the first sentence asserts that a certain individual thing exists, while the second asserts that something falls under this individual. The first sentence may or may not be true, but the second is most certainly false.[73]

'Julius Caesar exists' says nothing about predication, that is, about falling under a certain property. 'Something falls under Julius Caesar,' on the other hand, mentions predication explicitly. How, then, could the two sentences mean the same thing? One possible answer would be that 'exists' and 'something falls under' mean the same thing.[74] One could hold that

---

72. I shall neglect for the time being all the complications that arise from Frege's insistence that 'the concept *F* represents an object. This view forces him to hold that 'The concept *F* is realized' makes sense, even though it is about an object.

73. Although I have used terms like 'nonsense' and 'meaningful' freely, I would prefer to put the matter differently whenever it is important. I would prefer to say, for example, that the sentence 'Something falls under the individual thing *a*' makes perfect sense. However, knowing what the sentence says, I also know that it is false, as a matter of the categorial structure of the world.

74. That is, 'exists' and 'is,' as they occur in 'This *exists*' and 'this *is* green,' represent the same entity. Needless to say, I strongly object to this Kantian view. The nexus of exemplification is not the same entity as existence.

'exist' does not really stand for any separate notion; then it would follow that existence cannot be attributed to individual things. But what would lead a philosopher to conclude that the meaning of 'existence' is exhausted by that of 'falls under'?

Moore, in "The Concept of Reality," argues as follows:[75] (1) The sentence 'Lions are real' means the same as 'There are things which fall under the property of being a lion.' (2) Thus the expression 'real' (in this usage) does not stand for any conception at all, because (3) the only conceptions which occur in the proposition 'Lions are real' are (a) the conception of being a lion, and (b) the conception of falling under something; and obviously 'real' does not stand for either of these two conceptions. Moore's mistake is obvious; especially since he considers the sentence 'There are things which fall under the property of being a lion,' rather than 'Something falls under the property of being a lion.' He simply fails to mention the two further notions involved in the meaning of the sentence 'Lions are real' — the notions of existence and of an individual thing. These appear clearly in the words 'There are things (which).' Hence it is quite reasonable to hold that 'real' stands for a conception, namely, for the notion of existence. However, let us assume that Moore is right. If we then think of 'Julius Caesar exists' in analogy to 'Lions are real,' we must conclude that 'Julius Caesar exists' is nonsense, for 'Lions are real,' according to Moore, mentions only the notions of being a lion and of falling under something. Caesar is not a property and it makes no sense to say that something falls under him.

So far I have argued that existence belongs to everything, and therefore it cannot be nonsense to say that it belongs to an individual thing. Yet I have also agreed with Frege's idea that what we assert of the concept *square root of 4* in 'There is a square root of 4' cannot be asserted of an individual thing. My reason for agreeing with Frege's assertion is this: I take it that 'There is a square root of 4' is short for 'There is an entity which falls under the concept *square root of 4*.[76] The latter sentence involves not only the notion of existence but also that of predication. But it

75. G. E. Moore, *Philosophical Studies* (London, 1922), pp. 212–13.

76. To be more precise, it is short for 'There is an entity which is a square root of 4.' I added 'which falls under the concept' for greater emphasis. Notice that I speak of an "entity." I do so in order to avoid, at this time, the question of what numbers are.

is false to assert of an individual thing that something falls under it. However, Frege's reason seems to be different from mine. He assumes that existence is a concept of second level.[77] If so, then it would follow that concepts — but not objects — could fall under it. Existence, according to my view, is not of any definite type, and this makes it a rather unique kind of entity. Why does Frege consider it a concept of the second level?

I believe that Frege was misled because we are able to say something like 'The concept *F* is realized' instead of 'There are *F*s.'[78] Starting with sentences of the kind 'There are *F*s' as paradigm cases of existence statements, he thinks that such sentences somehow say that a concept is fulfilled, that it is not empty, that something falls under it. Now, the statement 'Concept *F* is fulfilled' looks like an ordinary subject-predicate statement, except that the subject itself is a concept. It looks like a statement of the form '*F* is *G*.' But what does it mean to say that concept *F* is fulfilled, that it is not empty, that something falls under it? I think that these are just clumsy expressions for the thought that there is something which is *F*. But the sentence 'There is something which is *F*' shows quite clearly that existence is not predicated of *F*; it is said to belong to some other entity, namely, some entity which has the property *F*. In the sentence 'There is some property which is *G*' existence is not a property of *G* but is said to belong to a property which has the property *G*.

That existence is not solely a property of concepts of the first level can also be seen from the following consideration. Frege seems to be saying quite literally that 'There are *F*s' expresses the same Thought as '(the concept) F exists,' for the latter sentence expresses existence as a property of a concept. It is clear, I submit, that the two sentences do not express the same Thought. To say that there are individual things which have the property *F* is not to say that the property *F* exists, although the two statements are equivalent.[79] If I am right then it follows that Frege must change his view in one of two ways. First, he might hold that 'There are *F*s' expresses that the concept *F* falls under the concept of being fulfilled. But then he must distinguish between this concept of being fulfilled, on the one hand, and the concept of existence, on the other. While 'There are

77. Compare: "Because existence is a property of concepts the ontological argument for the existence of God breaks down" (*F*, p. 65).
78. I disregard once more Frege's view that 'the concept *F*' represents an object.
79. Just as I shall try to avoid the word 'definition,' so I shall try to avoid the expression 'analytic truths.' The equivalence statement mentioned is not "analytically true," nor is it a logical truth. It is a truth of ontology or, as I shall say, a categorial truth.'

Fs' expresses that F falls under the concept of being fulfilled, 'F exists' expresses that F falls under the quite different notion of 'existence.' Second, Frege could distinguish between two notions of "existence." While 'There are Fs' predicates one kind of existence of F, 'F exists' says that F exists in still another sense. Since I do not think that this last suggestion makes much sense, only the first one seems viable.

I should mention that we must distinguish between the notion of existence and the quantifier *some*.[80] This distinction is often blurred when one speaks of the expression 'Some entities (are)' as the *existential* quantifier. It must be emphasized that the so-called existential quantifier has no more to do with existence than the so-called universal quantifier. To stress this point, one ought to read the sign '(x)' as 'All individual things (are such)' and the sign '$(\exists x)$' as 'Some individual things (are such).' The essential difference between these two expressions is that the first represents in part the quantifier *all* while the second represents in part the quantifier *some*. Existence is not represented in either case, but it is understood that the variables range over existents. If we wish to express this understanding, we can introduce a sign for the notion of existence, say, 'E,' and write '$(A\ Ex)$' for 'All existing individuals (are such)' and '$(S\ Ex)$' for 'Some existing individuals (are such).'

It is pointless to try to "define" existence in terms of the so-called existential quantifier. Consider, for example, a suggestion by J. Hintikka to "define" 'a exists' as '$(\exists x)\ (x = a)$.'[81] Hintikka writes:

What I have been arguing is that existence cannot be conceived of as an irreducible *predicate*. Even if we introduce a special predicate $Q(a)$ to express 'a exists,' it turns out to be definable in terms of the ordinary existential quantifier. In this sense, existence is expressed by the existential quantifier and by nothing else. Any primitive predicate of existence is *necessarily* redundant if the normal meanings of our logical concepts are accepted.[82]

If my analysis is correct, then it follows that existence is an irreducible notion (entity). Even though it is true that the two sentences 'a exists' and 'Some existing individual is identical with a' are equivalent, we cannot reasonably claim to have "defined" the notion of existence by means of the latter sentence, for that sentence contains the notion of existence. Nor is it

80. I shall speak of the word 'some' and also of what it represents as a quantifier.
81. J. Hintikka, "Studies in the Logic of Existence and Necessity," *The Monist*, L (1966), 55–76.
82. *Ibid.*, p. 66.

true that existence is expressed by the so-called existential quantifier. The expression '($\exists x$),' as ordinarily understood, is a complex expression that expresses a complex notion. The primary ingredient of that complex idea is the notion *some* (at least one). Another ingredient is the notion of an individual. Depending on whether we think of '($\exists x$)' as 'Some individuals (are such)' or as 'Some existing individuals (are such),' we may say that this expression "presupposes" or represents the notion of existence, respectively. Hence we may say that *a part* of the so-called existential quantifier expresses the notion of existence, not that the existential quantifier as such expresses this notion. Moreover, this part is also a part of the universal quantifier and hence is not at all confined to the so-called existential quantifier. Finally, since according to my view the notion of existence is a part of (or presupposed by) the notion of the so-called existential quantifier (as well as of the notion of the universal quantifier), we do not have to introduce it in addition and quite aside from the so-called existential quantifier. However, we must clearly keep in mind that we cannot "reduce" the notion of existence to some logical notion; rather, a certain complex notion contains among other things the notion of existence.

So much for the notion of existence. Let us return to the main question: Has Frege shown that concepts are unsaturated? First of all, has he shown that concepts occur predicatively whenever they fall under higher concepts? I agreed earlier that Frege has shown this in the case where a concept falls under the so-called second-level concept of existence. And the same result holds for the universal quantifier. If we assume that these two are the only second-level concepts and discard the possibility of higher-level concepts, then Frege has indeed proved his point. His strategy is now transparent. He wants to hold that all concepts — and only concepts — occur predicatively. If he is right, then it follows that a concept word can never replace a proper name and vice versa. In order to show that concepts always occur predicatively, he considers the two most obvious counterexamples, the sentences 'All mammals have red blood' and 'There is a square root of 4.' He shows for both cases that appearance is deceptive, that the relevant concept occurs predicatively. In order to show that a proper name cannot be replaced by a concept word, he considers once more a sentence of the form 'The concept horse is easily attained.' He has two options. He can claim, as he does, that this sentence expresses the intended Thought adequately. Then he must insist, in order to save his principle, that the expression 'the concept horse' does not represent a concept, since it obviously does not occur predicatively in this context. Or Frege could claim that the sentence is not as yet in the best possible form. He could then try to reformulate it so that it would become obvious that the relevant concept occurs predicatively. In other words, he could adopt for descriptions the same method which he applies to other apparent exceptions to his principle. We know that he does not follow this method in the case of descriptions of concepts, but we may ask ourselves whether it would be at all feasible.

Consider, then, a sentence of the form 'The F is G' — for example, 'The present king of France is bald.' I take it that 'the F' is merely short for 'the x which is F.' The whole sentence is thus a shorter way of saying 'The individual thing which is a present king of France is bald.' Now, where we have a description of a concept rather than of an individual thing, the relevant phrase has the form 'the f which is F.' Here 'f' is a variable while 'F' is a concept word (of higher level). It is clear that 'F' occurs predicatively in this context. But F is of course not the concept which we are describing. On the other hand, 'f does not occur predicatively; but it is a variable and not the name of a concept. Thus there simply is no straightforward answer to the question of whether the concept described occurs predicatively. If we consider the whole context of the form 'The f which is F is also G,' it is obvious that the expression 'the f which is F' does not occur predicatively. Nor does the situation change when we apply Russell's analysis. The expression 'There is an f such that any g is F if and only if g is identical with f' contains nothing which could be said to represent the concept described. The whole expression does not occur predicatively; as a matter of fact, the whole expression is a complete sentence and therefore cannot occur predicatively. We must conclude that a closer look at descriptions of concepts does not show that they are used predicatively. From this, however, we do not deduce that such descriptions must represent objects rather than concepts. We conclude instead that not all expressions for concepts occur predicatively, and hence that Frege's notion of the unsaturatedness of concepts is untenable.

Descriptions admittedly form quite obvious exceptions to Frege's principle, but there is also a less complicated case. Consider the sentence 'Midnight blue is a beautiful color.' With this sentence we are saying that a certain property has another property. The color midnight blue, however, is not predicated of anything, neither of a particular individual nor of individuals in general. Yet it is undoubtedly a concept. Thus it follows that Frege's doctrine is false; concept words and concepts do not always occur predicatively. One might try to save Frege's view by insisting that the sentence does not adequately represent the intended Thought, that a better sentence would be 'An object's being midnight blue is a beautiful color.' But what reason could one adduce for this contention? One cannot say that, *because* concepts are always unsaturated, this is the proper way to write sentences of this kind. That concepts are always unsaturated must show itself ultimately in the Thoughts (or states of affairs) which we consider. But the Thought under discussion is already perfectly well expressed in the sentence 'Midnight blue is a beautiful color'; nothing needs to be added or changed. In this respect, there is a great difference between the present example and the earlier ones analyzed by Frege. The Thought commonly expressed by 'All mammals have red blood,' I agreed with Frege, is more faithfully mirrored in the sentence 'If anything is a mammal, then it has red blood.' Similarly, I agreed that the sentence 'There is a square root of 4' is merely short for 'There is an object (entity) which is a square root of 4.' However, the sentence 'Midnight blue is a beautiful color' is perfect as it stands, yet it contains a concept word which does not occur predicatively.

We cannot defend Frege's view by pointing to his distinction between falling under and falling within:

The relation of an object to a first-level concept that it falls under is different from the (admittedly similar) relation of a first-level to a second-level concept. (To do justice at once to the distinction and to the similarity, we might perhaps say: An object falls *under* a first level concept; a concept falls *within* a second-level concept.) [83]

One could perhaps argue that we must write 'Midnight blue (x) is a beautiful color' in order to bring out the idea that something falls within something rather than under something. But this will not do; whatever reasons there are for distinguishing between the two connections are the very same reasons for saying that 'midnight blue' must occur predicatively. Furthermore, it is not sound to distinguish between the two connections simply because different kinds of entities are connected; there

83. *BG*, p. 201; *T*, pp. 50–51.

is no better reason for this than there is for saying that concepts must occur predicatively.[84]

Notice that Frege's distinction between falling under and falling within is made in regard to first-level concepts on the one hand and quantifiers on the other. I extended it to second-level concepts, which are not quantifiers. By rejecting the distinction for this extension, I do not mean to deny that the connection between an individual object and a property is different from the connection between a quantifier and what it quantifies; on the contrary, I insist that there is a great difference between the two cases. I used an example which, as far as I know, never occurs in Frege's writing. The only second-level concepts in Frege's system are the usual two quantifiers and an operator expressed by 'the value-range of the concept *F*.' He never talks about properties of properties, the "ordinary" concepts of second level.

Are there properties of properties? Of course there are.[85] But let us assume for the moment that there are no predicative entities of higher than the first level. Let us assume that there are only the usual two quantifiers in addition to individual things and properties of the first level. In such a world, concepts would indeed be unsaturated. Or, rather, concepts would be unsaturated regardless of whether Frege is correct in holding that descriptions of concepts represent objects. This result of our investigation seems to speak very strongly for my explication of the notion of unsaturatedness. However, for the sake of completeness I shall briefly mention some other possible interpretations of this rather mystifying part of Frege's view.

According to one classical view, substances can exist independently, while accidents cannot. The precise meaning of this doctrine is not altogether clear; more often than not, though, what is meant is that substances can exist without any accidents, or without any specific accidents,

---

84. As it happens, Frege's distinction is, in fact, not only sound but of great importance. However, this is due to the fact that his second-level concepts are the quantifiers and not to the fact that they are of second level. The connection between a quantifier and a concept which it quantifies is indeed radically different from the nexus of exemplification which holds between individuals and properties and between properties and properties of such properties.

85. On the issue of elementarism compare H. Hochberg, "Elementarism, Independence, and Ontology," *Philosophical Studies*, XII (1961), 36–43; and G. Bergmann, "Synthetic *A Priori*," in *LR*.

while accidents are not independent of substances in the same way.[86] What we must note is that substances are always thought of as complex entities, composed of matter and form. Frege's distinction between saturated and unsaturated entities may perhaps be compared with the distinction between independent and dependent entities. However, there are many things which speak against this interpretation. Most important, it seems to me, is the fact that Frege's objects, unlike substances, are not complex entities but are, as some say, "bare individuals." I shall return to this point shortly.

What first comes to mind when one reads about unsaturated entities is the idea that an entity is called unsaturated because it needs to be supplemented by another entity in order to yield a state of affairs. A concept is unsaturated because it needs to be connected with an object in order to yield a state of affairs (or Thought). But this interpretation cannot be correct, for it implies that objects as well as concepts are unsaturated. An object by itself is not as yet a state of affairs; it needs to be supplemented by a concept in order to yield a state of affairs.

There remains one further possibility. In his famous papers on logical atomism, Russell claims that understanding a predicate is quite different from understanding a name.[87] According to Russell, two conditions must be fulfilled in order to understand a (logical) proper name: (a) one must be acquainted with the individual named, and (b) one must know that the label is the name of that individual. The understanding of a predicate involves more. One must understand the form of a proposition; one must know what it means to say that something is so-and-so. For example, when one understands the predicate 'red,' he understands propositions of the form 'red (x).'

Why is there this alleged difference between understanding a proper name and understanding a predicate? Russell only hints at an answer. At one point he alludes to the theory of types; at another he claims that a predicate can never occur except as a predicate. He adds: "When it [the predicate] seems to occur as a subject, the phrase wants amplifying and explaining, unless, of course, you are talking about the word itself." Now

---

86. For an explication of some of the many notions of independence see E. B. Allaire, "Existence, Independence, and Universals," *Philosophical Review*, LXIX (1960), 485–96, reprinted in *EO*.

87. In *Logic and Knowledge*, p. 205, Russell explains that his view on what we mean by understanding the words that we use as predicates is derived from Wittgenstein.

Russell here seems to be very close to Frege's view, as we interpreted it, that concepts (and concept words) are unsaturated, If so, Russell's view suffers from the same shortcomings as Frege's doctrine.

Russell's mention of the theory of types suggests another idea he may have had. In order to understand a predicate, one must understand the form of propositions into which the predicate can enter. In other words, one must understand what kinds of expressions will yield well-formed sentences when combined with the predicate under study. What is well-formed, in this sense, depends of course on the theory of types. For example, the predicate 'red' can combine with a proper name 'a' to yield the sentence 'red(a),' because the predicate is of the first type while the proper name is of zero type.[88] Thus, in order to understand the predicate 'red,' we must not only understand what the predicate represents but must also understand the expression 'red(x),' because this expression tells us, by means of the variable, with what kind of sign one can complete the predicate in order to get a well-formed sentence. When we write 'red(x)' we reveal a "formal property" of red, namely, that it can combine with a certain other kind of entity.[89]

The so-called theory of types, consists of two very different parts. First, there is a division of entities into different categories. Individual things are said to be of type zero, properties of individual things are of type one, properties of such properties are of type two, and so on.[90] Second, the theory specifies a number of laws which hold for the different categories. For example, according to one of the categorial laws, an individual thing can only yield a state of affairs when combined with a property of the first level.[91] It cannot combine with another individual thing or with a property of the second level. Another categorial law states that the connection of exemplification is asymmetrical: an entity of level n can exemplify an

88. I assume here that an expression is of the same type as the entity represented by the expression.

89. For a discussion of Wittgenstein's view on propositional functions, formal and proper concepts, and related topics see E. B. Allaire, "The *Tractatus*: Nominalistic or Realistic," in *EO*.

90. The type distinction is thus simply a piece of ontology, namely, the distinction between such categories as individuals, properties of individuals, properties of properties of individuals, and so on. It amounts to nothing more than a formal insistence that properties of individuals are not individuals, that properties of properties of individuals are not properties of individuals, etc.

91. For the sake of simplicity, I leave out relations. What I say here should be said more precisely, but I hope that this does not distract from my point.

entity of level $n + 1$, but not vice versa. The general idea, I trust, is clear. What I wish to emphasize is the fact that the type distinction and the type laws are not wholly dependent on each other. Given that the world consists of such-and-such kinds of entities, one cannot in general tell what laws hold for them.

When we write 'red(x)' instead of 'red,' we do not merely indicate that red is of a certain category, assuming that the shape of the sign tells us this much; we also implicitly give a categorial law for this type. The expression tells us that this kind of entity may be exemplified by individual things. In an artificial language the shape of an expression would tell us (a) whether it is a constant or a variable, and (b) of what type the constant or variable is. The shape would not tell us as yet how to combine the one expression with other expressions so that we get a well-formed sentence. We can add this further information either in the form of explicit type rules, that is, categorial laws, or by adding to the sign the appropriate variable(s) at the appropriate place(s), with the understanding that a well-formed sentence will have to be of this form. This, then, is the whole and sole point of writing 'red(x)' rather than 'red.' Only in this sense does the understanding of a predicate involve an understanding of the form of a proposition.

However, the theory of types does not have the consequence which Russell thinks it has. And it does not lend any support to Frege's contention that concepts are unsaturated.

First of all, note that Russell mentions the form 'red(x)' but not the form 'ϕ(red).' If understanding a predicate means understanding the forms of all propositions in which the predicate can occur, then we must be given the form 'ϕ(red)' as well as the form 'red(x).' But the form 'ϕ(red)' is just the kind of expression in which a predicate does not occur predicatively. Nor would it be proper to write something like 'ϕ(red(x))' instead, for such an expression would represent 'ϕ' as a predicate of states of affairs rather than as a predicate of properties. The 'x' is not needed in order to indicate the type of 'red.' The type of an expression is never shown by a variable but always by the shape of the expression itself. The variables do not tell us what type of sign we have before us, but rather how to get from the sign to a well-formed sentence. Thus, 'red(x)' tells us that we get a well-formed sentence if we complete the predicate by adding a constant of zero type level; 'ϕ(red)' tells us that we get a well-formed sentence if we add to the predicate a constant of second level at the appropriate place.

Second, and more important, it turns out that there is no difference between proper names and predicates. Russell is wrong; there is no difference between understanding a proper name and understanding a predicate. From the shape of a proper name in an artificial language, we can tell only that it is of zero type, and not how to form sentences from it. In order to indicate the type rules for individual things, we must write something like '$f(a)$.' This expression tells us that we get a well-formed sentence from the proper name 'a' if we write in front of it a constant of the first level. Thus, there are categorial laws for individual things as well as for properties. If it is true that in order to understand the predicate 'red' one must understand the form 'red(x),' then it is also true that in order to understand the proper name 'a' one must understand the form '$f(a)$.' In this sense, proper names and their referents are as "unsaturated" as predicates and what they represent.

Let us return to Frege's line of thought in "Über Begriff und Gegenstand." At the very end of his article, Frege introduces an entirely new idea; he takes to the offensive, as it were. First, though, he admits that there is a difficulty with his view: "By a kind of necessity of language, my expressions, taken literally, sometimes miss my thought; I mention an object, when what I intend is a concept." [92] Let us consider, Frege proposes, what happens if we do not accept this somewhat awkward view. What happens if we do not admit that there are unsaturated entities? What happens if we take Kerry's view that objects and concepts are relative rather than ontological kinds? Can we then avoid the awkwardness involved in mentioning an object, when what we intend is a concept? Frege does not think so. He believes that the difficulty is merely shifted from one place to another.

Take the sentence 'a is green.' According to Frege, the object a falls under the predicative concept *green*. The nonpredicative object a "holds together" with the predicative entity green. The object a and the concept *green* can form a complex Thought only because the concept is unsaturated. Several objects could not "stick together" in this manner and hence could not form a Thought. The unity of a Thought, the difference be-

92. *BG*, p. 204; *T*, p. 54.

tween a list of entities and a Thought, forces us to acknowledge the exist-ence of unsaturated entities.[93]

Granted that the unity of a Thought necessitates a distinction between saturated and unsaturated entities, do we have to agree that concepts are unsaturated? Could we not hold that the concept *green* is of the same on-tological kind as the object *a*, but the Thought that *a* is green consists not only of these two entities but also of a link that connects them? Then we could represent the Thought by the sentence '*a* falls under green.' Frege agrees that this analysis is sound, but he insists that it cannot succeed without unsaturated entities. In addition to object and concept, the analy-sis yields the connection of falling under. But this connection, according to Frege, cannot be another saturated entity; for we would then have to postulate a fourth entity which would "collect" *a*, green, and the connec-tion of falling under into a Thought. Hence, we may hold that concepts are saturated, but then we have to say that there is the unsaturated entity of the connection of falling under.

According to Frege, these facts find an expression in language. '*a*' and 'the concept *green*' do not hold together, do not yield a sentence, because neither '*a*' nor 'the concept *green*' is a predicative expression. We can write '*a* falls under the concept *green*.' However, this formulation intro-duces a phrase which is used predicatively, namely, the expression 'falls under.' This shows, on the grammatical level, the need for unsaturated entities. As soon as we change 'falls under' into 'the connection of falling under,' we need a fourth expression in order to form a sentence.

I have emphasized repeatedly that Frege's grammatical point is not con-vincing without an ontological argument to back it up. My answer to Frege's argument is this: '*a*' and 'the concept *green*' do not yield a gram-matical sentence, it is true, but we can easily change this situation by add-ing the phrase 'falls under.' Similarly, '*a*' and 'green' do not yield a sen-tence in English; we must add the word 'is.' We have to add these two expressions because of the ontological fact that the corresponding Thought contains a connection in addition to *a* and green. Both sentences represent the Thought — or, as I would say, state of affairs — that *a* is connected with green (in a peculiar manner). However, contrary to Frege's opinion, 'the connection of falling under' does not represent any-

93. Frege stresses the unity of a Thought since he does not acknowledge states of affairs. I hold that a state of affairs has that same kind of unity.

thing different from 'falls under,' or, for that matter, from the expressions 'is' and 'the copula.' It is a mistake to conclude, as Frege does, that 'the connection of falling under' represents something different from 'falls under' because the expression '*a* the connection of falling under green' is ungrammatical.

What about the other point of Frege's argument? We discussed Frege's contention that concepts are predicative, and we rejected it, because we believe that there are (ordinary) properties of properties. Now an entirely different issue has arisen. The question is whether there is the connection of falling under. That the two issues are different can easily be seen, for the new issue arises independently of our stand in regard to the predicative nature of concepts. Let us assume that Frege is right, that concepts always occur predicatively. We are then faced with the question of whether such predication always involves a connection between the concept and some other entity. From this point of view it may seem that Frege's attack is directed against the existence of a connection between objects and concepts. It may appear that he argues against a connection of exemplification, because such a connection would only lead to an infinite regress.

I do not think so, however. It seems to me that Frege talks more often than not as if there is the connection of falling under; sometimes, though, as in the present context, he also talks as if the unsaturated concept connects directly with an object. It seems that he did not make a final decision in this matter; perhaps he regarded it as being of minor importance. From the context of the argument under analysis it is clear why he might do so. Although he insists that there must be unsaturated entities that account for the unity of a Thought, he intimates that we may think of either the concept or the connection as unsaturated. Elsewhere, I have argued that Frege is wrong in thinking that one could give a complete and accurate analysis of a Thought (state of affairs) without acknowledging the existence of the connection of exemplification.[94] Without this it remains an ontological mystery how a number of "nonrelational" entities could possibly form a complex entity. We may formulate as a principle of ontology that there is no complex entity without at least one connection. Since unsaturated concepts, no matter how we interpret their unsaturated-

94. *SM*, pp. 77–78. Compare also pp. 153–63 for a discussion of how entities hang together in a state of affairs.

ness, are not connections (or relations), they — together with objects — cannot account for complex Thoughts.

Frege's insistence that at least one part of a Thought must be unsaturated in order to explain the unity of the Thought strongly suggests one more interpretation of the notion of unsaturatedness. Frege may reason as follows: Every Thought must contain at least one entity which connects the other ingredients of the Thought but which is not itself connected with these further components. Put differently, every Thought must contain an entity that connects with the other entities without the need for a further connector. According to Frege, concepts are such entities; they connect with objects, but need no further entity to be so connected. To say that concepts are unsaturated is to say that they have this property. If one holds that concepts are not unsaturated in this sense, then he must hold that some other entity is unsaturated. For example, one may then consider that the connection of falling under connects objects and concepts without being connected with them through a further entity. If one holds that even the connection of falling under is saturated, then one needs a fourth type of entity which must be unsaturated in order to connect the other three — object, concept, and connection of falling under. And so on. Frege's point may be that one cannot account for the unity of Thought — or for any other complex entity — unless he admits that there is one kind of entity which differs from all other kinds in that it connects entities without being connected with them. If one holds that every entity needs to be connected to another entity by a third entity — if, in other words, all entities are saturated — then one cannot escape from an infinite regress. Frege's consideration shows that one can only avoid the regress by agreeing with him that there are unsaturated entities. Frege's argument shows a way out of the Bradleyan predicament. It shows that the Bradley regress cannot arise if one acknowledges the existence of at least two ontological categories — entities that require a connector in order to be connected with other entities, and entities that do not. What Bradley showed, though he did not see it and thus reached the wrong conclusion, is that two kinds of "relations" must be distinguished — saturated and unsaturated.

If Frege's analysis of Bradley's famous thesis is correct, and I think it is, then he has successfully refuted Kerry's view. He has shown that a

Thought must consist of at least two kinds of entities. Hence he has shown that one *can* use the terms 'object' and 'concept' in an absolute rather than a relative fashion. But notice that at least three issues are in danger of being confused with one another. First, there is the question of whether there is an ontological distinction between objects and concepts, a distinction which might be expressed by saying that, while something may fall under a concept, nothing can fall under an object. An object can never occur predicatively. Second, there is the question of whether concepts always occur predicatively. I think that a concept can, but must not necessarily, occur predicatively. Third, there is the issue of whether there must be entities which connect without requiring a connector.[95] Even if one agrees with Frege that there are such entities, thereby avoiding the Bradley regress, one is not forced to agree with him that concepts are those entities. As a matter of fact, one can agree with Frege's diagnosis of the lesson of Bradley's regress and yet disagree with him completely about the nature of concepts. For example, I agree with Frege that objects, because they cannot occur predicatively, are ontologically different from concepts. I disagree with him on the issue of whether concepts are always predicative. Since I took this to be the main import of the saturated-unsaturated distinction, I could express my view by saying that concepts are not unsaturated. Finally, I agree with Frege again when it comes to the proper response to the Bradley regress, except that in my opinion, the falling under connection, and not the concept, is the connector that needs no connection.

To sum up: (1) Starting from the expression for a judgmental content — '*a* falls under *F*' — Frege claims that such a content consists of at least two kinds of entities — an object and a concept. It contains an entity which can fall under other entities but under which nothing else can fall; and it contains an entity which can fall under other entities and under which entities can fall. (2) Certain considerations lead Frege to erroneously hold that every definite description represents an object. (3) Certain reasons lead him to maintain, again mistakenly, that every concept occurs predicatively. (4) Finally, Frege considers the problem of the Bradley regress. He correctly observes that the regress shows that a complex entity must consist of at least two ontological kinds. But he seems to

95. A state of affairs, however, cannot be "reduced" to such an entity and additional entities. Even a list of *all* the ingredients of a state of affairs is not a sentence. We must add to the list a statement to the effect *that* these ingredients form a state of affairs.

believe also that, having shown the need for these two ontological kinds, he has automatically defended his distinction in terms of saturatedness between concepts and objects.

OBJECTS

ONE OF FREGE's greatest philosophical achievements is his distinction between objects and concepts. His characterization of these two categories of entities not only opened the way toward a more powerful logical system but also prepared the ground for a better understanding of the nature of relations, quantifiers, and descriptions. Frege was one of the greatest logicians, because he broke with the tradition of classical logic. He was also one of the greatest ontologists, because he broke with the tradition of substance philosophy. These two achievements are related; Frege's quantificational logic, I believe, reveals the logical structure of the world because it has no room for substances.

However, just as Frege's view of concepts is flawed by his insistence that concepts are unsaturated, so his view of objects is marred by the belief that classes are objects on a par with individual things. In spite of this mistake, however, his view on objects contains a whole series of important truths. For example, Frege makes all the necessary distinctions between the connections that obtain between individual things and classes on the one hand and individual things and concepts (properties) on the other. Moreover, he distinguishes between these relations and the spatial part-whole connection. Individual things, he is fully aware, are not substances with natures but are what other philosophers have called "bare" entities.

A class of entities may consist of individual things, or of properties, or of relations among individual things, and so on. I shall primarily talk about classes of individual things, but I shall take for granted that what I say can be applied to classes of other kinds of entities. According to Frege, every function has a value-range. The value-ranges of concepts are called extensions. Hence one may think that extensions are the same as classes. Indeed, Frege often talks as if there is no difference between what he calls the extension of a concept and what others call the class determined by the concept. It also appears from other passages in Frege that value-ranges in general and extensions in particular are not the same as classes. Consider, for example, the concept *square root of 4*. It seems that the extension of this concept, in Frege's sense of 'extension,' is not the ordinary class consisting of the two numbers 2 and −2. Rather, the extension seems to be the class consisting of the ordered couples (2, true), (0, false), (−2, true), etc.[96] In the following discussion, I shall pretend that value-ranges and extensions are ordinary classes rather than classes of ordered couples or other "extraordinary" classes. This pretense should not significantly detract from what I have to say, and it will greatly facilitate my exposition.

Frege, as I said, claims that extensions are objects. This claim is built on the alleged fact that expressions which represent extensions are saturated.[97] We are now faced with a choice. We can continue to think of objects as individual things, such as the black pen on my desk, the sun, or the highest mountain. If we do, then it is patently obvious that classes of individual things cannot be objects. A class or group of individual things is just that, namely, a class of individual things; it is not an individual thing. From this point of view, Frege is simply mistaken when he says that classes are objects. On the other hand, we could argue that Frege's insistence that classes are objects shows that he does not confine the term 'object' to individual things. Rather, by 'object' he means an entity which is saturated and which differs in this respect from all concepts. There are then all kinds of objects, as different from each other as night and day, but all these kinds of entities have at least in common that they are not unsaturated, that they are not concepts.[98] It is clear, I think, that this is what Frege actually means by the term 'object.'

Even if we admit that individual things and classes of individual things are both saturated, so that it is important to have a term that covers both kinds, there is still no reason to confuse individual things with classes. Nor does Frege ever confuse the two categories — at least, not explicitly. One may think, though, that an implicit confusion must be involved in Frege's claim that extensions are admissible arguments for all first-level concepts.[99] If one distinguishes sharply between individual things and

96. On the notion of a value-range, compare R. Wells, "Frege's Ontology," *The Review of Metaphysics*, IV (1951), 537–73; and M. Furth, "Exposition of the System" (introduction to his partial translation of the *Grundgesetze*) in *The Basic Laws of Arithmetic* (Berkeley and Los Angeles, 1964).

97. Compare, for example, *FB*, pp. 18–19; *T*, pp. 31–32; and also *GG*, II, 254.

98. According to Frege, truth-values are also objects.

99. This claim leads to the famous Russell paradox. Compare on this matter Furth, *Basic Laws of Arithmetic*, pp. xliv–xlvii; Sobocinski, "L'Analyse de l'antinomie russellienne par Lesniewski," *Methodos*, I (1949), 220–28; W. V. Quine, "On Frege's Way Out," *Mind*, LXIV (1955), 145–59; and P. Geach, "On Frege's Way Out," *ibid.*, LXV (1956) 408–9.

classes, though granting that both are saturated, then it appears quite obvious that the latter never fall under such concepts. On the other hand, if we assume that Frege did not even implicitly confuse the two categories, then the question arises as to why he thought that all saturated entities can occur as arguments of first-level concepts. What is there, according to Frege, in or about saturatedness that qualifies saturated entities for the position of being an argument of a first-level concept? When Frege considers a distinction between individual things and extensions of individual things in terms of the concepts under which the two kinds may fall, he seems to reject such a distinction solely on the ground that it would lead to too many complications.[100] But why this should speak decisively against such a distinction is not clear; after all, the world is complicated, and if we wish to describe its structure we have no choice but to make the description as complicated as required.[101]

Now let us turn to another topic. So far, I have distinguished between individual things, classes, and concepts. Frege, we saw, calls both individuals things and classes objects, because they are saturated entities. One might reasonably contend, as we also saw, that he does not always distinguish as sharply as necessary between individual things and classes. But one cannot claim, I think, that he confuses concepts with classes. In this respect, Frege is on the side of the angels; he does not, like many contemporary philosophers, blur the distinction between properties on the one hand and classes of individual things on the other. However, he claims that there is a connection between concepts and extensions. Frege describes this connection by saying that the expression 'The extension of the concept F is the same as the extension of the concept G' has the same reference as the expression 'For all individual things, a thing falls under F if

100. Compare the *Nachwort* of the second volume of *GG*. This has been translated and appears in Furth, *Basic Laws of Arithmetic*.

101. Frege notes that a type theory for extensions and concepts would involve functions that could take as arguments entities of different types; functions, in other words, which would not belong to a definite type. He mentions identity as such a function. He argues that we cannot assume that there are as many different kinds of identity as there are type levels, because "identity is a relation given to us in so specific a form that it is inconceivable that various kinds of it should occur." (Appendix to *GG*, p. 254). I agree completely with Frege that there are entities which do not belong to any type. Identity, as Frege correctly remarks, is one such entity; others, in my view, are the quantifiers — the ordinary ones as well as numbers.

and only if it falls under *G*.'[102] He calls this assertion an undemonstrable logical law.[103] If we recall that, according to Frege, the referents of sentences are truth-values, we can reformulate the basic law so as to yield the familiar version that the extension of concept *F* is the same as the extension of concept *G* if and only if the same entities are both *F* and *G*. This law, I submit, does not show in any sense that there are no classes, but at most properties or concepts. Rather, since it is quite obviously a law that states a connection between extensions and concepts, its very truth presupposes the existence of both extensions and concepts. As I said, Frege never thinks otherwise.

How does our view that classes exist square with the widely accepted view that there are no such entities? How does it stand up under Russell's claim that classes are logical fictions because so-called class expressions are mere conveniences of language?[104] There are several individual things on the desk before me, among them a black pen and a red book. These individual things exist, and the group of things on my desk exists as well. As certainly as there are individual things and properties of such things, just as certainly are there classes of individual things. Whoever denies this truism must be wrong in some respect on some issue somewhere, or else he must use some crucial term with a special meaning. Let us look at Russell's position.

Russell first explains what he means by saying that classes are not among the ultimate furniture of the world. He envisions a complete symbolic language which contains a definition for everything definable and a simple sign for everything indefinable. He claims that this language would not contain a sign for the property of being a class in general or signs for particular classes in particular. Why didn't Russell simply say that there are no classes? Why did he explain his view in terms of an artificial language with its distinction between defined and undefined signs? I am convinced that Russell wished to hold that classes do not exist. However, such a bold assertion would be justifiably suspect. It would be as implausible as such philosophical pronouncements as "time is unreal," "perceptual objects exist only as long as they are perceived," and so on. To lend some plausibility to his view — to take the sting out of it, so

102. Since Frege thinks of sentences as names of truth-values, he uses an identity sign instead of the 'if and only if.'

103. Compare *FB*, p. 10; *T*, p 26. This is, of course, the basic law V of *GG*.

104. Compare B. Russell, *Introduction to Mathematical Philosophy* (London, 1919), pp. 181–83; also *PM*, vol. I.

to speak — Russell speaks of *definition*. The very clear problem of the existence of classes is thereby disguised. Since I shall discuss the notion of definition later in great detail, together with such related notions as analysis and reduction, I shall not go into the matter at this point. Instead, let us ask whether Russell could reasonably hold that a language is "complete" (in his sense) if it does not mention classes, even though there are such entities? Obviously, Russell must say that the language would not be complete under these conditions. Otherwise, ontology would reduce to a trick not to be taken seriously; one could show of anything that it does not exist by refusing to talk about it in an artificial language. Hence we have to ask once more whether there are classes before we can decide whether any artificial language is complete.

Second, Russell claims to have shown that we cannot regard classes as kinds of individuals. I take him to be saying that classes are not individual things, and I agree with him. Russell also claims that classes cannot be regarded as heaps or conglomerations, and I believe again that he is right, for reasons which I shall mention presently when discussing Frege's analysis of the part-whole relation. But he does not conclude from these considerations, as he should, that classes are not the same as some other kind of entity but form a distinct category, as it were. Instead, he asserts that we can identify classes with concepts (propositional functions).

Russell argues as follows: (1) Every class is defined by some concept, namely, the concept under which the members of the class fall. (2) Since there are other concepts which are formally equivalent to a given one, it is impossible to identify a class with a definite concept. (3) Even though this identification is impossible, it is still possible to define a class expression. To say that the class determined by the property F has the property G is to say that there is a property H which is formally equivalent to F and which has the property G.[105] We can take Russell's "definition" in one of two ways, depending on how we interpret the claim that to say one thing is to say something else. Russell, we must remember, uses this so-called definition to defend his claim that classes do not exist. This defense must rest on a very strong notion of what it means to say something in different ways: the very same thing must be expressed in two or more different ways. But in this sense of saying the same thing, the two sides of Russell's "definition," I submit, do not say the same thing. The left side mentions, among other things, the (categorial) property of being a class; the

105. For a symbolic formulation, compare "definition" 20.01 of *PM*.

right side says nothing about a class. How, then, can the two sides just be different linguistic formulations of the very same thing? Furthermore, Russell tries to show afterwards that his "definition" is correct. He presents a rather intricate justification for it. But what possible justification of that nature could show that certain words of English happen to be used for the very same things as certain other words? Would not a simple appeal to linguistic intuitions suffice? These two facts suggest, I believe, that the two sides of Russell's "definition" do not say the very same thing and, hence, do not show that there are no classes. Rather, they indicate that Russell's "definition" formulates a very interesting and important *discovery*. What Russell discovered is not that certain words of English are used for the same things, but rather that there is a certain connection between classes and properties. What he discovered is not a linguistic fact but a categorial one. His "definition" is really an equivalence statement in disguise. It asserts that a certain statement about a class is true, if and only if a certain statement about a property is true. This, I think, is the only viable description of the situation. (I shall delay the detailed discussion of the matter until later.) Grant for the moment that my analysis is correct. Grant that Russell's so-called definition is, in reality, an equivalence statement. Then it is obvious, I submit, that the very truth of this equivalence statement presupposes that there are classes in addition to concepts; otherwise, how could a statement about classes be true?

Before we leave Russell's discussion of classes, let me mention one point for future reference. Recall that Russell says that every class is *defined* by some concept. In the same context, he speaks of definite descriptions as definitions. He adds, though, that this is only one, albeit perfectly legitimate, sense of the term 'definition.' I shall never speak of definitions in this sense. I shall never say that a definite description of an individual thing is a definition of that thing. The point I wish to make is this: There is some similarity between a definite description of an individual thing and an expression of the form 'the class of individual things which have the property *F*': both are descriptions. There is also an obvious difference between descriptions of individual things and descriptions of classes: individual things are described in terms of properties which *they have*, while classes are described in terms of properties which *their members have*. I shall return to this difference shortly.

Frege, we saw, distinguishes between classes (extensions), individual things, and concepts. However, we also find passages like this one: "The extension of a concept is constituted in being, not by the individuals, but by the concept itself; i.e. by what is asserted of an object when it is brought under a concept."[106] Frege sums up by saying: "I do, in fact, maintain that the concept is logically prior to its extension; and I regard as futile the attempt to take the extension of a concept as a class, and make it rest, not on the concept, but on single things." Assertions like these seem to imply an existential and/or logical dependence of classes on concepts. What does he have in mind?

In the first passage, Frege may be saying that classes exist not because there are individual things but rather because there are concepts (under which individual things fall). So interpreted, what he says is surely false. If there were no individual things, there certainly could be no classes of such things. This is not to deny, though, that unless there are properties, individual things do not form classes. In a "world" in which there are individual things but no properties of individual things, there are no classes of individual things.[107] Hence, unless there are both individual things and properties, there are no classes of individual things. This consideration suggests another interpretation. What Frege may have in mind, though not too clearly, is that classes cannot be "given" except through concepts under which their members fall. This formulation is admittedly rather vague. We are no better off if we say instead that classes can only be "defined" through concepts. But another idea may be of some help. Russell, as we saw, thinks of the description of a class as a definition of that class. He distinguishes between two kinds of definitions of classes, namely, between definitions by intension and definitions by extension.[108] What he means is quite clear, aside from the notion of definition. We may talk about a class either by listing its members or by mentioning the concept under which its members fall. The former corresponds to Russell's "definition" by extension, the latter to "definition" by intension. Frege, we may think, claims that classes can only be "defined" by intension, never by extension.

Russell, by comparison, makes a somewhat different claim. He holds

106. "Kritische Beleuchtungen einiger Punkte in E. Schröders Vorlesungen über die Algebra der Logik," *Archiv für systematische Philosophie*, I (1895), 451; *T*, p. 102.

107. There are no "ordinary" classes of individual things, that is, for the category of individual things would of course exist.

108. *Introduction to Mathematical Philosophy*, pp. 12–13.

that "definition" by intension is more *fundamental* than "definition" by extension. This is shown, according to him, by two circumstances: (1) extensional definitions can always be reduced to intensional ones, while (2) intensional definitions often cannot even in principle be reduced to extensional ones. To show that (1) is the case, Russell introduces the property of being identical with some individual thing. The class consisting of, say, *a*, *b*, and *c* can be defined, according to Russell, in terms of the property of being identical with either *a* or *b* or *c*. Whether we agree with Russell depends, I think, on whether we are willing to talk about such a *property* as that of being identical with something. I do not think that such properties exist. For example, there is no such property as being identical with *a*, where *a* is some existing individual. Of course, there is the fact that *a* is identical with itself; and both *a* and the connection of identity exist. But in addition to these entities there exists no further entity — belonging to the category of properties — that could be called the property of being identical with *a*. (The belief that there are such properties as being identical with *a* or as being both green and round rests, I think, on the mistaken dogma that all forms — so-called open sentences — determine properties.) But even if we grant that this property does exist, we must not lose sight of the fact that "ordinary" properties of things are completely different from the so-called property of being identical with something. They are so different, in fact, that we should not speak of both as properties. Furthermore, we must not think that we have replaced a label by a description, for the so-called predicate 'being identical with *a*' contains the label '*a*.' Similar considerations hold for descriptions of classes, even though classes are described not by means of properties which they have but rather by means of properties which their members have.

At any rate, I think that it must be admitted that a class may be *described* in either of the two ways mentioned by Russell.[109] If so, then Frege would be wrong, if he were claiming that classes can only be described by intension, to use Russell's term. However, I think that Frege has something quite different in mind when he says that a class is constituted in being not by its members but by the concept under which its members

---

109. In my view, the definite description 'the class of individuals with the property *F*' mentions (at least) the quantifier *the*, the category *class*, the category *individual thing*, and the property *F*. We could abbreviate it as '(TC_x) Fx' in analogy to the description of an individual '(Tx) Fx.' To the description of a property '(Tf) Ff,' corresponds the description of a class of properties '(TC_f) Ff.' And so on.

fall. I think that what he has in mind is a certain objection against what he calls the domain calculus.[110]

Consider an area on a plane surface, say, the area formed by the pattern of a chessboard, consisting of thirty-two white and thirty-two black squares. Each of these sixty-four squares is a *spatial* part of the chessboard.[111] Each of the sixteen blocks of four adjacent squares, composed of two white and two black squares, is also a *spatial* part of the chessboard. A *spatial* part, we shall say, is a part of a *spatial* whole. For example, the chessboard is a spatial whole which contains the sixty-four squares as spatial parts. A block of squares is a whole, containing four squares as parts. It is obvious, for instance, that the spatial part-whole nexus is such that if an area is part of another area, and the second area is part of a third, then the first area is a part of the third area. Now notice the following facts: (1) The chessboard as a spatial whole consists of the sixty-four squares. It also consists of the sixteen blocks of squares. And it consists of the two halves, each formed by thirty-two squares. And so on. If we are asked to analyze the chessboard into its spatial parts, we can take any kind of area as a spatial part. There is no such thing as *the* spatial analysis of the chessboard. (2) If we consider any spatial part of the chessboard, this part in turn consists of spatial parts; it also forms a spatial whole. For example, we may first analyze the chessboard into sixteen blocks of squares. These blocks are spatial parts of the whole that is the chessboard. Then we may also analyze each block into four squares. The squares are then spatial parts of the whole that is the block. In short, every spatial part is itself a whole. (3) Consider the four double rows of squares that form the chessboard. The first two of these double rows form the lower half of the chessboard; the other two form the upper half. Together, the two halves form the whole chessboard. Consider now the first and the third double row, and let us say that they form a "parallel." The second and the fourth double row also form such a parallel. The two parallels together form the chessboard.

Next, let us compare the notions of spatial part, spatial whole, and the spatial part-whole nexus with the notions of element, class, and element-

110. I do not reproduce Frege's actual arguments of his article on Schröder, but report what I take to be their general thrust.

111. It goes without saying that these spatial parts are not sense-impressions. To claim, as Moore sometimes does, that sense-impressions are part of the surface of a perceptual object is to confuse spatial with ontological analysis. Compare also D. Lewis, "Moore's Realism," in *Moore and Ryle: Two Ontologists* by D. Lewis and L. Addis (The Hague, 1965).

class nexus, respectively. (1) The class of sixty-four squares consists of these sixty-four squares; the squares are elements of this class. But it does not consist of the sixteen blocks of squares; that is, these blocks are not elements of the class of squares. Rather, they are elements of the class of sixteen blocks; the class of squares is not the same as the class of blocks. Hence there is such a thing as *the* analysis of a class into its elements. (2) A member of the class of squares is not itself a class. Hence an element of a class need not be a class. Of course, there are classes of classes, but the class of sixty-four squares is a class of individual things.[112] (3) Consider again the double rows of squares. There is the class of the first two double rows; call it (*a,b*). Call the class of the econd pair of double rows (*c,d*). The class of these two classes is ((*a,b*),(*c,d*)). There are also the two classes of parallels, namely (*a,c*) and (*b,d*). Finally, there is the class of these two classes: ((*a,c*), (*b,d*)). But the class of pairs of double rows is not the same as the class of parallels of double rows, even though each of these two classes of classes "forms" the chessboard.

The chessboard is an individual thing, not a class of things. The situation is quite different when we say that the chessboard is a spatial whole; there are individual things and there are classes, but there are no spatial wholes in addition to spatial things. To say that the chessboard is a spatial whole is to say that it is a spatial entity, a spatial individual. Furthermore, to say that an individual thing is spatial is to say that it has spatial properties — a certain shape, for example — and that it stands in spatial relations to other things — it contains squares, for example. It is now clear that the spatial part-of relation is not the same as the element-of nexus. Most obviously, a part is always a spatial part of an *individual thing*, while an element is always an element of a class. Furthermore, as we have seen, while one and the same thing can be spatially analyzed into different parts, a class always yields the same elements; everything that is a spatial

---

112. I thus admit or, rather, insist that there are classes of classes. That makes me, in Goodman's misleading terms, a Platonist. A nominalist, on the other hand, is then someone who admits nothing but a part-whole nexus for entities. I do not think that this kind of nominalism constitutes a viable philosophical position. Since there are classes, no description of the categories of the world could be complete without mentioning them. In answer to Goodman's admonition to the Platonist: "Don't do anything I wouldn't do," we would have to say: "But then I couldn't do ontology." As ontologists we try to describe *all* the categorial features of the world. We do not try to "reconstruct" some of them in terms of others. We do not try to "reduce" some categories to others. Compare, for example, N. Goodman's *The Structure of Appearance* (Cambridge, 1951), and his "A World of Individuals," in *The Problem of Universals* (Notre Dame, 1956).

part of something has itself spatial parts, but not everything that is an element of a class is itself a class; and no two individual things have the same spatial parts, although two different classes may have the same ultimate elements.[113]

We must therefore distinguish between at least three different "connections" which an individual thing may have to something else. First, an individual thing *exemplifies* properties and relations. For example, the chessboard is square and to the left of a book. Second, an individual thing relates *spatially* to other individual things. For example, the chessboard is spatially related to one of its squares. Third, an individual thing is an *element of* a class of things. For example, the chessboard is a member of the class of all chessboards in the world.

After these preliminaries, let us now return to Frege. He means to argue, I think, that a class does not "consist" of its elements in the same sense in which a chessboard "consists" of sixty-four squares. In the first case we deal with the unique element-of nexus; in the second, with a complicated spatial relation. This is the real point of his remarks to the effect that a class is constituted in being not by individuals but by a concept.[114] A class, according to Frege, must not be conceived of as a spatial heap of things. In short, spatial analysis must not be confused with the analysis of a class into its elements.

Spatial analysis must not be confused with ontological analysis either.[115] In ontology we try to list all the categorial kinds of entities there are and attempt to state the categorial laws that hold for them.[116] Take the chessboard again. What kind of entity is it? According to Frege's view as well as mine, it is an individual thing, which exemplifies certain properties, stands in certain relations to other individual things, and is an element of a class of things. But notice that there can be no *ontological* analysis of this chessboard. We can describe its properties, but to so describe an individual thing is not to analyze it into its ontological constituents. An individual thing has no further ontological constituents; otherwise, it

113. Similar considerations apply to temporal parts and wholes.

114. Compare, especially, pp. 452–55 of his review of Schröder (*T*, pp 103–6).

115. Where I speak of ontological analysis, Frege, Wittgenstein, and Russell often speak of logical analysis. Our aim is more often than not the same. The logical atoms which Russell tried to discover are the ontological kinds I try to describe.

116. To put the matter succinctly, ontological analysis consists of the analysis of states of affairs into their categorial constituents. The crucial "part-whole" relation in ontology is neither a spatial nor a membership relation, but the unique connection that holds between states of affairs on the one hand and their constituents on the other.

would not really belong to a category. We can also give a spatial analysis of the chessboard, but this is not ontology. When we say, for example, that the chessboard consists of sixty-four squares, we have not "reduced" the chessboard to a more fundamental kind of entity. The squares themselves are individual things, just as is the whole chessboard. They, in turn, have properties and stand in relations to other things. An elephant is as much an irreducible *individual thing* as the head of a pin.

Anyone who thinks that the chessboard must be analyzable into further categories makes one of three mistakes: (1) He may believe that the chessboard is a class of things which needs to be analyzed into its elements. (2) He may think that a description of the chessboard constitutes an ontological analysis of it.[117] (3) Or he may confuse a spatial analysis of the chessboard with an ontological one. All three of these mistakes have occurred in the history of philosophy and whole philosophical traditions have been built on some of these confusions. I shall mention two paradigm cases.

□

Wittgenstein, in the *Notebooks*, tries to determine what the simple objects of logic are.[118] In his characteristic manner, he pursues several lines of thought simultaneously. His paradigm of a complex entity could well be our example of the chessboard. Although he talks about parts of his visual field, it seems quite clear that it is the spatial, not the egocentric, feature that determines his choice of the example. As prime examples of simple entities, Wittgenstein thinks of points (of the visual field).[119] This conception of what it is to be complex and simple sets the stage for the problems which he has to face.

The most obvious problem is this: If a chessboard is a complex object which has to be analyzed into such things as squares, then there seems to be no end to its analysis; for each square can be further analyzed into spatial parts, and each such part can be further analyzed into spatial parts, and so on. We seem to be forced to conclude that the chessboard consists of points, of *minima sensibilia*.[120] But if it consists of infinitely many

---

117. To say, as I do, that the chessboard is an individual thing is not to describe it in the ordinary sense but to assign it to a category.

118. L. Wittgenstein, *Notebooks 1914–1916*, ed. G. H. Wright and G. E. M. Anscombe (New York, 1961).

119. *Ibid.*, p. 45; relevant points are mentioned on p. 67.

120. *Ibid.*, pp. 45, 51.

points, then it seems to be impossible to give a complete analysis of it.[121] Moreover, we should be able to see these points. However, is it not quite obvious that we see no such thing?[122] We see the chessboard, we see the squares, and we see parts of these squares, but we do not see the ultimate entities of which the chessboard supposedly consists.[123] And if we do not see the simple entities of which a complex entity consists, how do we know that the entity is complex to begin with?

Wittgenstein is torn between two views. On the one hand, he is firmly convinced that spatial things such as chessboards, pencil strokes, and steamships are complex. Such is the hold of the mistaken view that analysis must be spatial analysis. On the other hand, he also realizes that we do not ordinarily treat such things as if they are complex. We seem to regard these things as simple.[124] It is not just a trick of language that we can refer to such things by simple names.[125] Perhaps, Wittgenstein muses, a certain square of the chessboard is a simple entity insofar as we do not perceive any single point of it separately.[126] At any rate, the fact that we can represent things by simple names speaks against their complexity.

Caught on these two horns of a dilemma, Wittgenstein tries to find a way out. He suggests at one point that the whole question of whether or not there are simple entities is nonsense.[127] At another point he seems to play with the idea that simplicity is a relative notion.[128] But his final thoughts on the matter seem to evolve along the following lines. He believes that the quest for analysis makes sense, yet he feels forced to concede that all the entities which we see are complex, so that he is unable to give an example of a simple entity.[129] However, we are acquainted with complex entities, and we are also acquainted with simpler parts of such entities; hence we can know simple objects as the end-product of analysis.[130] In other words, the notion of a simple entity is contained in the two notions of a complex entity and of analysis.[131] This result does not as yet tell us whether there are actually simple entities. Granted that we have the notion of a simple entity, we still have to ask whether there actually are indivisible entities.[132] Perhaps there is no limit to analysis, but Wittgenstein rejects this possibility. He argues that if there are no simple entities,

121. *Ibid.*, p. 62.
122. *Ibid.*, pp. 48, 50, 65.
123. *Ibid.*, p. 50.
124. *Ibid.*, pp. 43, 53, 69.
125. *Ibid.*, pp. 47, 60, 67.
126. *Ibid.*, p. 64.

127. *Ibid.*, p. 45.
128. *Ibid.*, p. 70.
129. *Ibid.*, p. 50.
130. *Ibid.*, pp. 46, 50.
131. *Ibid.*, p. 60.
132. *Ibid.*, p. 62.

then the world would have to be indefinite and could not have the fixed structure which it has.[133] At another point, he argues that there must be simple entities, because otherwise sentences about things could not have a definite sense.[134] However, the reason why there must be simple entities remains rather vague in the *Notebooks*, as vague as it is in the *Tractatus*.[135]

It is obvious that the two horns of the dilemma can be avoided as soon as one realizes that there is a difference between spatial and ontological analysis. A spatial analysis of the chessboard gets us to *smaller* individual things but to individual *things* nevertheless. Why does Wittgenstein confuse the two? Frege, we emphasized, distinguishes between the spatial part-whole relation on the one hand and such connections as predication and class membership on the other.[136] Wittgenstein does not. This is the answer. Yet it occurs to him that there may be a difference, for he raises the question: "Is spatial complexity also logical complexity?"[137] His answer, in this context, is not too certain: "It seems to be yes." What finally convinces him is a curious identification of logic and geometry expressed in the following remark: "The complexity of spatial objects is a logical complexity, for to say that one thing is part of another is always a tautology."[138] No remark could better bring out the difference between Wittgenstein's and Frege's views.

There is an interesting similarity between Wittgenstein's ultimate reason for rejecting ordinary spatial things as ontological simples and his reason for rejecting shades of colors as simple entities.[139] In both cases he believes that certain statements are analytic, or logically necessary, and it is this belief which prevents him from giving examples of simple entities. Wittgenstein, as we just saw, held that sentences about spatial relations among areas (or volumes) are analytic. Since they are analytic, he reasons, spatial analysis is logical analysis. Spatial analysis, however, does not yield perceptible simples. Hence we cannot point at anything and claim that it is a simple entity. The crucial statement in regard to colors, on the other

133. *Ibid.*

134. *Ibid.*, pp. 46, 63, 64.

135. *Tractatus Logico-Philosophicus*, trans. D. F. Pears and B. F. McGuiness (New York, 1961). Compare esp. §§ 2.02, 2.021, 2.0211, 2.0212, 2.026, 3.23.

136. Frege, Wittgenstein, and Russell would undoubtedly call these connections *logical* connections.

137. *Notebooks*, p. 45.

138. *Ibid.*, p. 62.

139. For a detailed discussion of the issue of incompatible colors see E. B. Allaire, "The *Tractatus*: Nominalistic or Realistic?" in *EO*.

hand, concerns the incompatibility of two colors: no surface can be both red and green all over at the same time. Wittgenstein asserts that this is a logical truth.[140] If so, then it follows from the explication of the notion of logical truth in terms of truth-tables that either red or green, or both properties, cannot be simple. But if simple shades of colors are not examples of simple entities (properties), what properties could be? As a consequence, Wittgenstein is unable to give an example of a simple property.[141] In the *Tractatus*, then, Wittgenstein still believes that there are simple entities; but, since he mistakes laws about spatial things and color properties (and relations) for logical (ontological) laws, he is unable to give examples of simple things and simple properties.

This unsatisfactory state of affairs seems to have led Wittgenstein to later repudiate the whole notion of ontological analysis. According to most interpreters of his later philosophy Wittgenstein shows in the *Investigations* that the concepts of absolute complexity and of absolute simplicity, as allegedly used in the *Tractatus*, are groundless. It is argued that a thing may be called simple only relative to a certain purpose, a certain point of view, or in regard to a specific comparison.[142] Whether something is simple or complex is said to depend on the context in which it is considered.[143]

It is quite true, for example, that chemical analysis yields different simple elements than does physical analysis. It is also obvious that it is not always clear what kind of analysis or what kind of simple entity someone has in mind. What is rather surprising is the claim that these obvious facts speak against the view of the *Tractatus*. There can be little doubt that in the *Tractatus* Wittgenstein is not concerned with chemical elements or elementary particles. What he tries to discover are *logical* simples or, as I would prefer to say, *ontological* simples. Hence there exists a definite frame of reference for the question of whether there are simple entities. As far as I can see, in the *Tractatus* Wittgenstein does not at all use an absolute notion of simplicity, whatever that may be. Quite to the contrary, he is searching for the ontological categories of the world. He does confuse spatial with ontological simplicity, as we have seen, but —

---

140. *Tractatus*, § 6.3751.

141. Compare also Wittgenstein's "Remarks on Logical Form," *Aristotelian Society*, supp. vol. IX (1929), 162–71.

142. Compare, for example, G. Pitcher, *The Philosophy of Wittgenstein* (Englewood Cliffs, N.J., 1964), pp. 178–80.

143. *Philosophical Investigations* (Oxford, 1953), § 47.

and this is the crucial point — he confuses the two not because he thinks in terms of absolute simplicity but because he thinks that spatial relations are logical connections.

The real question, then, is not whether there is such a thing as absolute simplicity, whatever that may be, but rather whether there is ontological simplicity. Wittgenstein seems to confuse these two different questions in his later philosophy. Since he believes that there are no absolutely simple entities, he comes to believe that there are no ontological simples. Hence he comes to believe that there is no such enterprise as ontology. The confusion between spatial and ontological analysis, however, is still part and parcel of Wittgenstein's later view. He uses the notion of spatial simplicity to make the point that things are only relatively simple. A white square of a chessboard, he says, is relatively simple when compared with the whole board. One infers that he would say that it is not absolutely simple, because it can be divided into smaller parts. But is not the shade of white of the square a simple entity? Wittgenstein answers that one may consider it simple, but that one may also think of it as composed of pure white and pure yellow. His answer shows that the notion of ontological analysis eludes him. Granted for the sake of the argument that a shade of white may be thought of as composed of pure white and pure yellow, this does not mean that one and the same entity can be conceived of as belonging to different ontological categories. The shade of white is a *property* of individual things, but so are the two colors of which it is supposed to consist. The task of ontology is to list all the categories such that every entity we come across belongs to one of these categories. For the purposes of ontology, it is therefore irrelevant that a shade of white may be conceived of as composed of pure white and pure yellow. If anything, this fact may reinforce the ontologist's conviction that properties form a category.

Frege distinguishes between spatial relations among areas on the one hand and class membership and class inclusion on the other. This is not all. He further distinguishes between all these connections and the one that obtains between an object and a concept under which that object falls. This connection, in turn, is distinguished from the connection between a second-level function and a first-level function. It is also distinguished from the relation of identity. In holding that all concepts are related to objects through the falling-under nexus, Frege rejects all substance-philosophies. Objects have no natures, they are "externally" related to the concepts under which they fall.[144] Hence Frege's objects are of the same kind as the so-called bare particulars some contemporary philosophers defend.[145] To say that an entity is "bare" is merely to say that it has no nature and not, of course, that it has no properties.[146] But to say that individual things do not have natures is also a roundabout way of saying that they form a category, that they are not ontologically complex. Recall now one of the mistakes I mentioned earlier, the view that a description of an individual thing constitutes an ontological analysis of it. This mistake, I believe, is an essential ingredient of all substance-philosophies. Let me explain.

Consider the black pen on my desk. According to my view it is an individual thing. According to the Aristotelian tradition it is a substance.[147] Certain properties of the pen — for example, its color — are called accidents. But substances are also said to have natures (essences). To say that the thing on my desk is a pen is to mention its nature, to say what the essence of that substance is. Is the connection between a substance and its accidents the same as that between the substance and its nature? According to the Aristotelian tradition there is a difference. An accident, it is held, is only externally related to a substance; one and the same substance may be related successively to quite different accidents. A substance remains what it is, regardless of what accidents it has. On the other hand, a nature or essence is not externally connected with a substance. Its relationship with the substance is much more intimate.

According to Frege — and many other philosophers — concepts (properties) cannot be classified as either accidental or essential. All the concepts under which an object falls are equally essential or inessential to that object. As a matter of fact, it is more nearly correct to say that they are all equally inessential, for, the nexus between object and concept — the

144. For the time being, I shall use 'object' for individual things. We must keep in mind, though, that Frege's objects also comprise such entities as truth-values and value-ranges.

145. Compare, for example, *ME* and *LR*; see also *EO*.

146. Sellars does not seem to appreciate this point when he argues that the sentence 'Universals are exemplified by bare particulars' is a self-contradiction. See W. Sellars, "Particulars," in *Science, Perception, and Reality* (London, 1963).

147. Any discussion of this view is severely hampered by the unfortunate tendency of its proponents to slide back and forth between discussing nonmental entities and discussing concepts and propositions in the mind. I shall always talk about nonmental entities in the following discussion.

falling-under relation — is quite similar to the connection which allegedly holds between substances and accidents. Of course, when I speak of the *external* connection between object and concept or between individual thing and property, I merely wish to contrast it with whatever connection there is supposed to be between a substance and its nature. Exemplification is *sui generis*. Hence we do not have to defend the existence of exemplification against possible objections by the Aristotelian; we can insist that it is the very same relation which, according to the Aristotelian, holds between substances and their accidents. What is at stake is the essence of that other connection, which supposedly holds between substances and their natures. One of the most basic reasons why substance-philosophies are untenable is that there is no such connection.

As it has been put by Aristotelians, to say that the thing on my desk is a pen is to say what it really, truly, and essentially *is*. It is not to say that the thing has the (external) property of being a pen. This formulation strongly suggests that the connection between substance and nature is that of *identity*.[148] To say that the thing on my desk is a pen is not to predicate an entity (a property) of *another* entity (an individual thing). Rather, it amounts to a re-identification of entities which only the mind has momentarily separated.[149] However, this way of putting things is not satisfactory, for what could it mean to say that the mind separates an entity from itself? At any rate, if it is correct that a certain substance and a certain nature are identical, then it follows that there is only one entity, which is variously called a nature or a substance. Consequently it is not correct to say that a substance *has* a nature; one must say that a substance *is* a nature.

Let us assume, then, that the statement 'The thing on my desk is a pen' is taken to be an identity statement. Is it an analytic or a synthetic statement? According to Frege's view and mine, it is, of course, a synthetic statement. According to the Aristotelian view it must be analytic, for if it is not analytic to say that a thing is what it is, then nothing else will be.[150] Furthermore, to say what a thing is, according to Aristotelian tradition is

148. Compare, for example, the following works by Henry B. Veatch: *Realism and Nominalism Revisited* (Milwaukee, 1954); and also "On Trying to Say and to Know What's What," *Philosophy and Phenomenological Research*, XXIII (1963), 83–96; and "The Truths of Metaphysics," *Review of Metaphysics*, XVII (1964), 372–95.

149. *Realism and Nominalism Revisited*, pp. 18–19.

150. Compare Veatch's attempts to explain why analytic statements do not appear to be analytic. For a criticism of these attempts, though not from my point of view, see M. S. Gram, "Realism and Necessity Reconsidered," *Review of Metaphysics*, XIX (1966), 565–77.

to "define" the thing; and "definitions," again according to the tradition, state necessary rather than accidental truths. But do we not all feel that the statement 'The thing on my desk is a pen' is synthetic? Even the Aristotelian sometimes admits that we do, but he tries to convince us that our first impression is false, that if we look closer we shall see that statements which appear to be synthetic are in reality analytic. His arguments do not appear to be sound.

Be that as it may, notice that the Aristotelian's problem is similar to the one which Frege later faces in regard to identity. However, according to Frege, the statement 'The morning star is the same as the evening star' does not merely appear to be synthetic, or informative; it actually is. Frege does not deny that certain identity statements are synthetic; on the contrary, he insists that they are. He must then explain how this is possible. Of course, the real difference between the Aristotelian and the Fregean is that the former treats certain statements as identity statements, while the latter thinks of them as predicative statements.

Aside from the difficulties just mentioned, there is an argument that conclusively proves that the statement under consideration cannot be an identity statement. If it were, then it would follow from this statement and another true statement like 'The thing on your desk is a pen' that my pen is your pen — that is, that there is one pen rather than two. Is there any answer to this objection? Can the Aristotelian still maintain that substance and nature are identical?

At this point the Aristotelian usually brings into play a new consideration. He asserts that every substance is its own nature, so that no two substances are the same nature. The fatal argument, he points out, assumes the opposite. Since the word '(a) pen' occurred in both premises, we took it for granted that the same entity was mentioned in both premises. In order to emphasize that the two natures are different, we must distinguish between them terminologically. We may write, for example, 'pen$_1$' and 'pen$_2$.' The thing on my desk is of the nature pen$_1$, while the thing on your desk is of the nature pen$_2$. But why do we have to assume, as the Aristotelian insists, that we are talking about different entities when we say that the thing on my desk is a *pen* and that the thing on your desk is a *pen*? After all, we do not distinguish in English between 'pen$_1$' and 'pen$_2$'; one word suffices. The only reason the Aristotelian gives is that otherwise we shall have to conclude that there is only one pen. While we take for granted that 'pen' represents the same entity in both premises in order to refute the identity thesis, the Aristotelian takes the identity thesis for granted in order to refute our assumption. Indeed, it has been argued that a word like 'pen' cannot represent a universal, because otherwise my pen and your pen would have to be the same substance, that is, the same entity. One concludes, therefore, that natures cannot be universals.[151] What is overlooked is the fact that this argument against a Fregean who accepts universals works only if one can establish *on independent grounds* that the identity thesis is correct.[152]

According to the Aristotelian, there are two substances involved: the thing on my desk and the thing on your desk. The two expressions 'pen$_1$' and 'pen$_2$' represent these different substances. But these two expressions must represent complex entities, as is shown by the fact that we cannot omit from them either the word 'pen' or the indices. If we omit 'pen,' then we no longer have an expression for *what* the two things are, for their nature; if we omit the indices, then we are faced with the unacceptable conclusion that the two pens are one pen. Substances, it transpires, must be complex entities.[153] We might be tempted to say that a substance consists of form and matter; the word 'pen' indicates the form of the substance, and the index indicates its matter. If we make this move, then we have to face the whole dialectic of thing and property once more, and we shall also have to face the realism-nominalism issue on another level. For we may now ask whether forms are universals while matter constitutes the individuating factor. Moreover, we must also ask how form and matter are related. Obviously they cannot be identical; if we assume that they are, then we merely introduce another round of arguments of the type mentioned earlier. And it really makes no sense, within the Aristotelian tradition, to hold that form and matter are the same. However, if we assume that the connection between form and matter is not that of identity,

151. The term 'universal,' as I use it here, is not necessarily a mental entity, a concept in the mind. Rather, a universal is an entity which is predicative, that is, an entity which can be exemplified by individual things. Individuals, though they can exemplify many universals, are not universals, because they are not exemplified by anything.

152. Compare, for example, F. Copleston, *A History of Philosophy* (Garden City, Image Book ed., 1962), II, pt. 1, 168.

153. Alternatively, the Aristotelian ontology has been defended by the thesis that identity between properties is not the same as identity between individuals. See, for example, I. M. Bochenski, "The Problem of Universals," in *The Problem of Universals*. I do not think that this thesis can be maintained. Sameness, it seems to me as it seemed to Frege, is the same for all kinds of entities; every entity of any kind is what it is and nothing else. That this impression is correct is shown by the fact that no coherent explication of that other kind of identity has ever been given.

what else could it be? Structurally speaking, we might just as well say that pieces of matter are individual things (objects), that forms are properties (concepts), and that the former exemplify the latter.[154]

Of course, an Aristotelian cannot accept this interpretation, for, according to it, the expression 'the thing on my desk' represents a piece of matter. The Aristotelian insists that the thing on my desk is a substance and not just a *bare* piece of matter. But a substance, as we have seen, is a complex entity, said to consist of matter and form. An expression like 'this pen' may be thought to show this fact most clearly. There is a piece of matter, represented by 'this,' and there is a form, represented by 'pen.' The connection between matter and form, it is true, is not mirrored in the expression. How could we make it explicit? Consider the sentence 'This pen is black.' I am prepared to argue that this sentence says the same as the sentence 'This thing, which is a pen, is black.' If so, then there can be no doubt as to what the connection between matter and form must be. It is nothing else but the nexus of exemplification. But if a substance turns out to be a piece of matter exemplifying a certain form, then it is what other philosophers have called a *state of affairs*.

Whether an Aristotelian agrees with this diagnosis depends on how seriously he takes the view that a substance consists of matter and form. Some Aristotelians, it appears to me, wish to stop the argument on the level of substance, nature, and accident. As a result, they are forced to hold, in some form or another, that substances are simple and yet complex.[155] We have seen why they must be complex. By holding simultaneously that they are simple, these Aristotelians try to keep the lid on the Pandora's box containing the issues of individuation and universals.

The most crucial difference between the Aristotelian and a Fregean is this: According to the Fregean, an expression like 'the pen on my desk' represents a "bare" object, a "simple" individual thing. It does not represent a complex entity consisting of an individual, exemplification, and a property. In particular, it does not represent a state of affairs. According to the Aristotelian, on the other hand, such an expression represents a sub-

154. The matter-form relation, I hasten to add, seems to me to be thought of in analogy to the spatial part-whole relation rather than to the exemplification nexus. This, I think, is one of the features of the matter-form schema which is directed against Platonism.

155. It is at this point that the Aristotelian takes refuge in all kinds of spurious doctrines. He may introduce irrelevant epistemological considerations. For example, he may say that concepts in the mind are *applicable* to many things. Or he may espouse the untenable thesis that there are common names. Compare, for example, *SM*; and also my paper "Common Names," in *EO*.

stance, that is, an entity which according to our analysis must be complex. The crucial step which leads to the Aristotelian view is the assumption that we do not just describe an "external" property of a thing when we say that it is a pen, but that we thereby mention a *constituent* of the thing. I wish to emphasize that this step is in the wrong direction, because it is sometimes taken by philosophers who, in other respects, belong to the tradition of Frege and Russell rather than to that of Aristotle and Aquinas.

Assume that there are two black pens on my desk. According to some philosophers, the general dialectic of sameness and difference forces us to hold that each of the two pens consists of a particular (individual entity) and (at least) a universal.[156] Each pen must contain a particular, because no other view solves the problem of individuation. Each pen must also contain a universal, because no other view explains the fact that the pens have the same color. Furthermore, particulars are said to exemplify universals. A particular's exemplification of a universal is a state of affairs. Hence each pen, it is said, is really a state of affairs.[157]

Something must have gone wrong, it seems to me. A pen on my desk is an individual thing, or, as Frege would say, an object. It is not at all a state of affairs. That the pen is black, that it is on my desk, that the thing on my desk is a pen — all these are states of affairs, but the pen itself is not. What has gone wrong, I suggest, is that one assumes implicitly that the properties of an individual thing are *constituents* of the thing. Sometimes, this assumption occurs quite explicitly. Allaire, for example, claims that the entity represented by the expression 'the pen on my desk' is, *at the minimum*, its (nonrelational) properties. He continues:

'The pen on my desk' denotes a *thing*. The issue is whether or not a thing also contains a particular, an entity which is different in kind and wholly distinct from properties. If that is the way the issue is best expressed, then we can easily explicate this fundamental ontological question: What is a thing? It means: Does a thing consist of just its properties or does it also contain a particular? [158]

156. Compare, for example, G. Bergmann's *ME* and *LR*; see also *EO*.
157. I used to hold this view myself. Compare, for example, *SM*.
158. E. B. Allaire, "Ontology and Acquaintance: A Reply to Clatterbaugh," *Philosophy of Science*, XXXII (1965), p. 279. I have changed the example so that it is the same as in the discussion here.

If I am right, then the pen on my desk *is* not (at the minimum) its properties. It is not (at the minimum) *identical* with its properties. It does not *consist* (at least) of properties. Rather, the pen on my desk *has* properties; it *exemplifies* properties. To say, for example, that the pen on my desk is black is to describe the pen as *having* a certain color; it is not to mention a *constituent* of the pen. In what sense of 'consist' could one reasonably claim that the pen consists of properties?

For the reasons explained earlier, one cannot hold that the pen is the same as its properties nor that the pen consists of properties in the same way as it consists of spatial parts. By saying that the pen consists of properties, we cannot mean that it has properties as a class has members. The view that the pen is simply a class of properties is untenable.[159] But consider a state of affairs, say, that the pen on my desk is black. We may say that this state of affairs consists (at least) of an individual thing, the pen, and a property, its color. This sense of 'consists,' I believe, is irreducible.[160] That it is neither the spatial nor the membership notion is clear. Now *if* the pen were the same as some such state of affairs as that the thing on my desk is a pen or that the pen on my desk is black, *then* it would make sense to say that it consists of properties. But it is obvious to me that the pen is not such a state of affairs.

The same confusion between individual things and states of affairs occurs in certain formulations of the problem of individuation. Consider again two black pens. As it has been put, the pens are numerically distinct but qualitatively the same (in regard to color, or in regard to being pens). Hence they must consist, one argues, in part of particulars and in part of universals. But to say that the pens are qualitatively the same is not to say that they are the same in some *part* or *constituent*. Rather, it merely means that they *have* the same color or that they *are* both pens. It means that these two individual things *exemplify* certain properties. I agree, however, that, unless there were properties, individual things could not *share* such properties; and unless there were individual things, there would be no *different* things to share them. In brief, I agree that there are both "particulars" and "universals" as categorial kinds. Furthermore, I

159. Compare, for example, H. Hochberg, "Things and Descriptions," *American Philosophical Quarterly*, III (1966), 1–9. The membership relation must not be confused with quite a different relation, namely, the so-called coexemplification relation which may be said to hold among all the properties of the pen.

160. On it rests the notion of ontological analysis, as I mentioned in footnote 116 above.

agree that there are states of affairs. In fact, there is only one point on which I disagree with the ontological view under discussion. According to that view, such ordinary things as pens or chairs are states of affairs which consist of particulars and universals, while I believe that they are individual things (particulars).

The disagreement may appear to be trivial, but I think that it has at least one important consequence. If one believes that a pen, for example, is a state of affairs which consists of properties and a particular, then he has a difficult time answering the epistemological question of how we are acquainted with particulars. This is the reason why some philosophers who agree that there are particulars cannot agree on whether or how we are acquainted with them.[161] Other philosophers eventually reached the conclusion that particulars cannot exist, because we are not acquainted with them.[162]

What is the epistemological problem? Everyone agrees that we see such things as pens, chairs, and mountains. Everyone agrees that we see certain properties of pens, chairs, and mountains — for example, their colors. But almost no one claims that he can see particulars. Yet, particulars are presumably "contained" in pens, chairs, and mountains. In arguing against an ontology of particulars, one usually reasons that, no matter how attentively one looks, one sees pens, chairs, and mountains; one also sees their colors; but one does not see particulars. Of course one doesn't. One does not see particulars *in addition* to pens and their properties, because pens are particulars, or, as I prefer to say, individual things. If you admit that you see such things as pens, mountains, and chairs, then you have admitted that you see particulars. Of course, to say that we see an individual thing when we see a pen is not to claim that we think of ontology when we see a pen. Neither the word 'individual thing' nor the notion of an ontological category needs to flash through our mind when we see a pen. What we see when we see a pen is the kind of entity which a philosopher,

---

161. Compare, for example, G. Bergmann, "Synthetic *A Priori*," in *LR*; E. B. Allaire, "Bare Particulars," in *EO*; Allaire, "Another Look at Bare Particulars," *Philosophical Studies*, XVI (1965), 16–21; K. Clatterbaugh, "General Ontology and the Principle of Acquaintance," *Philosophy of Science*, XXXII (1965), 272–76; and E. B. Allaire, "Ontology and Acquaintance: A Reply to Clatterbaugh," *ibid.*, pp. 277–80.

162. See, for example, a series of articles by H. Hochberg: "Universals, Particulars, and Predication," *Review of Metaphysics*, XIX (1965), 87–102; "On Being and Being Presented," *Philosophy of Science*, XXXII (1965), 123–36; and "Things and Descriptions," *American Philosophical Quarterly*, III (1966), 1–9.

with his extraordinary interests, calls an object, an individual thing, or a bare particular.

I claim that we see Fregean objects, bare particulars, or individual things. But how can I prove it? Well, we see this fountain pen on my desk; and this fountain pen is an individual thing. Hence we do see individual things. No doubt, to some philosophers, this proof will appear too easy, but I do not know how else to argue for the existence and perception of individual things. Many further points, of course, need to be discussed. But after everything has been said and done, after all the actual and possible confusions of other positions have been dispelled, what better way is there to defend an ontology of individual things than to show that we see individual things whenever we open our eyes?[163] The burden of proof, I believe, rests with Frege's opponent. If the pen on my desk is not an entity which differs in significant respects from the properties it has and the relations in which it stands to other things, then I would like to know just what kind of entity it is supposed to be.

To sum up some of our most important results: Frege's objects — excluding truth-values and other extraordinary entities — are simple entities. They do not in any sense of the term consist of entities of further categories. They form a category. A pen on my desk has spatial parts, but these spatial parts are not its ontological constituents. Frege insists that the spatial analysis of an object must not be confused with ontological analysis. Spatial analysis does not yield entities of different categories; it merely yields smaller individual things. And though it may be true that spatial analysis has no lower limit, the same does not hold for ontological analysis.

Being simple, Fregean objects have no natures or, rather, are no natures. Nor do they contain properties of any kind. Hence they are what other philosophers call bare particulars and what I call individual things. In this connection, I argued that such entities as pens or chairs do not contain objects or individual things. My argument, I think, may shed some light on the epistemological problem of how we are acquainted with objects in particular and categorial kinds in general.

163. I disagree sharply with the claim that one can defend the existence of an ontological category by dialectical means alone. Ontology, as I understand it, aims at a description of the categorial features of the *perceptual world*.

REDUCTION

'l HE PROBLEM OF IDENTITY comes to the fore in the *Grundlagen*, but Frege does not propose a solution. We know, of course, that he solves it to his own satisfaction in a later paper. We might, therefore, have delayed the discussion of identity until the next chapter, but a number of considerations persuaded me to close this chapter with a section on identity and analyticity. Foremost among these is the fact that the problem of identity becomes so important in the *Grundlagen* that Frege's inability to solve it there threatens his attempt to lay the foundations of arithmetic. His analysis of the concept of number and his attempted proof that arithmetic is analytic rest so firmly on the notion of identity that, without a clear understanding of this notion, these other achievements seem to be built on quicksand. It seems to me that the *Grundlagen* contains more than one sign of an uneasy awareness of the unfinished task of solving the problem of identity.

However, it is not easy to explain the problem as it appears in the *Grundlagen*; too many other problems threaten to intrude. Nor is it easy to explain some of Frege's philosophical moves without taking a stand on some very fundamental issues. I shall start out with a brief description of Frege's conception of the basic problems of the philosophy of arithmetic. Then I shall discuss his answer to the question: What are numbers? Next, I shall describe Frege's attempts to derive arithmetic from logic. In this context, we shall have to consider his successive attempts to define numbers. I shall make several important assumptions, without any extensive argument, in order to show the significance of the attempted definitions for the derivation of arithmetic from logic. This will reveal the importance of identity for Frege's enterprise.

The structure of the *Grundlagen* leaves little doubt that, according to Frege, two problems constitute the philosophy of arithmetic. The first problem concerns the nature of numbers, the second the nature of arithmetical propositions. To ask what numbers are is to ask, within a philosophical context, to what category numbers belong. Consequently, the question divides, for Frege, into two, more specific ones. First, are numbers mental or nonmental entities? Second, are numbers objects or concepts (functions)?

The second main problem is whether and in what sense arithmetical propositions are necessary. This divides into two specific questions. First,

108

are arithmetical propositions analytic or synthetic? Second, are they known *a priori* or *a posteriori*?

I think that Frege's solution of the first problem is partly right and partly wrong. I agree with him that numbers are not mental entities, but I think that he is wrong in holding that they are objects. In regard to the second main problem, we shall see that the question of whether arithmetic can be reduced to logic allows for a straight answer if we sufficiently clarify the notion of reduction. Frege's technical achievements in this field are generally recognized and uncontroversial. Up to a point, he did indeed succeed in showing that arithmetic is analytic and hence known *a priori*. I shall try to show precisely where that point is.

Numbers, according to Frege, are nonmental objects. That they are not subjective mental entities I shall always take for granted, but I do not think that they are objects, in Frege's sense of the term. Rather, they are concepts of the second level (as Frege would say), or quantifiers (as I shall say).[164]

It must be stressed that Frege comes very close to saying that numbers are concepts within which other concepts fall. He very nearly says that in my terminology numbers are quantifiers. See, for example, the following passage:

If I say 'Venus has 0 moons,' there simply does not exist any moon or agglomeration of moons for anything to be asserted of; but what happens is that a property is assigned to the *concept* "moon of Venus," namely, that of including nothing under it. If I say 'The king's carriage is drawn by 4 horses,' then I assign the number 4 to the concept "horse that draws the king's carriage." [165]

What Frege seems to be saying here and at other places is this: When I say that Venus has some moons, I assign a property to the concept *moon of Venus*, namely, the property of including some (individual) things under it. Similarly, when I say that Venus has 0 moons or that Venus has 5 moons, I assign to the concept *moon of Venus* the properties of including nothing or of including 5 things under it. Now, the so-called property

164. We must keep in mind that Frege's concepts of second level are quantifiers, not ordinary properties of properties. According to Russell and other philosophers, numbers are properties of properties (or classes of classes), but this is not the same as the view that they are concepts within which concepts fall, as expressed in Frege's terminology.

165. *F*, p. 59.

of including so many things under it is not an ordinary property of properties. This fact appears quite clearly when we turn to the symbolism of *Principia Mathematica*. For example, that there are some moons of Venus, that the property of being a moon of Venus is such that some things fall under it, is expressed in the well-known manner by means of the "existential" quantifier. On the other hand, the fact that, say, green is a color, that the property green has the property of being a color, is not expressed by means of a quantifier at all. In order to distinguish between these two different cases, it will be best to avoid speaking of the *property* of having so many things fall under a property. If we make this distinction, we shall be less tempted to think of numbers as properties of properties (or classes of classes). If we keep in mind that the "property" of having a certain number of things fall under a property is like the "property" of having some things fall under a property and not like a property of properties like color, we shall be able to see clearly that numbers belong to the category of quantifiers and not to the category of properties (or classes). And only if we realize that numbers are quantifiers can we understand why numbers do not belong to a type hierarchy. Just as we mean the same thing by 'some' (or 'all') when we speak of some individual things, some properties, some properties of properties, and so on, so we mean the same thing by '4' when we say there are 4 individual things, 4 properties, 4 properties of properties, and so forth. Just as there is only one quantifier represented by 'some,' so there is only one number represented by '4.'[166] Numbers as quantifiers are indifferent to the type distinction.

Even though Frege comes very close to holding what I consider to be the correct view, there can be no doubt that he wishes to hold that numbers are objects rather than concepts of the second level. He realizes, of course, that a sentence like "The content of a statement of number is an assertion about a concept" may give the mistaken impression that he views numbers as higher concepts. Hence he tries to dispel this impression by claiming (a) that the sign '0' is only an element of the predicate 'the number 0 belongs to,' (b) that we speak of *the* number 0, using the definite article, and (c) that it is impossible to speak of 0's, 1's, 2's, etc., in plural.[167] He also mentions that arithmetical statements are essentially identity statements.

166. As I use the expression, the *quantifier* 'some' is only part of the expression 'some entities.' For example, the familiar symbols '(x)' and '$(\exists x)$' are in my opinion complex: They contain an expression for a quantifier and an individual variable.

167. *F*, pp. 68–69, 80n.

Frege's first claim does not go very far in showing that numbers must be objects rather than concepts of second level. We may say such things as 'The number 2 belongs to the confept *F*.' We may also leave out the word 'number' and say instead: 'There are 2 things which are *F*.' And this we could abbreviate, in analogy to the abbreviation for 'There are some things which are *F*,' by the expression '$(2x)\ F(x)$.' As a matter of fact, if we have to choose among different possible ways of saying that there are 2 elephants in the zoo, the very best way of saying this is the one which I just used, rather than the stilted Fregean sentence 'The number 2 belongs to the concept *being an elephant in the zoo*.' I take it, though, that the expression 'There are 2 elephants in the zoo' is merely short for the expression 'There are 2 things which are elephants in the zoo,' just as 'There are some elephants in the zoo' is short for 'There are some things which are elephants in the zoo.'

At any rate, from the fact, if fact it is, that '2' is only a part of the predicate 'the number 2 belongs to,' it does not follow that this part represents an object. It does not follow from the fact that 'green' is part of the predicate 'the color green belongs to' that 'green' represents an object. Nor does it follow, of course, that 'green' does not represent an object. The real question is what the expression 'the number 2' represents. This leads us to Frege's second claim.

His second reason stands or falls with the soundness of his contention that the definite singular article always indicates a proper name rather than a concept word. I have already discussed this part of Frege's philosophy and have tried to show that it is not sound. A definite description need not be the description of an object; there are also definite descriptions of concepts. In the case of the expression 'the number 2,' we have neither a description of an object nor a description of a concept (of first level). Rather, we have a description of a quantifier.[168] This description describes the entity which is represented by the numeral '2.'

If numbers were first-level concepts, then we would expect to be able to form a plural for number words. Since number words do not allow us to form a plural, as Frege correctly observes, we may conclude that numbers are not first-level concepts. But we must not infer from this conclusion that numbers are objects. There remains the possibility that they are con-

168. We could not formulate such a description within the framework of *PM*. Nor, of course, could we say by means of *PM* many of the things which have been said here. For example, we cannot talk about entities in general. The price we pay for the unlimited expressive power of English is a certain amount of ambiguity and the possibility of formal paradox.

cepts of the second level (quantifiers). Indeed, it is equally impossible to form a plural for a quantifier like 'some' or 'all.' In general, it is impossible to form a plural for all those entities which do not have other entities falling under them, that is, for entities which are not predicative. We can speak of tigers because there are (individual) things which are a tiger, and we can speak of colors because there are properties which are a color. But we cannot speak of 2's or 3's, because there are no entities which are — in the sense of exemplify — a two or a three. Frege's third reason shows not that numbers must be objects but that they cannot be concepts of the first level. Numbers are not ordinary properties either of individual things or of other properties.

Frege seems to reason that numbers must be objects since they are mentioned most prominently in identity statements where they are not predicated of anything.[169] I do not consider this a very convincing reason. First of all, it is not clear, as Frege believes it is, that concepts must always occur predicatively. I think it is possible to conceive of the statement '2 + 2 = 4' in analogy to the statement 'blue and yellow yield green' insofar as the predicative nature of properties is concerned. Second, even if we assume that ordinary concepts always occur predicatively, the same rule may not hold for concepts of second level. Taking as our paradigm of such a concept the quantifier *some*, it seems to me that quantifiers never occur predicatively and also that we may have an "arithmetic" of ordinary quantifiers.[170] Consider, for example, the three "logical" quantifiers *all*, *some*, and *none*. Let us agree to mean by 'some' at least one, but not all.[171] We can then formulate the following true statements: all — some = some, some — some = some or none, some + some = some or all, and so forth. Since quantifiers do not belong to certain types, it makes no difference whether we think of these statements as applicable to individual things, or properties, or properties of properties.

However, there is the possibility that Frege's fourth and last reason must be interpreted differently than in the last paragraph. At a later stage of his philosophical development, Frege holds that there can be no iden-

---

169. *F*, pp. 68–69.

170. Frege's concept of second level is not precisely the same as what I call a quantifier. In order to avoid misunderstandings, let me emphasize again that from my point of view such a second-level concept is really a complex entity consisting of a quantifier and some category.

171. This is not a "definition" of 'some.' We all know what the word means. My explanation is intended to exclude certain doubtful cases, in order to have a more precise notion.

tity statements for concepts. If we assume that this law holds for concepts of any level, and if we further assume that arithmetical statements are really identity statements, then it follows that numbers must be objects rather than concepts.[172] Now, if Frege's reason for holding that identity does not obtain between concepts is simply the one mentioned above, that expressions in identity statements do not occur predicatively, then we have no new argument for his contention that numbers are objects. But Frege may have still another reason, and if so, then he would also have another argument for his contention. We shall return to this possibility later.

None of the four reasons so far considered sounds convincing. Also, some of Frege's most telling arguments seem to show that numbers are not objects but concepts of the second level. We may therefore suspect that some hidden reason is responsible for Frege's insistence that numbers are objects. Frege actually "defines" the number which belongs to the concept *F* as the *extension* of the concept *similar to F*. Numbers are "defined" as extensions, and extensions, according to Frege, are objects. Hence one could claim that it is his "definition" of numbers which forces him to insist that they must be objects. The reasons which we have just analyzed may be adduced to defend this particular kind of "definition." Looked at in this way, the order of presentation of Frege's case that numbers must be objects is not the same as his actual line of reasoning; what really convinces him are not the considerations just criticized, but rather the *success* of his "definition" of numbers as extensions.

In a footnote, Frege remarks that he could have "defined" numbers not as extensions of concepts but as concepts.[173] He also notes that this way of "defining" numbers would have invited two objections: first, that a definition of numbers as concepts contradicts his assertion that numbers are objects rather than concepts; and second, that two concepts can have the same extension without being identical. However, Frege also claims in that footnote that both objections can be met. He does not explain how, nor does he give us the slightest clue. Can we reconcile the footnote with the interpretation of the last paragraph?

One could reasonably argue that the two objections cannot, in fact, be met within the general framework of Frege's theory. Thus Frege really has no choice; numbers must be extensions and, hence, objects. To be

---

172. Assuming, of course, that Frege's division of entities into concepts (functions) and objects is exhaustive. I do not think that it is, but this is not at issue here.

173. *F*, p. 80.

more accurate, the second objection cannot be met, and thus the first objection will not arise. It is therefore the second objection which ultimately forces Frege to insist that numbers are objects. Assume that the number of *F* is "defined" as the concept *similar to F*. The number of *G* is then the concept *similar to G*. Assume further that there are as many things which are *F* as there are things which are *G*. Then the number of *F* is the same as the number of *G*. According to the "definition," however, *F* and *G* do not have the same number; for the concept *similar to F* is quite obviously not the same concept as the concept *similar to G*, even though the two concepts have the same extension.[174] According to the objectionable "definition," no two concepts could have the same number.

There is a possibility that we have misinterpreted Frege's remarks in the footnote. By saying that he could write 'the concept *similar to F*' instead of 'the extension of the concept *similar to F*,' Frege might not mean at all that numbers could be "defined" as concepts rather than objects. We must recall that an expression like 'the concept so-and-so' represents, according to Frege, an object and not a concept. Therefore, what he may mean is that numbers can be "defined" as objects without having to be "defined" as extensions; for we may safely assume that expressions of the type 'the concept *F*' do not represent extensions or classes.[175] If this is what Frege has in mind, then he can perhaps answer the second objection. While it is quite obvious that the concept *similar to F* is different from the concept *similar to G*, it is not equally obvious that the two expressions 'the concept *similar to F*' and 'the concept *similar to G*' must represent different objects.[176] Perhaps one may hold that these two expressions name the same object.

Be that as it may, according to either one of our two interpretations of the footnote, Frege seems to be forced to "define" numbers as objects. Hence there remains the possibility that the success of his "definition," rather than the reasons which he explicitly mentions, persuaded Frege that numbers are objects.

174. Always assuming, of course, that there are such entities as the concept *similar to F* and the concept *similar to G*. What I said earlier about the so-called properties of being identical with *a* and being both green and round holds naturally also for such properties as the ones just mentioned.

175. R. Wells calls these strange objects *concept-correlates*. (Compare his article "Frege's Ontology," *Review of Metaphysics*, IV [1951], 537–73.) Frege never explains in detail what kinds of entities they are.

176. This is one of the places where I cannot make my point and at the same time do justice to Frege's view about the definite article.

By stating that numbers are nonmental objects, Frege has completely answered the philosophical question of what numbers are. He has assigned numbers to a certain category of entities, and that is all a philosopher needs to do in this context. His attempts to "define" numbers belong to an entirely different enterprise. They are important for his program of deriving arithmetic from logic and, hence, for his attempt to clarify the nature of arithmetical propositions. This fact will become more obvious as we proceed in our present inquiry. But in anticipation of one of my main contentions, I wish to stress at this point that there is a fundamental difference between claiming that numbers belong to a certain category and "defining" them in the Fregean manner. We deal here, if I may put it so, with two kinds of analysis. On the one hand, there is ontological analysis, which aims at a list and description of the ontological kind of entities. On the other hand, there is logical analysis, whose aim is to find out what states of affairs are logically equivalent to what other states of affairs. The so-called reduction of arithmetic to logic involves this second kind of analysis.

In the *Grundlagen*, Frege's aim is to make it "probable that the laws of arithmetic are analytic judgments and consequently *a priori*. Arithmetic thus becomes simply a development of logic, and every proposition of arithmetic a law of logic, albeit a derivative one."[177] The "reduction" of arithmetic to logic thus rests on the idea that arithmetic is analytic. The connection between this notion of reduction and the concept of analyticity becomes clear from Frege's explanation that a proposition is analytic if and only if, in finding the proof for it, "we come only on general logical laws and on definitions, . . . bearing in mind that we must take account also of all propositions upon which the admissibility of any of the definitions depends."[178] I take it that this explanation is reasonably clear as far as the conception of logical laws is concerned. I think that most philosophers can agree what these logical laws are, namely, the usual theorems of the higher functional calculus (with the exceptions, of course, of the axiom of infinity and the axiom of choice). In any specific case, we can always consult Frege's logical system as outlined in either the *Begriffsschrift* or the *Grundgesetze*, or we can turn to *Principia Mathematica*.

---

177. *F*, p. 99.
178. *Ibid*., p. 4.

However, the role which definitions play in Frege's explication of analyticity is not clear at all. Frege mentions that definitions may depend on certain propositions. But how could they? If by means of a definition we merely confer a well-known meaning or sense to an arbitrary sign, then it is hard to see how there could be any propositions which would prevent us from going about this arbitrary and purely conventional business of introducing shorter expressions for longer ones. It seems that Frege must mean by the term 'definition' something other than a mere abbreviation. If so, then it is not the unproblematic notion of a linguistic convention by means of which we assign some meaning to an expression which either has had no previous meaning or is supposed to have had no meaning. Frege describes definitions as being fruitful, as having to prove their worth, as being admissible or not, and so forth.[179] This raises the question of how he conceives of them if he does not consider them abbreviations.

In the *Grundlagen*, there is no clear view on definitions.[180] This is partly owing to the fact that neither is there any clear view on identity, for Frege believes that the two notions are intimately connected. Every definition, he implies, turns into a judgment of identity.[181] In other words, he seems to hold that definitions are always identity statements. Hence we may expect to get a clarification of the former notion through the latter.

In order to clearly see how confused Frege was in the matter of definitions, consider his assessment of their function.[182] Pointing out that the definitions of the *Grundlagen* do not simply specify a concept in terms of a list of characteristics, he tries to explain their role by means of a geometrical illustration. Let concepts be represented by certain well-demar-

179. However, we also find the following remark in the *Grundlagen*: "The definition of an object does not, as such, really assert anything about the object, but only lays down the meaning of a symbol" (p. 78). Compare also the following passage from the *Grundgesetze*: "In order now to introduce new signs in terms of those already familiar, we require the *double-stroke of definition*, which appears as an iterated judgment-stroke coupled with a horizontal:

$$'|\!\!|\!\!-'$$

and which is used in place of the judgment-stroke where something is to be, not judged, but abbreviated by definition. We introduce a new name by means of a *definition* by stipulating that it is to have the same sense and the same denotation as some name composed of signs that are familiar" (p. 27).

180. We shall see that such a view emerges only much later in an unpublished manuscript.

181. *F*, pp. 78–79. In his review of Husserl's *Philosophie der Arithmetik*, Frege says: "Since every definition is an identity statement [*Gleichung*], one can not define identity itself" (*Zeitschrift für Philosophie und philosophische Kritik*, CIII (1894), p. 320).

182. *F*, pp. 100–101.

cated areas in a plane. A concept defined by a list of characteristics corresponds to an area common to all those areas which represent the defining characteristics. No new line is drawn. We merely trace already existing lines in such a way that the new area contains several of the original areas. What Frege has in mind is quite obvious. Consider the two concepts (characteristics) *red* and *square*. We can introduce a new sign 'rere' with the stipulation that it shall be short for 'red and square.' Thus, instead of saying 'such-and-such is red and square,' we can always say 'such-and-such is rere.' That nothing new emerges in this process is quite obvious. Frege wishes to contrast the "fruitful" definitions of the *Grundlagen* with this kind of linguistic convention, but he does not succeed. The type of definition employed in the *Grundlagen*, he says, is a matter of drawing boundaries which did not previously exist. "What we shall be able to infer from it, cannot be inspected in advance; here, we are not simply taking out of the box again what we have just put into it." Now, if we assume that the whole plane is divided up into areas and that these areas represent simple concepts, then it would be impossible for us to draw any new boundary lines. We cannot assume that the lines which enclose simple concepts can be filled in by us; for we do not "create" simple concepts but merely "discover" them. When we discover that a certain complex concept consists of certain simple concepts, we do not draw boundaries which did not previously exist; we merely trace within the larger area certain lines which are already there. But nothing essentially new emerges in this process either. We merely take out of the complex concept, if I may put it so, what it contains. We find out, for example, that the area represented by the term 'bachelor' is contained in larger areas represented by such words as 'male' and 'unmarried.' This, too, is merely a linguistic matter. Other people in the past have found it convenient to abbreviate a longer expression by the shorter word 'bachelor.' Just as we may introduce new abbreviations, so we may ask ourselves on other occasions whether a common expression already is an abbreviation and, if it is, what it abbreviates. Obviously, these two processes must be distinguished. Nonetheless, it is common to say that one defines a term both when one introduces for the first time a new expression for a complicated common expression and when one reports that someone else has already abbreviated a complicated expression by a shorter, common one.

Perhaps there are other interpretations of Frege's illustration. I find it highly significant that he resorts to using a metaphor when he tries to explain the nature of fruitful definitions. Perhaps we can glimpse what their nature is, not from Frege's explication but from the actual definitions. Let us look at his attempts to define number.

Frege's first attempt follows a suggestion by Leibniz.[183] The individual numbers are "defined" by "defining," first, the numbers 0 and 1, and, second, the step from a given number to its successor.[184] The number 0 is "defined" as follows: The number 0 belongs to a concept if the proposition that *a* does not fall under that concept is true universally, whatever *a* may be. The "definition" of 1 is: The number 1 belongs to a concept *F* if the proposition that *a* does not fall under *F* is not true universally, whatever *a* may be, and if from the propositions '*a* falls under *F*' and '*b* falls under *F*' it follows universally that *a* and *b* are the same. Finally, the third "definition" runs as follows: The number (n + 1) belongs to a concept *F* if there is an object *a* falling under *F* and such that the number *n* belongs to the concept *falling under F, but not a.*[185]

In order to see how these "definitions" may be used to "reduce" arithmetic to logic, let us recall the following well-known additional steps that must be taken. By means of the "definitions" just mentioned, one can "define" the rest of the integers. For example, the number 2 is "defined" as the successor of the number 1. In this manner, every numerical expression like 'a concept has a certain number' can be "replaced" by an expression which consists solely of logical signs, that is, variables, connectives, identity, and the two standard quantifiers. Next, one "defines" the usual arithmetical operations. Addition, for example, is "defined" as follows: The sum of the two numbers *n* and *m* belongs to a concept *F*, if there is a concept *G* and there is a concept *H* such that (a) any individual falls under *F* if and only if it falls under *G* or *H*, (b) there is no individual which falls both

183. *Ibid.*, pp. 67–69.

184. I shall have to use in my exposition such highly problematic terms as 'definition' and 'reduction,' but I shall continue to indicate on occasion that these terms are problematic by putting them in quotation marks.

185. According to my view, these three "definitions" are really the following three equivalence statements:

(1) $(Af) [(ox) f(x) \equiv (Ax) \sim f(x)]$

(2) $(Af) [(1x) f(x) \equiv (Sx) (y) [f(y) \equiv (x = y)]]$

(3) $(Af) [(n + 1x) f(x) \equiv (Sx) [f(x) \& (ny) (f(y) \& y \neq x)]]$, where it must be added that '*n*' ranges over numbers, that is, certain quantifiers.

under G and H, and (c) n belongs to G and m belongs to H. By means of this "definition," we get, for every arithmetical expression which "predicates" the *sum* of two numbers of a concept, another expression which does not contain the arithmetical notion of a sum. Finally, consider an arithmetical statement like '$1 + 1 = 2$.' By means of the previous "definitions" we can now "transform" this arithmetical truth into a logical statement.[186] Moreover, and this is the crux of the matter, this logical statement is a logical truth.[187]

However, Frege does not think that his three "definitions" are satisfactory. He objects, first, that the last "definition" presupposes that we know what the expression 'the number n belongs to F' means. The definition presupposes that we already know what numbers are. Hence we can never, by means of the three "definitions," decide "whether any concept has the number *Julius Caesar* belonging to it, or whether that same familiar conqueror of Gaul is a number or not." [188] Frege is, of course, perfectly correct. The third "definition" (and also our "definition" of sum) contains not only logical terms but also the arithmetical notion of being a number. This fact can also be described in the following way. The definiens of the third "definition" (and of our "definition" of sum) contains not only the usual (logical) variables but also the sign 'n.' This variable is supposed to range over numbers; it is not one of the usual logical variables ranging over individual things, properties of individual things, etc. The definiens of the third "definition" (and of the "definition" of sum) is not a purely logical expression. Of course, instead of accepting the third "definition," as Frege himself points out, we could construct a series of "definitions" — "defining" first the expression 'the number $1 + 1$ belongs to F,' then the expression 'the number $1 + 1 + 1$ belongs to F,' etc. But this would not provide us with a "definition" of the notion of being a number.

Frege's second objection is that the three "definitions" do not allow us to prove that "if the number a belongs to the concept F and the number b belongs to the same concept, then necessarily $a = b$. Thus we should be unable to justify the expression '*the* number which belongs to the concept F,' and therefore should find it impossible in general to prove numerical

---

186. This is not quite accurate, as we shall see in the next paragraph.

187. I call a statement a logical truth if it is true and if it mentions nothing but the usual logical entities: connectives. Compare pp. 141–42 below.

188. *F*, p. 68.

identity, since we should be quite unable to achieve a determinate number."[189]

This objection rests on Frege's dogma that numbers are objects. According to Frege, "It is only an illusion that we have defined 0 and 1; in reality we have only fixed the sense of the phrases 'the number 0 belongs to' [and] 'the number 1 belongs to'; but we have no authority to pick out the 0 and 1 here as self-subsistent objects that can be recognized as the same again."[190] In order to understand Frege's thoughts, it is necessary, I think, for us to realize that his point could be made equally well for expressions like '0 belongs to' and '1 belongs to.' Even though the first two "definitions" contain descriptions of numbers in the definiendum, that fact is not essential for Frege's objection. What is essential is the fact that the definiendum contains the phrase 'belongs to.' This expression has not previously been explained; it is not one of the familiar connections like the relation of falling under a concept or the relation of falling within a higher concept. This, I believe, is the reason for Frege's claim that the first two "definitions" do not "define" the numbers 0 and 1 but instead "define" certain concepts. Assume for a moment that my view is correct, that numbers are quantifiers. In this case, one could claim that the first two "definitions" suffice to "define" 0 and 1, for, in addition to 0 and 1, the definiendum contains only familiar notions — in particular, the familiar notion of the connection between a quantifier and what it quantifies. Similarly, assume that numbers are properties of properties. In this case, too, we could claim that the numbers 0 and 1 are "defined." The definiendum contains merely the familiar connection of exemplification between a number and a property. If my interpretation is correct, then it follows from the alleged fact that the first two "definitions" do not "define" numbers but "define" certain concepts instead, that we have as yet no way of understanding numerical equations, that is, identity statements like '$1 + 1 = 2$.'

These considerations raise a question: What kind of a connection is there between a number (conceived of as an object) and a concept? One of the obvious answers is that the connection is unique. In addition to all the other relations which exist, there is this unique relation between a concept and the number of entities which fall under the concept. Another obvious move would be to say that '1 belongs to' is one unanalyzable predi-

189. *Ibid.*
190. *Ibid.*

cate, so that there can be no question about the referent of any part of this predicate. This view is unacceptable; it implies that there are no numbers. If '1' is to be the name of an entity, then '1 belongs to' must be a complex expression, and we may ask what the expression 'belongs to' represents. This leads to another possibility. One could claim that '1 belongs to F' is just another way of writing '1 = the number of F,' so that the two expressions have the same meaning.[191] If so, then there seems to be no special relation of belonging to; there is merely the familiar connection of identity. But notice that the reformulation of '1 belongs to F' contains not only the identity sign but also a description. The only way in which we can reformulate expressions like '1 belongs to F' in terms of identity is by means of a description like 'the number of F.' This shows, first of all, why Frege has to search for a "definition" of such expressions as 'the number of F.' It shows, second, that our original question about the nature of the relation of belonging to has not really been answered. We must realize that 'the number of F' is merely short for 'the number which belongs to F.' And this latter description mentions again the problematic relation of belonging to.[192] As far as I know, Frege never concerned himself seriously with the question. Later, in the *Grundgesetze*, he abbreviates the expression 'the number of the concept F' by a sign of the form 'NF.' Thus he uses a functor rather than a definite description, shifting the problem to a different level.[193]

Before we proceed to Frege's next "definition" of number, let us see whether we can draw some inferences about his notion of a definition. His first objection, it will be recalled, is that his "definition" does not "define" the notion of number; it presupposes it. From this objection, it may appear that Frege thinks of a "definition" as introducing a sense or meaning for the "defined" expression. He seems to be saying that we cannot assume that we know what 'number' means until we have "defined" the term. A "definition," in short, presents us with the meaning of an expression. But this interpretation does not agree with another feature of Frege's

191. Compare Frege's remarks in *F*, p. 69.
192. Compare this with the description 'the color of my pen.' This description could be reformulated as 'the color *exemplified* by my pen.'
193. On this level, nothing less than the existence of functions proper — as distinguished from concepts — is at stake. I side with Russell rather than Frege: ontologically speaking, so-called functions are really relations.

"definitions." In all three "definitions," Frege uses the phrase 'if, then.'[194] Hence all three "definitions" are really nothing but compound sentences, and, as such, they contain only expressions which have a prior meaning. Frege's so-called definitions turn out to be true statements, and true statements, almost everyone agrees, do not "introduce" the meanings of words; they presuppose them. This is the source of tension in Frege's conception of definitions. At times he thinks of them as mere abbreviations for longer expressions, so that it is a matter of linguistic convention that the definiens and the definiendum have the same meaning. At other times he thinks of definitions as statements which are true or false, but not as a matter of convention.

We can discern this tension also in connection with Frege's second objection. Frege complains that by means of his "definitions" we cannot prove a certain statement. But how can he possibly expect to get new "theorems" from a set of "definitions"? For example, if we introduce the mark 'number' — which is supposed to have no prior meaning — as an abbreviation for a longer expression, how will we now be able to prove anything that was not provable before?[195] Conventional abbreviations neither add to nor detract from our knowledge. They are always expendable. On the other hand, if we think of "definitions" not as abbreviations but as adding to our inventory of premises, then we cannot also think of them as introducing meanings. "Definitions" are then indistinguishable from other true statements. There is, for example, no cause for Frege's complaint that his "definitions" do not tell us what the word 'number' means; it is only an illusion to believe that his first "definition" tells us what the sign 'o' means.[196] It only tells us something about this number; it is a true statement about o. If we did not understand the meaning of 'o' in Frege's "definition," then we could not understand the whole "definition," because we could not understand the consequent of the conditional. But, of course, we do understand the meaning of 'o,' and we do understand what the conditional says, and so we may be impressed by Frege's discovery of such an important truth.[197]

194. I shall often assume that the logical connection involved is the biconditional rather than the conditional.

195. With the exception, of course, of the equivalence statement that is a direct consequence of the abbreviation.

196. Or what the expression 'the number o belongs to' means.

197. Compare, for example, his "definition" of the notion of being a successor in the *f*-series, *F*, pp. 92–93.

Frege cannot have his cake and eat it too. Either the definiens and the definiendum have the same meaning (always as a matter of linguistic convention, explicitly stated or implicitly understood), or they do not. In the first case, we can say that we have given meaning to an expression. But in this case, nothing new can ever be proved. In the second case, the "definition" may enable us to prove something new. But it will no longer be a matter of convention whether to accept the "definition." In fact, I can see no valid reason why we should call such statements 'definitions.'[198] Rather, we should speak of theorems, or statements, or true propositions. By calling true statements 'definitions,' one gives the impression that their truth is a matter of convention, and hence that their status as basic propositions is unproblematic. Moreover, as everyone knows, every abbreviation can be turned into a statement that is true by virtue of the convention involved in the abbreviation. Some philosophers say that such a statement is a necessary truth, that it is analytic. It is true by virtue of the meaning of the terms involved, as it is so misleadingly put. Now, if one thinks of certain true statements as definitions, one may also come to believe that these statements are analytic truths, that they are necessary truths. Hence by the simple expedient of calling certain equivalence statements definitions, one accomplishes the remarkable feat of turning true statements into analytic ones. I shall return to this point again.

Consider Frege's second attempt to "define" numbers. He views the problem in the light of certain considerations about the manner in which we are acquainted with numbers: "How, then, are numbers to be given to us, if we cannot have any ideas or intuitions of them? Since it is only in the context of a proposition that words have any meaning, our problem becomes this: to define the sense of a proposition in which a number word occurs."[199] With an eye on his later "definition" in terms of similarity among classes, he turns to identity statements. Since numbers are objects, he reasons, identity sentences must have a sense for them. Then he announces what seems to be a general principle: "If we are to use the symbol *a* to signify an object, we must have a criterion [*Kennzeichen*] for deciding in all cases whether *b* is the same as *a*, even though it is

---

198. I believe that the term 'definition' is completely superfluous: we can always speak of abbreviations, true equivalence statements, and so on.
199. *F*, p. 73.

not always in our power to apply this criterion." [200] Frege therefore claims that we have to "define" the sense of the following proposition: 'The number which belongs to the concept F is the same as that which belongs to the concept G.' The content of this proposition, according to Frege, must be reproduced in different terms.[201] A successful "definition," then, would amount to a general criterion for the identity of numbers.

Frege's remarks about a criterion for deciding whether objects are the same, though clear enough in the context, seem to have misled some contemporary philosophers. These days, a criterion for sameness is often confused with the notion of sameness itself. Some philosophers think that the quest for a criterion of sameness for a certain kind of entity is a quest for the meaning of the word 'same' as applied to these entities, as if 'same' means different things when applied to different kinds of entities. These philosophers pretend not to understand what one means by saying that A is the same as B until one has explained to them what 'same' means when applied to entities like A and B. And to explain what 'same' means consists, in their opinion, in giving a criterion for the sameness of entities like A and B. However, there can be no explanation, explication, or "definition" of what 'same' means. Nor do we need one. We all know what the word mens; and, since we know what it means, we are sure that it does not mean one thing when applied to one kind of entity and something else when applied to another kind of entity. As 'criterion' is now often used, the only criterion for the sameness of A and B is that they are the same.

We may ask how we can decide under certain circumstances that A and B are the same, and how we may find out whether they are the same. Under what conditions is it reasonable to assume that A and B are the same? What kind of evidence tends to show that A is the same as B? These are reasonable questions; they ask for a criterion for the sameness of A and B. Such a criterion may be different for different kinds of entities, for the conditions under which different kinds of entities are the same may of course differ. Thus, to ask for a criterion of sameness for certain entities is to ask for the conditions under which these entities are the same; it is not to ask for a "meaning" or "use" of the word 'same'

---

200. Obviously, Frege means to say that we must have a criterion for deciding whether what 'a' represents is the same as what 'b' represents.

201. This could mean either that we must find an expression which is abbreviated by the identity statement or that we must find a statement that is (logically) equivalent to it.

as applied to these entities. The deepest root of the confusion between conditions for sameness and the meaning of the word 'same' is undoubtedly the more general confusion between the conditions under which a statement is true and the meaning of that statement. Shades of the verification theory of meaning!

Frege's actual "definition" of numbers shows quite clearly how the so-called criterion works. The number of F is the same as the number of G, according to his "definition," *if and only if* the concept F is similar to the concept G.[202] This "definition" provides us with a criterion; we know now under what conditions two numbers are the same — they are the same if the concepts of which they are numbers are similar. Similarity among concepts is a condition for sameness of the numbers of the concepts. Frege *discovered* this condition; he *discovered* this criterion. Of course, he did not discover it by a thorough study of German usage. Nor does his discovery tell us what it means to say that two numbers are the *same*. But we see now how the unclear notion of definition may contribute to the confusion between the meaning of 'same' and the conditions for sameness. If one thinks of a statement of certain conditions for sameness as a definition, then one may also believe that the definiens and the definiendum have the same meaning. If so, then one may claim that 'The number of F is the same as that of G,' means the same as the sentence 'The concept F is similar to the concept G.' Hence one may conclude that 'sameness' when applied to numbers means one thing; applied to other entities it means something else again. But so-called statements of criteria for sameness are not abbreviations. They are equivalence (or identity) statements.

Following up on his proposal, Frege suggests tentatively the following "definition": The sentence 'The number of F is the same as the number of G' is to mean the same as the sentence 'F is similar to G.'[203] This proposal can be justified, according to Frege, by showing that whenever F and G are similar, the two expressions 'the number of F' and 'the number of G' can be interchanged everywhere *salva veritate*.[204]

Notice, first, that Frege speaks here about two sentences as meaning the same thing. But it is clear, I think, that if the definiens means the same as the definiendum, then we need no further justification for the "defi-

202. Frege actually proves this equivalence from his "definitions"; see *F*, pp. 85–86.
203. *Ibid.*, p. 76. Frege actually gives this "definition" for directions rather than for numbers.
204. *Ibid.*, p. 77.

nition." Notice, second, Frege's particular choice of words; he does not say that the first sentence means the same as the second, but rather that the first sentence *is to mean* the same as the second. He implies that we give some meaning to the first sentence, just as we confer a meaning to an expression when we introduce it as an abbreviation of another expression. But if we *give* the meaning of the second sentence to the first sentence, then it makes no sense to speak of a justification for the "definition" in terms of substitutivity *salva veritate*, for this is automatically guaranteed by our stipulation. On the other hand, if such a justification is in order, then we cannot think of the "definition" as conferring, by convention, a meaning to an expression. Rather, we must think of the first sentence as having a meaning independently of the meaning of the second sentence, so that we can test whether or not substitution of one meaning for the other preserves the truth-value of the context. We must think of the two sentences as being equivalent or, rather, as being perhaps equivalent. In short, if a justification in terms of substitutivity is called for, then the so-called definition states an equivalence; and if the so-called definition confers a meaning to a sentence, then a justification in terms of substitutivity is pointless.

Notice, third, that Frege proposes the test of substitutivity, because he accepts Leibniz' "definition" of identity.[205] However, my remarks about the "definition" of sameness between numbers in terms of similarity among concepts hold also for Leibniz' "definition" of identity. This "definition" does not tell us what 'same' or 'identical' means.[206] Rather, it tells us under what conditions two entities are the same; it is an equivalence statement. Things are the same as each other if and only if one can be substituted for the other without loss of truth.[207] This equivalence, to make my point once more, does not tell us what 'same' means; it merely tells us under what circumstances two entities A and B are the same.[208] It states, if you prefer, a criterion for sameness. Assume, for example, that we wonder whether or not the thing A which we saw yesterday is the same as the thing B now before us. After some checking, we become convinced that B has the same properties (and relations) as A. We then con-

205. *Ibid.*, pp. 76–77.
206. I do not distinguish between identity and sameness.
207. I follow here Frege's formulation of Leibniz' "definition."
208. Of course, *two* entities are never the same. Behind this awkward formulation lies a deeper point. As we shall see later, the importance of the notion of identity arises in connection with variables.

clude that B is indeed the thing which we saw yesterday. Of course, we may be mistaken; B may just look very much like A. And, of course, we cannot check all the properties of B; nor may we be able to remember many properties of A. We may even have to be satisfied with indirect evidence that A and B both have a certain property F. But all these complications do not detract from the principle of the matter; if we decide that A and B are the same, we do not apply or presuppose a "definition" of sameness, but we do act on the basis of our belief in the proposition that A and B are the same if and only if they share all properties (and relations).

That the so-called Leibniz definition does not provide us with the meaning of 'same' can also be seen from another consideration. In order to decide whether A and B are the same, we must find out, for example, whether B has the *same* property F which, as we recall, A has. Hence we must already know the meaning of 'same' in order to apply the "definition" to the case of A and B. Nor can it be objected that 'same' means one thing when used in connection with predicates and quite another when used with names of things. The Leibniz "definition" does not only hold for individual things; it also holds for properties of individual things, for relations among individual things, for properties of properties of individual things, and so on. And the meaning of 'same' which is involved is the same for all these kinds of entities.[209]

Frege's second proposal does not satisfy him either. He raises the same objection: The second "definition" attempt does not yield a "definition" of the notion of number and hence does not allow us to decide whether, say, England is a number.[210] The proposed "definition" does not allow us to decide whether a certain entity is identical with the number of F if the entity is not described by an expression of the form 'the number of . . . ,' but is instead named by a proper name like '4.' For example, by means of the "definition" we cannot decide whether the sentence 'The number of planets $= 9$' is true.

While explaining this objection, Frege makes some further remarks about the nature of "definitions." In one paragraph he seems to hold two incompatible views. On the one hand, he appears to hold that "definitions" are mere abbreviations which do not assert anything about an object but

209. This does not agree with Frege's view. As we shall see, he holds that identity does not obtain between concepts but only between objects.
210. *F*, pp. 77–78.

merely fix the meaning of a new expression: "The definition of an object does not, as such, really assert anything about the object, but only lays down the meaning of a symbol."[211] On the other hand, he also implies that a "definition" not only adds to our stock of expressions for well-known meanings but also adds to our stock of such meanings and hence allows us to draw new conclusions. The discrepancy between these two notions is, however, concealed by the fact that Frege identifies the "meaning" of an expression at times with the object represented by the expression, and at other times with the way in which this object is given.

□

The third and last "definition" proposed by Frege rests on the following intuitive ideas. The concept F will be similar to the concept G if and only if the class determined by the concept *concept similar to F* is the same as the class determined by the concept *concept similar to G*. In other words, two concepts are similar if and only if the concept of *being similar to the one* determines the same class as the concept of *being similar to the other*. This fact suggests to Frege the following "definition": The number which belongs to the concept F is the extension of the concept *similar to the concept F*.[212]

Frege makes use of the following facts: (a) Similarity is an equivalence relation. (b) Therefore the relational property of standing in this relation to something is an equivalence property. (c) The number of F is the same as that of G if and only if F and G are similar. Informally, he may have reasoned as follows: Similarity between F and G amounts to identity between the extensions of the concepts *similar to F* and *similar to G*. But so does identity of number; similarity between F and G amounts to identity of the number of F with the number of G. We may therefore try to identify the two sides of the two identity statements: The number of F is then identical with the extension of the concept *similar to F* and the number of G is identical with the extension of the concept *similar to G*. This "identification" will have to show its worth by being fruitful. "[Definitions] that could just as well be omitted and leave no link missing in the chain of proofs should be rejected as completely worthless."[213]

Before I discuss Frege's further steps in his derivation of arithmetic

211. *Ibid.*, p. 78.
212. *Ibid.*, pp. 79–80. I have translated Frege's *gleichzahlig* as 'similar.'
213. *Ibid.*, p. 81.

from logic, let us recall some of the well-known ingredients of his "definition" of numbers in terms of extensions. In this way I shall be able to explain, though rather briefly, my own views about this matter.

There are, first of all, a number of mere *abbreviations*.

A(1) Let us say, for short, 'the two-place relation R is *one-many*' instead of 'the two-place relation R is such that for each second-place member of R there is exactly one first-place member of R which bears the relation R to that second-place member.'

A(2) Let us say, for short, 'the two-place relation R is *many-one*' instead of 'the two-place relation R is such that for each first-place member of R there is exactly one second-place member to which the first-place member bears the relation R.'

A(3) Let us say, for short, 'R is *one-one*' instead of 'R is both one-many and many-one.'

A(4) Let us say, for short, 'the two-place relation R is a *correlator* between the two properties F and G (or between the two classes C_F and C_G)' instead of 'the two-place relation R fulfills the following four conditions: (a) R is one-one, (b) the things which are F (which are elements of C_F) are first-place members of R, (c) the things which are G (which are elements of C_G) are second-place members of R, and (d) if any individual thing, say, a is F (is an element of C_F), then the individual thing b which is related to a by R is G (is an element of C_G), and conversely.'

A(5) Let us say, for short, 'F and G are similar (C_F and C_G are similar)' instead of 'there is a correlator between F and G (between C_F and C_G).'

A(6) Let us say, for short, 'R is an *equivalence relation*' instead of 'R is both symmetric and transitive.'

A(7) Let us say, for short, 'the property F is an *equivalence property with respect to R* (the class C_F is an equivalence class in respect to R)' instead of '$F(C_F)$ fulfills the following two conditions: (a) R holds between any pair of things which are F (which are elements of C_F), and (b) if any individual with the property F (belonging to C_F) bears R to another individual, then the second individual is also F (belongs also to C_F).'

Next, I list a series of true statements in which these abbreviations occur.

T(1) If R is an equivalence relation, then the relational property of standing in the relation R to something (the class determined by this property), is an equivalence property (equivalence class) with respect to R. (This follows from the fact that if R is both symmetric and transitive, then the relational property fulfills conditions (a) and (b) of A(7).)

T(2) Similarity is an equivalence relation. (This follows from the fact that it is both symmetric and transitive.)

T(3) The relational property of being similar to a given property (the class determined by the property of being similar to a given class) is an equivalence property with respect to similarity (is an equivalence class with respect to similarity). (This follows from T(1) and T(2).)

The following true statements allow us to "connect" numbers with the abbreviated notions listed earlier.

N(1) (a) There are 0 individuals which are F (which are elements of C_F) if and only if it is not the case that there is an individual which is F (which belongs to C_F).[214]

(b) There is 1 individual which is F (which belongs to C_F) if and only if there is an individual x such that any individual y is F (belongs to C_F) if and only if y is x.

(c) And so on.

N(2) (a) 0 is a number.

(b) 1 is a number.

(c) And so on.

N(3) Let N be any one of the numbers 0, 1, 2, 3, etc., then:

(a) if there are N individuals which are F (which belong to C_F) and N individuals which are G (which belong to C_G), then F and G (C_F and C_G) are similar. (This follows from N(1) and the meaning of 'similar.')

(b) if there are N individuals which are F (which belong to C_F) and F is similar to G (C_F is similar to C_G), then there are N individuals which are G (which belong to C_G). (This, too, follows from N(1) and the meaning of 'similar.')

(c) if there are N individuals which are F (which belong to C_F), then there are N individuals which are G (which belong to C_G) if and only if F and G (C_F and C_G) are similar. (This follows from (a) and (b).)

N(4) The "property" of there being N individuals with a given property (the class determined by the "property" of there being N individuals

214. For the sake of brevity, I formulate these and similar statements just for individuals.

belonging to a given class) is an equivalence property (equivalence class) with respect to similarity. (This follows from N(3) (c) and A(7).)[215]

N(5) The class of classes which are similar to a given class C_F is the same as the class of classes which have the same number N of individuals as C_F. (This follows from N(4) and T(3).)

With these abbreviations and theorems in mind, let us take another look at Frege's "definition." Let us assume, for the sake of the discussion, that it makes sense to speak of the *property* of there being so-and-so many things which exemplify a given property — or, in other words, that numbers are in some sense properties of properties.[216] If so, then it is true that a given "numerical property" U is coextensive with another property, namely, the property of being similar to a certain property. Frege makes use of this fact in his "definition"; he "identifies" the "numerical property" with the class determined by that number. From my point of view, several things have to be stressed.

First, Frege's so-called definition is a statement rather than an abbreviation. It corresponds, *after a fashion*, to N(5). Frege reverses the order of introduction; he does not, as I did, base N(5) on certain statements about numbers. But this does not matter for my point; whether we think of N(5) as a theorem or as some kind of axiom, it is in either case not an abbreviation.

Second, Frege's "definition" — viewed as a statement — turns out to be false when taken literally. At least this is so if we take it that Frege "identifies" "numerical properties" with classes, for properties are one kind of entity, classes quite a different kind. I would not know how to argue for this difference without using premises which may appear much less plausible than my contention. That a class of individual things is different from a property which these things have is obvious to me. If this is obvious, and if numbers are properties of properties, then they could not possibly be classes. Of course, Frege would not really accept the assumption that numbers are properties (concepts). He would insist that they are objects. But his "definition" does not settle this issue. We cannot assume

215. I put 'property' between double quotation marks in order to indicate the problematic nature of this use. If I am right, then there is really no such property.

216. To repeat, in my opinion they are as little properties of properties as are the quantifiers *all* and *some*. In addition, as I mentioned earlier, there is the objection that even if natural numbers were properties of properties there still would be no such property as *there being N individuals which exemplify a certain property*. Recall that I claimed that forms ("open sentences") do *not* in general determine properties.

that numbers are what Frege's "definition" says they are, namely, classes. Such an assumption is only warranted when we deal with mere abbreviations, and Frege's "definition" is a statement of identity.

Third, there is, nonetheless, a sense in which Frege's "definition" is successful. If we "identify" the "numerical property" of being the number of F with the class determined by the property of being similar to F, we do not just "identify" any property with any class. Rather, we "identify" a property with a class determined by this property.[217] The "definition" works because many statements about properties are *equivalent* to statements about the respective classes determined by these properties. In many contexts we can substitute predicates for the corresponding class expressions *salva veritate*, and vice versa.[218] This does not mean, however, that properties are classes. It merely means that certain statements about properties are equivalent to certain other statements about classes.[219]

Fourth, granting for the moment that numbers are objects, and overlooking the difficulty of how to describe them, Frege's "definition" comes to this: Based on certain truths about equivalence properties with respect to similarity, Frege's "definition" is an identity statement with two descriptions. The left side describes a number as the number of the concept F, the right side describes that number as the extension of a certain (relational) concept. In short, it is claimed that a certain description describes the same object as another description. This claim may or may not be true. Claims of this sort are certainly not just matters of convention. Frege is therefore right when he says that his "definitions" must be justified. I would prefer to say that they must be shown to be true or, if accepted as axioms, explicitly claimed to be true. But the need for a justification is precisely the factor which prevents us from calling such statements "definitions." At any rate, since Frege's "definition" turns out to be an identity statement with two descriptions, the importance of the notion of identity for Frege's "reduction" of arithmetic to logic is quite apparent.

To round out Frege's approach, I shall briefly mention some further steps of the "reduction."

217. To be more precise, we "identify" a property with the class determined by another property which is coextensive with the first.

218. These are, of course, the so-called *extensional* contexts.

219. The question arises whether they are *logically* equivalent to each other. I shall try to answer this below.

(1) Frege explains the expression 'the concept F is similar to the concept G' in the familiar fashion, corresponding to our A(5) and the abbreviations that lead to it.

(2) He then "defines" the property of being a number as follows: "The expression 'N is a number' is to mean the same as the expression 'there exists a concept such that N is the number which belongs to it.' "[220] Frege's formulation implies that he has a mere abbreviation in mind, but the true state of affairs is quite different. The word 'number' does not occur at any place as an abbreviation. It is always to be taken in its ordinary and unproblematic sense. With its ordinary meaning, it enters into the description 'the number which belongs to the concept F.' Since we understand this description, we are in a position to decide whether Frege's "definition" of the number of a concept is true. We are also in a position to decide whether Frege's "definition" of the concept *number* is true, for that "definition" is an equivalence statement which reads: For all entities n, n is a number if and only if there is a concept of which n is the number.

(3) Frege proves next that the number of F is the same as the number of G if (and only if) F is similar to G. This follows from his "definition" of numbers as extensions and the notion of similarity. It amounts to showing that if two concepts are similar, then any concept which is similar to either concept is similar to both. This amounts to producing a one-one relation which holds between, say, F and H, if a one-one relation holds between F and G and between G and H.

(4) In his next step Frege "defines" individual numbers. The number 0 is "defined" as follows: "0 is the number which belongs to the concept *not identical with itself*."[221] This corresponds roughly to our true equivalence statement N(1). However, it differs from N(1) in that Frege's "definition" is an identity statement involving a proper name and a description, rather than an equivalence; it also differs from N(1) in that Frege mentions a definite "property" under which, as we know, nothing falls. The first difference is transparent. The second gains its significance within the wider context of the "reduction" of arithmetic to logic: Frege thinks of the concept *not being identical with itself* as a purely logical concept. Hence he claims that only logical notions are involved in his "definition" of 0.

(5) There follows a "definition" of the relation of immediate successor

220. *F*, p. 85.
221. *Ibid.*, p 87.

(in the series of natural numbers): "The expression 'there exists a concept f, and an object falling under it x, such that the number which belongs to the concept f is N and the number which belongs to the concept *falling under f but not identical with x* is M' is to mean the same as 'N follows in the series of natural numbers directly after M.' "[222] Here again we have a true equivalence statement rather than a mere abbreviation, as Frege's formulation implies.

(6) Frege outlines a schema for the "definition" of the rest of the natural numbers and shows that 1 follows directly after 0. The schema is of the following kind: 1 is the number of the concept *identical with 0*; 2 is the number of the concept *identical with 0 or with 1*; and so on. Frege can now show that the number 1 follows directly after 0, since the number of the concept *identical with 0* follows directly after 0. We must note once again that Frege's "definitions" of '1,' '2,' and so on are not abbreviations but identity statements with proper names and descriptions.

(7) Finally, in sketching the proof for a certain theorem, Frege mentions the crucial "definition" of the ancestral relation of a relation R: "The proposition 'if every object to which X stands in the relation R falls under the concept F, and if from the proposition that d falls under the concept F it follows universally, whatever d may be, that every object to which d stands in the relation R falls under the concept F, then Y falls under the concept f, whatever f may be' is to mean the same as 'Y follows in the R-series after X.' "[223] Frege mentions in passing that only by means of this "definition" is it possible to reduce the argument from n to $(n + 1)$ to the general laws of logic.[224]

Since the general idea of this reduction is familiar, I shall only indicate its more important steps. But I shall bring out in my formulation that we are not dealing with abbreviations. Applying the general "definition" just mentioned to the special case of the series of natural numbers, we discover that Y follows in the series of natural numbers after X if and only if Y has all the properties which (a) belong to X, and (b) are such that, if they belong to any given number, they belong also to the number which follows in the series of natural numbers directly after the given number. Furthermore, it is also true that N is a natural number if and only if N is the number 0 or N has all the properties which (a) belong to 0, and

222. *Ibid.*, p. 89.
223. *Ibid.*, p. 92. Compare also *B*, p. 55; and *GG, I*, 59–60.
224. *F*, p. 93.

(b) are such that, if they belong to anything *m*, they also belong to whatever follows in the series of natural numbers directly after *m*. If one treats these true statements as "definitions" and reformulates the ordinary *principle of mathematical induction* on the basis of these "definitions," then the principle becomes a logical truth: If *F* is a property which (a) belongs to o, and (b) is such that, if it belongs to any number *m*, it also belongs to whatever follows in the series of natural numbers directly after *m*, then *F* belongs to everything which is either identical with o or has all the properties which (a) belong to o, and (b) are such that, if they belong to any object *m*, they belong also to whatever follows in the series of natural numbers directly after *m*.

This "proof" of the principle of mathematical induction leads us back to the main topic — Frege's plan of deriving arithmetic from logic. After having surveyed his main ideas, we can sum up the customary view of the derivation in a different way. Consider Peano's five axioms for arithmetic.[225] The whole of (finite) arithmetic, as one says, can be deduced from these axioms together with certain "definitions." Assume that this can indeed be done.[226] Now the axioms contain three nonlogical — that is, arithmetical — terms, namely, 'o,' 'number,' and 'immediate successor.' Frege, as we just saw, provides "definitions" for these three terms: the number o is "defined" in terms of the logical "property" of not being identical with itself; the natural numbers can be "defined" in terms of the ancestral of the relation of immediate successor; and the relation of immediate successor is "defined" as in (5) on page 133. If we use these "definitions" to replace the arithmetical terms in the five axioms, we get five sentences which no longer contain any arithmetical terms but consist entirely of logical expressions. We get five logical statements which may or may not be true. As it happens, the five sentences can be shown, on purely logical grounds,

225. Compare Peano's *Formulaire de mathématiques* (Turin, 1895).
226. Of course, we have good reason to suspect these further "definitions" as well. For example, it is claimed that, say, addition is "defined recursively" by the two sentences (1) '*m* + o = *m*' and (2) '*m* + the successor of *n* = the successor of (*m* + *n*).' That this is not an abbreviation for the notion of addition is obvious. (1) and (2) are simply two true sentences; their truth follows, among other things, from the common meaning of '+.' Recursive "definitions" are implicit "definitions" and hence, in my view, no "definitions" at all. If I show someone the sentences (1) and (2), but replace the familiar '+' by an unfamiliar sign, he may *guess* that the unfamiliar sign stands for addition, because he realizes that (1) and (2) are true, if they are so interpreted.

to be logical truths.[227] But this means that we can *derive* Peano's axioms from the laws of logic together with the appropriate "definitions" of the three arithmetical terms mentioned earlier. Furthermore, since the whole of (finite) arithmetic follows (logically) from these five axioms (together with certain further "definitions"), the whole of (finite) arithmetic follows from the laws of logic (and certain further "definitions").

Recall now Frege's purpose and his program. He wishes to show that arithmetic is analytic (and hence *a priori*). He holds that a proposition is analytic if and only if we can prove it from logical laws together with "definitions." He provides both the crucial "definitions" and the relevant logical laws, as we have seen. By means of these one can indeed prove all arithmetical propositions. Hence Frege does show that arithmetic is analytic and that it is therefore simply a "development of logic." [228]

We cannot fully appreciate his achievement unless we are completely clear about the role which "definitions" play in the "reduction." Assume for a moment that the crucial "definitions" were mere abbreviations. Assume, for example, that the mark 'o' is just short for the expression 'the number of the concept *not being identical with itself*.' Now, if all of Frege's crucial "definitions" were of this sort, then it would be a purely arbitrary, conventional, linguistic matter that we express certain propositions by means of what we call arithmetical signs, rather than by means of logical signs. The difference between these two kinds of signs would be a difference in shape only; they would differ only as perceptual objects. In the strictest possible sense, arithmetic and logic would constitute one and the same body of knowledge, expressed in two ways by different marks and noises. We would have the rather strange situation that two different groups of people, the logicians and the mathematicians, are doing the very same thing and hence doing it twice. The only difference between a logician and a mathematician would be that the former insists on writing down certain shapes while the latter, for some hidden reason, insists on using quite different signs. The difference between them would not be greater than that between a philosopher who publishes in English and a philosopher who publishes the very same ideas in German.

This is, of course, not the true state of affairs. Frege's "definitions" are not mere abbreviations. They are true statements. Consider, for example,

---

227. I neglect here the important fact that Peano's third axiom cannot be shown to be true unless we assume the axiom of infinity.
228. *F*, p. 99.

the "definition" of 'o': 'o = the number which belongs to the concept *not identical with itself.*' Here we have a true identity statement with a label for and a description of the number o. If we also believe the proposition 'the number of the concept *not identical with itself* = the extension of the concept of *being similar to the concept of being not identical with itself,*' then we can say that o = the extension of the concept of *being similar to the concept of not being identical with itself.* We have now an identity statement which contains a description of o in purely logical terms. In this manner, Frege "replaces" an arithmetical expression by a description which contains nothing but logical signs. In Frege's terminology, one object is presented both directly, by means of a proper name (in this case, an arithmetical sign), and indirectly, through a description in logical terms.

According to my view, the number zero is a quantifier, not a class. Now it is true that there are o entities which have the "property" of not being identical with itself. We may, for the sake of analogy, express this fact in the words 'o is the number of the "property" of not being identical with itself.'[229] But we cannot replace, in the Fregean fashion, the description by an expression which contains nothing but logical signs, for the number of that "property" is not identical with a class. Nor is it the "property" of being similar to that property. However, there is a statement which relates an arithmetical state of affairs to a logical one: 'For all properties f and g: the number of things which are f is the same as the number of things which are g if and only if f is similar to g.' This statement leads to another: 'For all properties f: o things are f if and only if f is similar to the "property" of not being identical with itself.' Thus we have established a "connection" between o on the one hand and logical notions on the other: an arithmetical statement, we have discovered, is equivalent to a logical one.

These considerations allow us to bring the difference between Frege's and our method of "reduction" into sharper focus. Talking once more in terms of Peano's axioms, Frege "coordinates" arithmetic to logic by means of certain *identity statements.* The first one is his "definition" of the number of a concept. From this identity statement and another one about the

229. To be precise, this is short for 'o is the number of entities which have the "property" of not being identical with itself.' This sentence describes o as the number of certain entities. This is a description not in terms of a property which something *has*, but in terms of the quantifier which *quantifies* certain entities.

number zero, he derives an identity statement which relates 'zero' to a logical description. Next, he considers two equivalence statements: the first involves the notion of immediate successor; the second, the notion of a natural number.[230] By replacing in these equivalence statements certain arithmetical expressions by (a) his description of the number of F in logical terms, and/or (b) his description of o in logical terms, he obtains sentences which contain nothing but logical signs and which are equivalent to certain arithmetical sentences. This second step of the "reduction" involves two things: "definitions" of certain arithmetical terms in terms of other arithmetical terms, and replacement of the latter terms by logical expressions in accordance with the "definitions" of 'o' and 'the number of F.' Hence there are several points at which the "reduction" is problematic in a way in which no abbreviational chain is ever problematic. (1) There is the "identification" of the number of a concept F with a certain class. (2) There is the "identification" of the number o with the number of a certain concept. (3) There is the assertion that a certain sentence about immediate successor is equivalent to another sentence which contains the expression 'the number of.' (4) Finally, there is the assertion that a certain sentence with the expression 'natural number' is equivalent to another sentence with the expressions 'o' and 'immediate successor.' Granted that substitution based on true identity statements is unproblematic, it would follow unproblematically if steps (1) and (2) were unproblematic, that o is the extension of a certain concept. Thus, the elimination of o in favor of logical terms would be unproblematic. Similar considerations hold for steps (3) and (4). This shows once more how important the notion of identity is for Frege's program. It also shows, I think, that the most crucial and problematic steps of the "reduction" are disguised as "definitions." I say *disguised* because I believe that philosophers generally take the attitude that one must not quarrel with what are, after all, *mere* definitions. Of course, one need not quarrel with a definition if that term hides nothing but a proposal for an abbreviation. But if the so-called definition turns out to be either an identity statement (involving descriptions) or an equivalence statement, then we can no longer treat it cavalierly.

According to my view, Frege's step (1) is false; step (2) appears in the form of an equivalence statement; and only steps (3) and (4) remain.

---

230. This is not precisely what Frege does, but he could have proceeded in this manner, since he had all the technical tools at his disposal.

The "reduction" of arithmetic to logic, in my view, comes to this:[231] Certain arithmetical statements are equivalent to certain logical statements. These equivalences allow us to formulate, for Peano's five axioms, five equivalent logical statements. The whole philosophical problem of the "reduction" centers around one and only one question: What is the nature and status of those equivalences that connect arithmetical with logical states of affairs? That these statements are not based on mere abbreviations seems to me evident.

Whether arithmetic is analytic (and hence merely an extension of logic), depends on the nature of the crucial "definitions" employed in the "reduction." One may be tempted to argue as follows: Since certain arithmetical expressions are mere abbreviations of logical expressions, certain equivalence statements in which these expressions occur are analytic. Since all arithmetical truths follow logically from these analytic equivalence statements together with the analytic laws of logic, the whole of arithmetic is analytic. We saw that this kind of argument does not hold, because the crucial "definitions" are not mere abbreviations. But the argument also implicitly assimilates two very distinct things by treating both abbreviation proposals and logical laws as analytic. A definition, in the sense of a proposed abbreviation, is neither true nor false; it is merely a stipulation. If we accept the stipulation, if we agree to use a shorter expression with the same meaning as a longer one, then we can also state an equivalence which will be true by virtue of our acceptance of the convention. For example, since we all accept the well-known abbreviation, the sentence 'For all individual things: an individual is a bachelor if and only if it is an unmarried male of marriageable age' is true. But it is only true because we accepted a certain linguistic convention. Let us call such truths *abbreviational truths*. However, is it not the case that the sentence follows from the logical truth 'For all things and for all properties: a thing has a property if and only if it has that property'? Of course it is. But it follows from this logical truth only in conjunction with the original stipulation. If 'A is a bachelor' were not an abbreviation for the longer expression, then the sentence would not follow from the logical truth. In short, abbreviational truths are true by virtue of arbitrary linguistic conventions about abbrevia-

231. A somewhat similar view is expressed in H. Hochberg, "Peano, Russell, and Logicism," *Analysis*, XVI (1956), 118–20.

tions, whereas logical truths rest neither on conventions nor on abbreviations. The logical sentence mentioned earlier is true because that is the way things and properties behave.

Since there is this difference between abbreviational and logical truths, one should not call both kinds analytic truths. Nor is this the only reason. As a matter of fact, I shall never use the term 'analytic' at all, just as I shall never use the term 'definition.' I believe that we can say everything we wish to say in philosophy without using either one of these unfortunate terms.

Before we return to Frege, let us take up one further point. Consider the sentence 'For all individual things: if an individual is green and round, then it is green.' This is not an abbreviational truth. It is often called a logical truth (tautology). I shall say instead that it *follows* from a logical truth, namely, from the logical truth 'For all individuals and for all properties f and g: if an individual has f and also has g, then it has the property f.' A logical truth, as I use the term, does not contain descriptive constants.

Frege himself criticizes Kant for using the term 'analytic' too narrowly.[232] For Kant, the paradigm of an analytic judgment is a judgment in which the predicate concept is contained in the subject concept. Furthermore, also according to Kant, a "definition" of a concept consists of a list of characteristics of the things which fall under the concept. From this point of view, all definitional truths are analytic truths. Consider, for example, the statement 'All bachelors are males.' This is an analytic truth, because the predicate concept *male* is contained in the subject concept *bachelor*, which (at least) consists of the complex concept *unmarried male*. Hence 'Bachelors are males' is an analytic truth because 'bachelor' happens to be an abbreviation for 'unmarried male.' But what shall we say about the statement 'All unmarried males are males'? This, too, is an analytic judgment, yet it involves no abbreviation. Therefore, it is not the case that all analytic judgments are also definitional or abbreviational truths. As conceived by Kant, the term 'analytic judgment' is broader than the term 'abbreviational truth.' However, for Frege it is not broad enough. Frege holds that *all* logical truths are analytic truths, not only those which resemble 'For all f, for all g, and for all x: if x is both f and g, then x is f.'

232. *F*, pp. 99–101.

As I stated, I shall not use the notion of analyticity at all. Instead, I wish to distinguish between different *kinds* of truths (and, of course, falsehoods). At the top of the hierarchy are *ontological* truths. Ontological statements tell us what categories of entities there are and what the laws for these entities are. For example, that there are individual things, that there are properties, that there are logical connections, that there are spatial relations, that there are quantifiers, and so on — these are all ontological truths. It is also an ontological truth that individual things exemplify properties while properties do not exemplify individuals, that properties of individuals exemplify properties but not quantifiers, and that states of affairs are connected through logical connections but do not exemplify such connections. A system like that of *Principia Mathematica* does not "tell" us what the ontological truths are; it presupposes them.[233] That there are individual things and properties of individual things, for example, is *shown* by the fact that the system contains individual variables and property variables.

Logic, as commonly understood, consists really of two quite distinct theories: so-called sentential logic and so-called predicate logic. Sentential logic is about facts (states of affairs) and their connections in general. It rests on the ontological assumption that there are facts and connectives among them and elaborates the laws that hold for them. One such law states — to give the flavor of my point of view — that the conjunction of any two facts p and q — be they ontological facts, facts of arithmetic, facts of set-theory, or what have you — is equivalent to the negation of the fact that not p or not q. Predicate logic, on the other hand, is about entities and their properties, in general, and how they hang together.[234] Again, it is taken for granted that there are entities with properties. The theory merely formulates the laws that hold for all properties of whatever kind. One law states, for example, that if any entity c exemplifies any two properties f and g, then it exemplifies the property f. In short, while sentential logic is the general theory of facts, predicate logic is the general theory of properties.

233. For this point and some related ones, compare G. Bergmann's papers "Ineffability, Ontology, and Method" and "Generality and Existence" in *LR*.

234. Notice that I speak of *entities* rather than individual things. Predicate logic, as here conceived, does not only deal with individuals, their properties (including relations), properties of such properties, and so on. It holds equally well for properties of connectives, properties of quantifiers, properties of exemplification; in short, for any kind of property of any kind of entity (just as set-theory holds for all kinds of sets).

Set theory is about sets (classes), their elements, and their connections. The crucial notions are, of course, those of a class of entities, being a member of a class, and class inclusion. For example, it is a truth about classes that for any three sets of entities, if the class A is included in the class B, and the class B is included in the class C, then A is included in C.

Finally, arithmetical statements are about the quantifiers we call numbers and assert that certain relations — addition, multiplication, and so forth — hold among them.

Thus I distinguish between these five theories in terms of what they are about. Ontology states what categories there are and how they hang together. Given this framework, sentential logic tells us in detail how states of affairs behave, while predicate logic tells us how properties behave. Set theory deals with classes and how they are related to one another. Arithmetic states the relations among numbers.[235] In each of the last four fields, a certain category and certain connections are singled out for special attention: in sentential logic they are connections, such as *and* and *or*, and states of affairs; in predicate logic they are properties and the nexus of exemplification; in set theory they are connections, such as *being a member* and *being included in*, and classes; and in arithmetic they are relations, such as addition and multiplication, and numbers.

Now, Frege's "definitions" do not belong to any of these five kinds of statements. Rather, they form a new kind, for they establish connections between logical statements and arithmetical statements.[236] Frege's crucial "definitions" amount to true equivalence statements asserting that certain arithmetical statements are true if and only if certain logical statements are true.[237] They show a double dependency, if I may put it so, for they depend both on the logical structure of the world — as the logical statements do — and also on the arithmetical structure of the world — as the arithmetical statements do. These "definitions" are true because the logical

235. There are also statements about certain relations among specific properties and relations: 'Green is a color,' 'The relation *to the left of* is asymmetrical,' etc. Such statements, I believe, are paradigms of what philosophers have called synthetic *a priori* truths. Compare Bergmann's "Synthetic *a priori*" in *LR*; also the discussion below on pages 149–50.

236. Similar connections hold between statements of logic and statements of set theory. For example, it is true that for all x and for all f: x is f if and only if x is an element of the class of things which are f. In so-called validity theory, we use these equivalences between logical and set-theoretical statements in order to find out whether a certain logical statement is true on the basis of the truth-value of its equivalent set-theoretical statement.

237. This is only roughly true, of course. First, Frege's crucial "definitions" are identity statements, not equivalences; second, they sometimes involve classes. But I have used this simplification.

structure and the arithmetical structure of the world are related to each other in a certain way. But notice the following important point. The connection between a given logical state of affairs and the equivalent arithmetical state of affairs is itself a "logical" one, namely, the connection represented by 'if and only if.' Hence one might say that logical statements are logically related to arithmetical ones.[238]

If a certain arithmetical statement is equivalent to a certain logical statement, then we can substitute the former for the latter *salva veritate*, and vice versa.[239] More accurately, since the alleged "definition" is a universally closed sentence of equivalence, any substitution instance of the left side can be substituted for any substitution instance of the right side. For example, since we have the true statement 'For all f: o individuals are f if and only if it is not the case that there is an individual which is f,' we can replace a statement like 'o individual things are mermaids' or 'There are o mermaids' by 'It is not the case that there is anything which is a mermaid.'

Should we say that the crucial equivalence statements are logical truths? Should we say, for example, that 'For all f: there are o fs if and only if it is not the case that something is f' is a logical truth? If we do, then we can say that arithmetic can be reduced to logic in the sense that every arithmetical statement follows from logical truths alone. That certain logical statements are equivalent to Peano's axioms would be logically true. Since every arithmetical truth would be *logically* equivalent to a logical truth, the arithmetical statement would follow from the logical truth and the relevant equivalence statement. Of course, we can call the crucial equivalence statements logical truths, but what would be gained? As long as we completely understand the nature of the so-called reduction, it does not much matter how we describe it. On the other hand, since these statements contain not only logical terms but arithmetical expressions as well, I shall stand by my previous classification of truths and say that they are not logical truths. This is not to say, however, that they are therefore "synthetic" or "contingent" truths. Logical truths, in my terminology, must be

238. The earlier explication implies that there are two kinds of "logical" relations; the relations of sentential logic — that is, the so-called connectives — and the relation of predicate logic — namely, exemplification. It would, of course, be best to replace talk about logic by a distinction between, say, fact theory and property theory.

239. I should add: "in all logical contexts." Since the respective states of affairs are merely equivalent, but not the same, their sentences cannot be substituted *salva veritate* in so-called intentional contexts.

distinguished from several other kinds of truths and not just opposed to contingent ones. Of course, the crucial equivalence statements are not arithmetical truths either.

We can now summarize. Arithmetic cannot be "reduced" to logic if this means that arithmetical statements are mere substitution instances of logical truths and happen to contain certain abbreviations. Arithmetical expressions are not abbreviations of logical ones. But there is a reduction of arithmetic to logic in a different sense. It happens that, as a matter of logical connection between different kinds of states of affairs, certain arithmetical states of affairs are equivalent to certain logical ones. From this it follows that the respective sentences can be substituted for each other *salva veritate* as long as it does not matter that the respective states of affairs are merely equivalent but not the same. Hence, it does not matter for the validity of an argument whether one of its premises is a logical truth or an equivalent arithmetical truth. As one usually describes the matter, certain logical statements are "analytically equivalent" to certain arithmetical statements. That is as far as the "reduction" goes; there is no "reduction" of numbers to logical entities.[240]

Earlier, I claimed that the analytic-synthetic distinction is superfluous, perhaps even misleading. It may be objected that this distinction is primarily designed to mark a difference which I have not as yet mentioned. It may be claimed that we must consider this distinction from the epistemological angle, as it were. A statement is analytic, it may be said, if it is *uninformative* about *matters of empirical observation*. Since it is uninformative about such matters, we need not consult *experience* for its confirmation. An analytic statement is thus true independently of *what is the case*.[241]

240. Assume that we have an axiomatized theory of mental phenomena. Assume that it has five axioms in analogy to Peano's axioms. Assume, finally, that someone discovers five physiological statements which are equivalent to these five axioms. In this case we could say that psychology has been "reduced" to physiology. This does not mean, of course, that thoughts are "nothing but brain states." Neither does it mean that thoughts are *identical* with brain states, just as numbers do not consist of logical quantifiers and connectives. Compare also M. Brodbeck, "Mental and Physical: Identity versus Sameness," in *Mind, Matter, and Method, Essays in Philosophy and Science in Honor of Herbert Feigl* (Minneapolis, 1966).

241. Compare E. Stenius, "Are True Numerical Statements Analytic or Synthetic?" *Philosophical Review*, LXXIV (1965), 357–72.

Quite obviously, this kind of claim stands in need of further explication. I italicized some of the crucial terms. On at least one interpretation of these terms, logic, arithmetic, and set theory would all turn out to be *synthetic*. Surely logic is not independent of how the logical connectives behave; arithmetic is not independent of what is the case, as far as numbers are concerned; and set theory is not independent of the relations that hold among classes. Nor could we possibly know what the logical structure of the world is, or what its arithmetic and set theory is, unless we have had some experience of it. Without experience we could not know anything, not even that the world has a particular ontological structure.

I suspect that this interpretation will be rejected by some philosophers. What they have in mind, though perhaps somewhat dimly, is the notion that analyticity is a matter of linguistic convention, of how we use language. Experience, they would point out, is meant to be experience of the world, as contrasted with experience of the way we speak. It seems to me that this approach must finally lead to the conclusion that logical truths, as paradigms of analytic truths, can be seen to be true by an inspection of language alone. Perhaps even arithmetic would be considered analytic in this sense. However, what does it mean to say that we need consult only "semantic" matters and need not look at the world in order to see that a statement is analytically true? Language, of course, has syntax or grammar. It is also used diplomatically, tactfully, poetically, and so forth. But neither grammar nor etiquette is the same as logic, arithmetic, or set theory. Language as such tells us nothing about the world; it does not even tell us what language itself is all about. When we wish to know what linguistic expressions are about and whether they are true, then we have to turn to the world. This holds for logical and arithmetical sentences as well as for the laws of science.

Neither logical, arithmetical, nor set-theoretical truths are a matter of how we use language. In the most obvious sense of the expression, how we use language is a matter of convention, and neither logic, arithmetic, nor set theory are matters of convention. On the other hand, if the crucial expression is short for something like 'how we use language in order to say what is true,' then how we use language is of course no longer a matter of sheer convention. By the same token, though, we can no longer be said to use language without having an eye on the world. I cannot argue more eloquently or convincingly against conventionalism, be it of the positivistic or the Oxonian stripe, then Frege did. Nor do I think that my arguments would be any more effective than his. Conventionalism, I fear, is one of the lazy habits of the mind. At any rate, sound arguments alone will not affect it.

In saying that even logic is a matter of experience, I have, of course, used 'experience' in a very broad sense. Another plausible interpretation of the analytic-synthetic dichotomy rests on a somewhat narrower notion of experience. The logical truth that any state of affairs either obtains or does not obtain, as it is often put, does not tell us which particular state of affairs obtains. I have no doubt that one can make a distinction between the state of affairs represented by, say, '(p) $(p$ or not $p)$' on the one hand and certain other states of affairs like the one represented by 'It is raining now in Pittsburgh' on the other. As a matter of fact, my characterization of logical truths rests on the possibility of such a distinction. But how shall we deal with, for example, arithmetic? Take the sentence '$2 + 2 = 4$.' If we say that this is not a logical sentence but one of those "specific ones" like 'It is raining now in Pittsburgh' not contained in logic, then we have to say that it contains a synthetic statement. On the other hand, if we do not think that arithmetical statements rest on experience in the narrower sense, and are thus just like logical ones, then we may say that the sentence expresses an analytic statement. It all depends on where we wish to draw the line. There is a felt difference between logical statements, arithmetical statements, and set-theoretical propositions on the one hand and the laws of, say, chemistry on the other. This difference is sometimes expressed in terms of analytic versus synthetic truths. But the notions of experience and of empirical observation, I believe, are not too helpful when we try to describe the felt difference in greater detail. Statements differ in what they are about; this is the primary difference between logic, arithmetic, and set-theory on the one hand and geometry, physics, etc., on the other. The first three theories deal with the three *categories* of properties, numbers, and classes, respectively, while the natural sciences deal with *specific* properties and classes of things. The felt difference turns out to be a difference in generality, not a matter of experience and observation.

This leads us to the second aspect of our topic. So far, I have replaced the analytic-synthetic distinction by a whole series of distinctions — between logical and arithmetical statements, between logical and set-theoretical statements, between logical and scientific statements, and so on. All these distinctions rest on ontological distinctions between different kinds of states of affairs. There is also the openly epistemological question of whether arithmetic is known *a priori* or *a posteriori*. Granted, as I have alleged, that arithmetical statements are not "devoid of content," that they are not merely products of linguistic conventions, how do we verify such statements? Do we consult experience? If so, what kind of experience? Do we have to consult our senses? Or does the "eye of the mind" alone behold arithmetical truths? We have discussed Frege's answers to these questions. Since he holds that numbers are not sensory objects, he argues that they are presented, through judgments, to the understanding only. If we now somehow identify experience and sense experience, and if we further hold that *a priori* statements can be known to be true independently of experience, then it is clear that Frege's view amounts to saying that arithmetical statements are known *a priori*. On the other hand, if we use 'experience' so that all mental acts of whatever kind are covered by the term, then it is clear that according to Frege's view nothing could be known to be true *a priori*, that is, independently of all experience.

Frege conceives of the distinction between *a priori* and *a posteriori* statements in a different way.[242] According to him, an *a priori* statement is one that can be derived exclusively from general laws which themselves neither need nor admit of proof. On the other hand, *a posteriori* statements cannot be proved without the help of singular statements, that is, statements about individual objects. According to this explanation, all logical statements are *a priori*. Arithmetical statements are *a priori* statements if their proofs do not involve singular statements. Frege believes that he has made it at least plausible that arithmetic is known *a priori* in this sense, for he thinks that he has shown how arithmetical statements can be derived from general logical laws and definitions.

From our point of view, we are led to consider whether an arithmetical statement like '$2 + 2 = 4$' is known *a priori* or *a posteriori*. According to my analysis, this statement is equivalent to a logical statement, but this is something we must discover and cannot just decree. In order to discover that the two statements are equivalent, we must find out whether they have the same truth-value, and, in order to do this, we must be able to establish the truth-value of each statement independently of the other. How then do we show that '$2 + 2 = 4$' is true? We consider 2 entities of a certain kind F and 2 entities of another kind G and we realize that there

242. *F*, p. 4.

are 4 entities which are either F or G. Or we realize that 4 entities of a certain kind H consist of 2 entities of kind F and 2 entities of kind G. Notice that I do not say that we *perceive* that $2 + 2 = 4$, because I do not want to give the impression that this arithmetical truth *must* be established on the basis of the perception of perceptual objects. Nonetheless, I do not want to deny that it *can* be established in this manner. Numbers, in my view, are quantifiers of very different kinds of entities. As Frege observes, one can count ideas and thoughts as well as apples. Hence there is no reason why an arithmetical truth must be established on the basis of apples rather than thoughts. Nor is there any reason why perception rather than "inner awareness" should play a role. The truth of '$2 + 2 = 4$' is established by considering certain entities of a certain kind, but it does not matter what entities of what kind; nor does it matter how we are acquainted with these entities. All that matters is that the kinds we consider are quantified in the relevant manner.[243]

Do I hold, then, that we might reject the sentence '$2 + 2 = 4$' as false if we believe that a given couple of apples and another couple of apples do not add up to four apples? If I do not hold this, but instead maintain that we would never reject an arithmetical statement in the face of such an experience, am I not admitting that arithmetical truths cannot be based on such experience? If we admit that a certain statement cannot be refuted by experience, do we not also admit that it cannot be based on experience? And if it is not based on experience, what else but linguistic convention could be its source?

In the case of the two groups of apples, one would obviously recount rather than assume that the arithmetical statement has been shown to be false. This is so because we believe that the arithmetical statement is true. But if I do not know that $2 + 2 = 4$ and if I try to establish it for the first time, so to speak, I might make a mistake without noticing it. Hence, if on the next occasion I seem to find out that 2 things and 2 things add up to 4 things, I might think that I had made a mistake on this second occasion. Now let us leave these psychological considerations aside. The point of the question which I just raised seems to be this: It is implicitly assumed that according to my view arithmetical truths are established by *induction*

---

243. Since I hold, for reasons explained in *SM*, that all mental acts intend states of affairs, it follows that we are only acquainted with numbers as constituents of states of affairs. We never see the number 2 in isolation, if I may put it so, but see some state of affairs like that there are 2 apples on the table. But notice that the same thing holds for all other kinds of entities. For example, we never see individuals or properties in isolation either.

from individual cases, just as one may arrive at the conclusion that water boils when heated (under certain conditions) from having observed, on several occasions, that particular pots of water boil when they are heated. Since this law about water would be shown to be false if we discovered several pots of water that do not boil when heated, we could also show that the arithmetical law does not hold if we discovered apples that do not add up in the proper way. But since arithmetical statements are in fact not refutable in this "empirical" manner, the argument goes, my view must be false: arithmetical statements cannot be based on experience.

However, to say that the truth of '2 + 2 = 4' is based on experience is not to say that it is derived by *induction* from the observation of a number of individual cases. What happens is this: We consider two apples to the left of two more apples. We see that, altogether, there are four apples in front of us. We see, in other words, that 2 apples + 2 apples are 4 apples. To be sure, in this case we notice this relation among numbers in connection with apples rather than with nuts or peas. However, and this is the crux of the matter, what we are considering are the quantifiers of the properties, not the properties themselves. When we pay attention to these quantifiers, we notice that they are related in a certain way, namely, in the way expressed by '2 + 2 = 4.' Of course, we could not have noticed this connection without paying attention to the quantifiers, and we could not pay attention to the quantifiers without having seen the apples or nuts or peas. But the arithmetical statement is not about apples or nuts or peas. Perhaps I can put it this way: The statement '2 + 2 = 4' asserts that there is a certain connection between certain quantifiers, but not that there is a certain connection between certain apples, nuts, peas, or any other individual things. The law about water, on the other hand, says that if anything is water, then it will boil when heated. The statement '2 + 2 = 4' is not like the law about water, but rather is like the statement 'Navy blue is darker than canary yellow.' Assume that I happen to notice that navy blue is darker than canary yellow while looking at a navy blue sweater and a canary yellow pair of slacks. Would I then expect to find two further objects such that the first is navy blue, the second canary yellow, and yet such that navy blue would no longer be darker than canary yellow? Obviously not. The statement that navy blue is darker than canary yellow asserts a certain relation between two properties. This relation does not change with the particular individuals that happen to have the two properties. For this very reason, one would not try to "confirm" that navy blue is darker than canary yellow by considering further pairs of navy blue and canary yellow things. In short, a statement like this is not established by induction from individual cases. A statement which asserts a certain relation between two properties is neither established nor can it be refuted like a statement which asserts that all individuals with a certain property invariably have another property. In the case of arithmetical statements, we are not dealing with properties like colors. Numbers are not properties but quantifiers. However, the general principle remains the same: an arithmetical statement asserts a relation between singular entities and is not a generalization about all entities of a certain kind. We now understand what is meant by saying that an arithmetical statement like '2 + 2 = 4' can be "established in *one* correct observation." We also see quite clearly in what sense arithmetical truths are a matter of experience and in what sense they are not. We cannot possibly know that 2 + 2 = 4 unless we are *acquainted* with some quantified entities, but we do not infer that 2 + 2 = 4 from a whole series of such acquaintances.

In this connection, it is interesting to note that statements like 'Navy blue is darker than canary yellow' are often said to be "necessary." For many philosophers, such statements are paradigms of what they call synthetic *a priori* truths. They are considered *a priori*, because they are supposed to be irrefutable by experience. One correctly reasons that there is no experience of a *particular* pair of navy blue and canary yellow individuals that could refute the statement that navy blue is darker than canary yellow. But then one confuses an experience of a particular pair of individual things with experience in general and concludes that no experience whatsoever could refute the statement. Since no experience can refute it, one argues, the statement cannot be based on experience; hence it must be known *a priori*. But why should one stop here? Why not conclude that the statement is analytic? Indeed, why not? Some philosophers take this additional step. Since the statement is allegedly irrefutable, they claim that it is true by virtue of our use of color words. Whatever is true by virtue of the meaning of terms, that line of reasoning goes, is analytic. That navy blue is darker than canary yellow is said to be due to the fact that we use the expressions 'navy blue,' 'darker,' and 'canary yellow' in the way we do; or, rather, since we use these expressions in the way we do, we are supposedly willing to say that this statement is true, while the sentence 'Navy blue is lighter than canary yellow' is false. Of course, this does not explain *why* we should be willing to assert the one sentence and not the other, but this objection does not faze a linguistic philosopher. His philosophy provides a quick answer: We say that certain sentences are true and others false because that is the way we use the words 'true' and 'false.' Needless to say, I am not in sympathy with this style of philosophizing.

I have called attention to a certain similarity between arithmetical statements and statements about relations among properties. There are also profound differences. Arithmetic, if I may put it so, is much more fundamental than the laws about colors, tones, or shapes. In this respect it is akin to logic and set theory. To see why, we need to realize that colors, for example, are exemplified by only one category of entities, namely, individual things, and that there could be a world with individuals but without colors. Numbers, on the other hand, do not just quantify one kind of entity. Everything, including categories, can be counted. Hence there will be numbers in any world as long as it contains entities, no matter what kinds of entities these are. In particular, there would be numbers in a world which does not contain colors but is otherwise like ours, while there could be no colors in a world without numbers.

Arithmetical statements, according to our reflections, can be established through "experience." Not only can we *see* that there are 2 individuals which are apples, but we can also *see* that these 2 apples added to 2 more apples yield 4 apples. Thus we *learn* that $2 + 2 = 4$, although not through a process of induction. Hence, if so-called *a priori* statements are statements which can be known to be true without consulting experience, then arithmetical statements are not *a priori*. If all statements which are not *a priori* are called *a posteriori*, then it follows that arithmetical statements are known *a posteriori*.[244] However, as I have tried to emphasize, logical statements, the truths of set theory, and even ontological statements are also known *a posteriori*. The only exceptions are abbreviational truths; at least, we may reasonably hold that they are exceptions, because in their case we need no experience of the world in general but only of the way in which people facilitate communication by means of abbreviation.

However, if we turn to Frege's distinction between *a priori* and *a posteriori* statements, we may reach the same conclusion he does: arithmetic is known *a priori*, for arithmetical statements are not derived from singular statements about individual things. But we may also say, taking Frege's distinction quite literally, that they are known *a posteriori*, for

244. I do not hold, of course, that every arithmetical statement must be established by experience; some can be *deduced* from others.

they are not derived from logical laws and other laws alone. As it turns out, arithmetical statements fall outside Frege's dichotomy. They are "singular" statements and hence not *a priori*, but they are not singular statements involving individual things and their properties or relations, and hence they are not known *a posteriori*.

□

In conclusion, Frege's "reduction" of arithmetic to logic involves two steps. First, certain "definitions" establish a connection between arithmetical and logical terms. Second, by replacing arithmetical terms in arithmetical statements with their logical counterparts, true arithmetical statements are turned into true logical statements. The most crucial "definition" occurs in the form of an identity statement: 'The number of the concept $F =$ the extension of the concept *similar to the concept F*.' Assume, for the sake of simplicity, that all "definitions" needed for the "reduction" are of this kind. Then it is clear that arithmetic would be "analytic" if and only if both the logical truths and these identity statements are analytic. Since it is assumed — by "definition," as one says — that logical truths are analytic, the crucial question is whether the identity statements are analytic. Now, if one calls these identity statements 'definitions,' then one may fool oneself into believing that they must be analytic, for such is the general connotation of the term 'definition.' But we saw that only one kind of "definition" can be taken to be analytic, namely, abbreviational truths. However, the "definitions" proposed by Frege are quite obviously not abbreviational truths; they are true identity statements. Hence, in order to be able to decide whether arithmetic is analytic, we must first inquire whether identity statements are analytic. Now, some identity statements are substitution instances of the logical truth '(x) (x $=$ x).'[245] Hence they are analytic. But Frege's "definitions" are not of this kind. His crucial identity statements contain descriptions. Speaking intuitively, identity statements with descriptions seem to convey valuable information about matters of fact; they seem to extend our knowledge about matters of fact. If so, it becomes rather doubtful that they are analytic; but then it is also doubtful that arithmetic is analytic. In this way, Frege's whole enterprise of the *Grundlagen* awaits a satisfactory solution to the problem of identity.

245. Or they are substitution instances of similar logical truths about all properties of individuals, properties of properties of individuals, and so on.

Sinn und Bedeutung:
A Solution

T HREE IMPORTANT PHILOSOPHICAL PROBLEMS are
raised in the *Begriffsschrift*. We have seen how Frege solves two of
these problems in the *Grundlagen*. He takes a stand on the realism-
idealism issue by defending the dichotomy between mental and nonmental
entities, that is, between ideas and mental acts on the one hand and objects and concepts on the other. He also takes a position in the realism-
nominalism controversy by arguing for the distinction between objects
and concepts. As a result, Frege's later philosophy is realistic in two fundamental respects: he acknowledges the existence of mind-independent entities, and he also defends the existence of universals. These two views may
well be thought of as the cornerstones of Frege's system.

It has become evident that I share these views of Frege's on realism.
Hence I basically agree with his first two solutions. However, I do not
think that Frege was equally successful in dealing with the last and third
problem. I find his solution of the problem of identity, in terms of senses,
unacceptable. Moreover, I cannot agree with his view that truth and falsehood are objects referred to by sentences. However, Frege's detailed discussion of the sense-reference distinction yields such a wealth of new
philosophical insights that it seems to be of little moment that he adopted
just these two out of several plausible views.

IDENTITY

FREGE'S ATTEMPT to show that arithmetic is analytic rests on the dubious assumption that an identity statement like 'the number of the concept F is the same as the extension of the concept *similar to the concept F*' is analytic. There are, of course, identity statements which are generally considered to be analytic, i.e., statements of the form '$a = a$.' But all the identity statements that are important for Frege's reduction are of a different sort; they are of the form '$a = b$,' where at least one of the expressions is a description. As Frege realizes, such identity statements extend our knowledge and should therefore be classified as synthetic.

Considerations like these led Frege to re-examine the notion of identity. Identity statements assert some kind of "connection" or "relation" between entities; this much is clear. If we consider whether the relation holds between expressions or between referents of expressions, however, we are faced with the following dilemma. Assume, first, that identity statements assert relations between referents. If so, then the state of affairs represented by '$a = a$' is exactly the same as the state of affairs represented by '$a = b$,' assuming that a is the same as b. The two sentences say the very same thing, namely, that something is identical with itself. But if what the two sentences say is precisely the same, then they could not possibly differ in "cognitive value." One sentence could not possibly add to our knowledge more than the other. However, the sentence '$a = a$' does not extend our knowledge at all. Hence '$a = b$' cannot extend our knowledge either. Yet it seems intuitively clear that the two sentences differ in cognitive value: '$a = a$' does not tell us anything new, while '$a = b$' does.[1] Thus we seem to be forced to conclude that identity cannot be a relation between referents.

Let us then consider the second alternative. Assume that identity is a relation between expressions. Then the expression '$a = b$' tells us that the signs 'a' and 'b' happen to be used (in a certain language) to represent the very same entity. The identity statement would tell us something about linguistic conventions, but it would not tell us anything about the world. It seems intuitively clear, however, that identity statements like '$a = b$' often convey information about nonlinguistic matters. Their cog-

---

1. For the moment, closely following Frege's argument, I am not distinguishing between labels and descriptions. It is clear, though, that only identity statements with descriptions can be informative in the relevant sense.

nitive value, if I may so put it, is not that they tell us something about language but that they tell us something about the world. Hence we seem to be forced to conclude that identity cannot be a relation between expressions.

There seems to be no satisfactory answer to the question of how identity statements can be informative, if we consider only referents and expressions. Frege does not have to cast around long for a third factor that might play a role. Starting in the *Begriffsschrift*, he insisted that one and the same object can be presented *in different ways*. From the very beginning, Frege talked not only about expressions and their referents, when dealing with identity, but also about *ways* in which referents are presented. The so-called senses of "Über Sinn und Bedeutung" are simply the modes of presentation mentioned both in the *Begriffsschrift* and the *Grundlagen*. However, in the earlier works these modes of presentation are not acknowledged to be ontological constituents of the world. Frege's decisive step in this paper is his realization that he cannot explicate the nature of identity in terms of modes of presentation without in some way making room for such modes in his ontology. He must have argued that if one cannot give a satisfactory account of identity without mentioning modes of presentation, then there must be, in addition to expressions and their referents, such modes of presentation.

How do modes of presentation help us to avoid the dilemma just mentioned? First of all, one of our intuitions is correct: identity is a relation between referents rather than between signs. Hence it is indeed true that '$a = b$' represents the same content as '$a = a$.'[2] But this is not the whole story, for there are also senses. Since one and the same referent may be presented by different senses, an identity statement of the form '$a = b$' tells us more than one of the form '$a = a$.' What we learn from a true synthetic identity statement is not that an object is identical with itself but that one object is connected with two different senses. All informative identity statements, according to Frege, tell us that a certain referent is presented by two definite senses. They tell us not only that something is identical with itself but also that something is connected with something else.

We must try to make this general idea more precise. Let us represent the sense of 'a' by the expression '$a \diamond$,' and the sense of 'b' by '$b \diamond$.' We

2. I speak here of contents, but Frege would at this point say that the two sentences refer to the same truth-value. I neglect this further complication for the moment.

know, as a matter of logic or ontology that every entity is identical with itself. Referents are identical with themselves, and so, of course, are senses. Consider now the sentence '$a = b$' and assume that it is true. This sentence tells us not only the obvious fact that something is identical with itself, but it tells us also the not so obvious fact that to the entity a there correspond the two senses $a \Diamond$ and $b \Diamond$. Of course, that $a \Diamond$ is different from $b \Diamond$ is taken for granted. A sense, just like anything else, is identical with itself and different from anything else. The information which '$a = b$' conveys could be expressed by the sentence 'the entity a is connected with senses $a \Diamond$ and $b \Diamond$.'[3]

This consideration immediately leads us to the most important question: What is the nature of the connection between referents and their senses?[4] It is clear, I think, that this connection cannot be a linguistic one. Senses are not mental entities, nor are they linguistic entities. Senses exist, according to Frege, whether we talk about them or not. Of course, what expressions we select to express certain senses is a matter of convention. But given that a certain expression 'a' has been chosen to express a certain sense $a \Diamond$, it is no longer a matter of convention that 'a' refers to the referent which is connected with $a \Diamond$; for that connection is not a matter of convention. The connections between the realm of referents and the realm of senses are not established by language; they exist prior to and independently of language. But if the connection between sense and reference is not a linguistic one, what is it? Perhaps we shall find an answer if we first clarify the notion of a sense.

Let us return for a moment to the *Begriffsschrift*. Frege held at that time that we need a sign of identity, because one and the same content can be determined in different ways. In his example, a particular point is said to be *directly given in intuition* and to be given as the point B which has a certain property. From this example we might infer that (direct) intuition is one way in which something can be given, that intuition is

---

3. This, we might want to say, is the *sense* expressed by '$a = b$.' The sense of '$a = a$,' on the other hand, could be expressed by the sentence 'the entity a is connected with sense $a \Diamond$.' From this point of view, though, even the sentence '$a = a$' turns out out to be synthetic; for it is certainly not analytic that a is connected with $a \Diamond$ rather than, say, with $c \Diamond$. Must we then conclude that this sentence has no sense at all? Compare the discussion of labels and descriptions below.

4. A question already raised by Russell in his criticism of Frege in the famous paper "On Denoting," *Mind*, n.s., XIV (1905), 479–93.

one mode of presentation. We might also conclude that so-called modes of presentation are simply different kinds of mental acts. From this point of view, an object can be given through different mental acts, and these mental acts are the different ways in which the object is determined. Needless to say, this interpretation does not agree with Frege's repeated insistence that senses are objective, nonmental entities.

Since Frege implies that referents are somehow presented through the medium of what he calls the senses of expressions, one may think that senses play a role comparable to ordinary ideas. According to some philosophical systems, the "objects of the outside world" are known through ideas. These ideas are, of course, mental entities, while Frege's senses are nonmental; otherwise the latter are very much like the former. In particular, the connection between a sense and its referent resembles the relation between an idea and what it represents.

This interpretation does not quite agree with the example of the *Begriffsschrift*, where a point is given in direct intuition, which, I take it, means that it is not mediated in any way. In "Über Sinn und Bedeutung" Frege clearly states that senses always intervene between mental ideas and objective referents. This difference also occurs in a linguistic form. In the *Begriffsschrift* the point given in direct intuition is labeled with the letter 'A'; no further description is associated with this label. But in a footnote of his later paper, Frege claims that even proper names like 'Aristotle' have a sense.[5] He remarks that there may be different opinions about the sense of this proper name; one may take its sense to be *The pupil of Plato and teacher of Alexander the Great*, or one could take as its sense *The teacher of Alexander the Great who was born in Stagira*. Even though there may be these different opinions, it seems clear that Frege wishes to hold that some sense attaches to the proper name. If so, then we have a point when we try to compare representative ideas with senses.

I shall always distinguish between labels and descriptions. 'Aristotle,' for example, is a label, while 'The pupil of Plato and teacher of Alexander the Great' is a description. 'Green,' to use another example, is a label, while 'The color of the book before me on my desk' is a description. There are labels and descriptions for individual objects, properties of such

5. *SB*, p. 27; *T*, p. 58.

objects, and so on. So far, I think, my distinction is sufficiently clear. But a certain philosophical consideration threatens to spoil it. Russell, for example, holds that we cannot use labels for entities with which we are not acquainted. If someone uses the word 'Aristotle' but is not acquainted with the great philosopher, then he cannot be *using the expression as a label*. Rather, in his case, the word functions as an abbreviation for some description such as 'The pupil of Plato and teacher of Alexander the Great.' This means that we cannot tell from the expression itself whether it is *used as a label*; we must also know if the person who uses the expression is acquainted with its referent.

Properly understood, Russell's view is sound. Unfortunately, it has created many misunderstandings. In order to avoid at least some of these, I shall not use the term 'label' in the manner in which Russell uses the term 'logical proper name.' I shall continue to say that 'Aristotle' and 'green' are labels, regardless of whether these expressions are used by people who are acquainted with their referents.[6] Most of the labels of, say, English, have been attached to their respective entities by other people, people who lived long before us or people who live far away from us.[7] When we learn a language, we learn, among other things, which (arbitrary) labels are attached to what entities. Once we have learned what some of these labels represent, we can learn what others represent without being directly acquainted with their referents. We have learned, for example, what the word 'Aristotle' represents not by having ever met Aristotle but by having been told that there lived a great philosopher who was the pupil of Plato and the teacher of Alexander the Great and who was called Aristotle. A blind man, to use another example, may learn what the word 'green' represents by learning that it represents a property of a certain kind.[8] Thus it is simply a fact that we use labels, even when we are not acquainted with their referents.

What, then, shall we say about Russell's view on logical proper names? Consider once more the name 'Aristotle.' This is a label. It is not ordinarily *used* as anything else, even if the speaker is not acquainted with Aris-

6. Whenever we deal with a label of an individual thing the expression 'proper name' could be used instead.

7. We usually describe individual things but use labels for properties. This could be due to the fact that most individual things are not as important to a large number of people as most properties are.

8. A blind person, needless to say, is not even acquainted with the "immediate" properties of colors. He can only know that there is a property with certain causal effects.

totle. Since I never met Aristotle, all that I know about him I have learned by having had him described to me. I was told that there lived a person at such-and-such a place so-and-so many years ago; that this person was a pupil of Plato; that he taught Alexander the Great; and so on. I learned, among other things, that the person who had all these properties was called 'Aristotle.' In other words, I learned what label other people attached to that person. On the other hand, someone who knew Aristotle personally knew many properties of the great philosopher, not through description but through acquaintance. He may have known, for example, that Aristotle had a long nose, because he had seen Aristotle's nose; he had neither been told nor had he read somewhere that Aristotle had a long nose. Since he had seen Aristotle's nose, he also knew that there was a philosopher with a long nose, not because anyone had told him so but because he had seen such a philosopher. In short, we may know that there are certain entities and what they are, either from our own observations or from communication with others. There is, as Russell put it, knowledge by acquaintance and knowledge by description.

I think that by a logical proper name Russell means a label which is used by someone who is acquainted with its referent. The same expression, when used by someone who is not acquainted with its referent but who has had the referent described to him, is called an abbreviation of a description (for that person), namely, of the description which was used to describe the referent to him. Whether an expression is a logical proper name thus depends on who uses it. I prefer to make Russell's distinction in terms of acquaintance. My distinction between labels and descriptions does not depend on whether someone is acquainted with something. From the fact that someone uses a certain label, say, the proper name 'Aristotle,' it does not follow that he is or is not acquainted with its referent. We may, of course, distinguish these two possibilities. We may ask whether a person has met Aristotle or whether he has only heard or read about the great philosopher.[9] If he has only heard or read about him, then we know of course that the great philosopher was *described* to him.

9. Russell seems to be of two minds about logical proper names. Sometimes he seems to hold the view which I have so far attributed to him, namely, that an expression is a label if and only if it is simple and if it is used by someone who is acquainted with its referent. At other times, though, he seems to hold a narrower view — that a person can use an expression as a label *only as long as* its referent is actually present. Perhaps he merely means that one can only *attach* a label to what is present, and not that one cannot use a label that has already been attached. If so, then I agree with him.

To summarize, I shall distinguish between labels and descriptions. This distinction is relative to a given language.[10] It has nothing to do with whether a person who uses an expression is acquainted with its referent. However, we must distinguish between two cases: A person may or may not be acquainted with the referent of a given label. If he is not acquainted with the referent, then he can only know what that referent is by having had it described to him. Put differently, unless a person is acquainted with a certain entity, he can only know about it through a description. Hence there are many labels in English which are used by people who are not acquainted with their referents but who know what these referents are by having had descriptions of them. Finally, it is clear that one can only attach a label to something when that thing is present. To be more precise, one can only label something which is not first thought of through a description when that entity is perceived.

Frege, we recall, says that there may be different opinions about the sense of the proper name 'Aristotle.' I think that this remark somehow reflects the fact that we learn what the expression 'Aristotle' represents through a description. What Frege seems to have in mind is the fact that different people may have been introduced to the referent of 'Aristotle' through different descriptions. Assume that someone has been told that Aristotle was the pupil of Plato and teacher of Alexander the Great. Let us also assume for the moment that the expression 'The pupil of Plato and teacher of Alexander the Great' is a definite description. Frege seems to hold that the sense of 'Aristotle' is for that person the sense of 'The pupil of Plato and teacher of Alexander the Great.' For another person, the sense of 'Aristotle' may be given by another description of the Greek philosopher. In general, Frege's view seems to be that proper names get their senses through descriptions. Proper names, if I may put it so, have a sense only derivatively; descriptions are the primary sources of senses.

This interpretation agrees with the fact that senses are ways in which objects can be presented. In the case of a description, there is an intuitively

---

10. I shall argue below that this is really a distinction between words and sentences. Ontologically speaking, it is the difference between states of affairs on the one hand and entities other than states of affairs on the other. I hope it will not be objected that one can use single words — for example, in Latin — to represent states of affairs. The answer to this objection is obvious.

clear distinction between the entity described and the particular manner in which it is described. The same thing may be described in different ways. In the case of labels, though, there is no similar distinction. Even if we assume that there are two labels for the same thing, nothing in or about either one tells us more than the other about that thing. Labels are distinguished from each other only as marks or noises. There is no distinction between a label's referent and the way that referent is labeled by this particular label. This seems to show that labels have no senses. For example, 'Aristotle' represents a certain person but does not express a sense. How does this conclusion agree with Frege's remarks about the sense of 'Aristotle'?

Aristotle is (identical with) the pupil of Plato who taught Alexander the Great. Hence we may try to defend the view that all names express senses by assigning to proper names senses expressed by descriptions. But this attempt immediately runs into a difficulty. Since Aristotle can be described in many different ways, how can we know which of many possible senses to assign to the proper name? Or shall we say that it has all these senses? This difficulty clearly shows that proper names do not express senses in the same way in which descriptions may be said to do so. It reveals that any attempt to endow proper names with senses will be artificial and arbitrary. Proper names simply do not express senses. In the case of Aristotle, there is another consideration which may conceal this fact. Since it so happens that we all learned who Aristotle was by having him described to us, we can narrow down the possible senses; we can hold that the proper name has the sense of the description by means of which we were first told about Aristotle.[11] But this move only shifts the problem from one plane to another. It now turns out that a proper name has different senses when used by different people. With descriptions, on the other hand, no such relativity occurs.

That labels do not express senses is perhaps more obvious if we use a different example. Consider the sentence 'This is green.' Here 'this' functions as a label. It is not an abbreviation of 'The thing called *"this."* '[12] No one else may ever have called this thing 'this.' Or consider the word

---

11. Alternatively, one may even try to defend the view that the proper name has the sense of whatever description is on the mind of a person who uses the proper name at a given moment.

12. Of course, 'this' is a peculiar kind of label; what it labels depends on the circumstances. The referent of 'Aristotle,' by comparison, is always the same. The peculiarity of 'this' makes it useful when the listener is present, and completely worthless when he is absent.

'green.' It, too, is a mere label. It represents a certain color, but it does not express a sense, that is, it does not present this color in a particular manner.

If labels do not express senses, then how are we to explain, in the Fregean fashion, the cognitive value of a statement like 'Venus is the morning star'? If 'Venus' expresses no sense, then it cannot have a sense different from the sense of 'the morning star.' The statement cannot inform us that two senses happen to be connected with the same object. Rather, it must be telling us that a certain object is connected with a certain sense. Then we can explain why the statement is synthetic; for it is presumably not analytic that a certain object is connected with a certain sense. Thus we can distinguish between two kinds of synthetic identity statements: identity statements with two descriptions tell us that one and the same object is connected with two specific senses; identity statements with one label and one description tell us that a certain object is connected with a certain sense. I think that these considerations show that the problem of identity can be solved in the Fregean fashion, even if we assume that labels do not express a sense. The important ingredient of Frege's approach is the view that descriptions have senses as well as referents, not that all names have both a sense and a reference. There are excellent arguments for the contention that labels do not express senses, and we do not even need to assume that they do in order to solve the problem of identity in the Fregean style.

Suppose we wish to know whether Aristotle was the pupil of Plato who taught Alexander the Great, or in Fregean terms, whether a certain object is connected with a certain sense. If we assume that an object can only be presented to us through the medium of a sense, then there is no easy answer to our inquiry; the object in question would have to be presented to us through a certain sense, which raises the further question as to whether it is connected with this sense. To be more precise, in order to decide whether a given object is connected with a given sense, we would first have to know whether that object is connected with a certain sense. Hence, our question leads to an infinite regress, and in order to escape from it we must assume that an object can be given at least sometimes "directly," that is, not through a sense.

This objection to Frege's view is rather familiar. Recall that I compared Frege's senses with the ideas of the representative realist. This comparison was invited by Frege's assertion that senses intervene between mental ideas on the one hand and their objects on the other.[13] The representative realist has to face up to the same kind of objection. Unless we can decide that a given idea represents a certain object without having to know first that a certain idea represents that object, we can never find out whether any given idea represents a certain object.[14] This objection is as fatal to the representative realist view as it is to Frege's doctrine of senses as intervening between ideas and objects.

We must therefore reject at least two parts of Frege's doctrine. First, we must reject the view that *every* name expresses a sense. Insisting on a distinction between labels and descriptions, we may hold provisionally that descriptions express a sense while labels do not. Second, we must reject the related view that every object is somehow presented to us through a sense. Instead, we have to hold that objects can be presented to us directly. Let me put the matter in less abstract terms at the price of being no longer completely faithful to Frege's general approach. First, we must recognize that entities can be either named (labeled) or described. We must recognize, in other words, that there is a very fundamental difference between proper names and descriptions. Second, we must realize that we can perceive objects directly without having them first described to us.[15]

We arrive, then, at a modified Fregean view. Assuming that there are senses, and making a distinction between labels and descriptions, we may hold that descriptions both express a sense and have a referent, while labels only refer. The problem of identity, as posed by Frege, can be solved with this modified view. To see this, we must first distinguish between identity statements with labels and identity statements which involve at least one description. If we have a true identity statement with two labels, then we know that as a matter of linguistic fact one entity happens to be called by two different names. Such a statement does not provide us with any nonlinguistic information. In order to keep this fact in mind without having to mention it repeatedly, we shall talk about a language that contains only one label for any given entity. In such a language, all true identity statements with labels are of the form '$a = a$.' They are substitution instances of the logical truth that every entity is identical with itself.

13. Compare, for example, Frege's analogy of the telescope in *SB*, p. 30; *T*, p. 60.
14. For a detailed discussion of representative realism see *SM*.
15. I do not mean to say, of course, that direct realism is true.

Hence, all the true identity statements with labels are, in Frege's sense, analytic. In addition to such statements, however, there are also identity statements with descriptions. If such an identity statement is true, then it conveys new information. For example, that the morning star is the evening star is an interesting *astronomical* fact. Such statements are therefore, in Frege's sense, synthetic, and, as such, they give rise to the problem of identity. We may attempt to solve this problem in a Fregean fashion by distinguishing between a sense and a reference for descriptions.

□

This leads back to the main questions: What are senses? How are they connected with objects? I do not think that there are satisfactory answers to these two questions, but I shall not endeavor to go through all the conceivable answers, one by one, in order to show that they will not do. I am convinced that there are no satisfactory answers, because I am convinced that there are no such entities as senses. If this is so, then it is not at all surprising that senses must remain nebulous entities in Frege's system.[16] However, some philosophers will no doubt continue to defend Frege's distinction between sense and reference, if for no other reason than to draw spurious support for their own views. Some will undoubtedly identify senses with meanings, where meanings are thought of as attached to expressions independently of any referents. What should disturb these philosophers is the fact that Frege thinks of senses as entities. Others will think of senses as individual concepts.[17] This view, I believe, is closer to the spirit of Frege's philosophy. But by the same token it is also as unacceptable as is Frege's position; for as little as there are senses, just so little are there individual concepts. The problem of identity, we saw, is

16. Wienpahl has argued that Frege's senses are combinations of physical properties of expressions. Consider an identity statement with two descriptions. Wienpahl claims that the only differences between the two descriptions are (a) a difference in physical shape, and (b) a difference in referents of the components of the descriptions. He argues that the difference in sense cannot be the difference (b), for he holds that simple signs may have a sense. He concludes that it must be the difference (a) which constitutes the difference in sense (P. D. Wienpahl, "Frege's Sinn und Bedeutung," *Mind*, LIX [1950], 483–94).

I would object to this argument that simple signs do not have a sense; if anything has a sense, then descriptions and only descriptions have one. I would therefore claim that it is the difference (b) that leads to a distinction between different senses.

17. Compare, for example, R. Carnap, *Meaning and Necessity* (Chicago, 1947); also A. Church, "A Formulation of the Logic of Sense and Denotation," in *Structure, Method and Meaning: Essays in Honor of Henry M. Sheffer* (New York, 1951).

the problem of the nature of descriptions. And the nature of descriptions must be clarified without resource to such nebulous entities as senses, meanings, or individual concepts.[18]

Earlier, in the *Grundlagen*, before Frege introduces the distinction between sense and reference, he characterizes descriptions in the following manner: First, he says that descriptions *define* or *determine* an object by means of a concept. Recall that Russell, too, speaks of descriptions as defining their objects. Second, Frege points out that, in order to be able to determine an object by means of a concept, it is necessary to show that there is precisely one object that falls under the concept. Third, if this condition is not fulfilled, if it is not the case that precisely one object falls under the relevant concept, then the description has no *content* or *sense*.[19] We could rephrase Frege's last point by saying that a description which does not describe precisely one thing has no meaning. These remarks show that Frege is well aware of the distinction between labels and descriptions. He realizes quite clearly that descriptions, as distinguished from labels, are complex expressions. Nonetheless, Frege chooses to neglect this fundamental difference between labels and descriptions. Instead, he concentrates on the distinction between concept words and names of objects. Russell, by comparison, was not only aware of the difference between labels and descriptions but made the most of it in his attempts to solve a series of philosophical problems.

Assume that we are constructing a clarified "language" of the kind found in *Principia Mathematica*. We could decide to introduce only labels which actually represent something. We could also decide to introduce descriptions, irrespective of whether they represent precisely one entity. Finally, we could further decide not to use abbreviations of descriptions, with the result that a description could always be distinguished from a label by its complexity. If we encounter a "language" constructed according to these conventions, then we always know that *a* exists, provided we know that '*a*' is a label of the "language." In order to *say* that *a* exists, we would, of course, have to have an expression like 'exists.' But notice that sentences like '*a* exists' would be superfluous in our artificial "language."

18. The one philosopher who has always seen this clearly is, of course, Russell.
19. *F*, pp. 87–88n.

That *a* exists would not have to be *said*, since it is already *shown* by the occurrence of '*a*.' Hence we can get along without an expression like 'exists.' Similar considerations do not hold for English, which has not been so constructed that every simple expression has a referent; it contains labels which do not label anything. Hence it is not superfluous or uninformative to point out in English that Hamlet does not exist, while London exists.

Descriptions, we assumed, are admitted into the clarified "language" irrespective of whether they represent an entity. From the occurrence of an expression of the form 'the *x* which is *F*,' we cannot tell whether there is such an *x*. Now there are in *PM* certain theorems which hold only if the relevant description has a referent. For example, proposition 14.18 says: If the *x* which is *F exists*, then if all *x* are *G*, the *x* which if *F* will also be *G*. In order to express this proposition, Russell believes that he must introduce a new sign, corresponding to the English word 'exists.' He writes 'E! ($\imath x$) $F(x)$' for 'the *x* which is *F* exists.' [20] I wish to emphasize that this new sign is only needed — if it is needed at all — because we have admitted descriptions which do not describe anything.[21]

Every sentence in the artificial "language" that consists of labels will be either true or false. But what shall we say about sentences with descriptions which do not describe something? According to the rules of construction, these are perfectly well-formed sentences, and yet we hesitate to say that they are either true or false. Frege avoids this puzzle by "defining" a function, representing the definite article, in such a way that every description has a referent.[22] According to Frege, the description 'the *x* which is *F*' refers to a certain object, if there is precisely one such object which is *F*; otherwise, it represents the value-range determined by the concept *F*. By means of this "definition," Frege assures that every sentence of his clarified "language" has a truth-value, even if it contains a description which does not seem to describe anything. I have said that Frege avoids the puzzle, not that he solves it. The important question is this:

---

20. The peculiarity of 'E!' has often been noticed. I shall explain presently why there really is no need for such a sign.

21. For a quite different approach compare D. Hilbert and P. Bernays, *Grundlagen der Mathematik* (Berlin, 1934), vol. I. For an excellent discussion of the connection between our "classical" treatment of descriptions and the intuitionistic method of Hilbert and Bernays, see K. Schröter, "Theorie des bestimmten Artikels," *Zeitschrift für mathematische Logik und Grundlagen der Mathematik*, II (1956), 37–56.

22. Compare esp. *GG*, I, 18–20; and also *SB*, p. 42n.; *T*, p. 71n.

Do descriptions that do not describe precisely one entity represent any-thing? Frege believes that they do not. He therefore "postulates" or "de-crees" that they shall have a reference. Surely this will not do. If certain descriptions do not have a referent, we cannot just provide them with one. As Frege himself so often points out, it makes absolutely no sense to "pos-tulate" entities, be they numbers or, as in this case, referents of descriptions.[23] Frege must therefore still face the original problem: Given that certain descriptions do not refer to anything, do we not have to admit that there are (declarative) sentences which are neither true nor false? Of course, there are a number of ways out, and I shall propose one presently, but to "assign" referents to descriptions is not a solution.

After these introductory remarks, let us turn to a more systematic dis-cussion of descriptions. I shall start with Russell's theory of descriptions, not only because it is well known but also because my own view is simply a version of it. To refresh our memory, let us note the following impor-tant points of Russell's approach. First, Russell takes expressions like 'the horse in front of my house' to be short for expressions like 'the thing (in-dividual) which is a horse in front of my house.' Consequently, he repre-sents the former by the expression '$(\imath x)\ F(x)$.' I fully agree with this step. It seems to me that expressions like 'the horse in front of my house' ex-press the very same thought (or part of a thought) as expressions like 'the individual thing which is a horse in front of my house,' just as I am con-vinced that expressions like 'all men' and 'some men' are merely short for 'all individual things which are men' and 'some individual things which are men,' respectively.[24] Second, Russell claims that '$(\imath x)\ F(x)$' is an *in-complete symbol*, that is, an expression which does not represent an entity. His notion of an incomplete symbol implies that any sentence which con-tains the expression '$(\imath x)\ F(x)$' is capable of being *analyzed* into a sen-tence that no longer contains this expression. Finally, Russell holds that

23. I do not mean to say, however, that it makes no sense to *assume* that there are certain entities, when one is not sure.

24. However, there is well-known asymmetry between 'all men' and 'some men.' 'All' and 'some' are, in my view, words for quantifiers of individuals, properties, etc. Hence, if I want to say that all men are mortal, I must do so by talking about all *individual things*. I do not want to say, of course, that all individual things are men (and are mortal). I must therefore say that all individual things, *if* they are men, etc. A similar consideration does not arise for the quantifier *some*. It makes no difference whether I say 'some things which are men are mortal' or 'some things are men and are mortal.'

every sentence which contains a description as the subject term can be "translated" into a sentence of the form

$$(\exists x) \, ((y) \, (F(y) \equiv (x = y)) \, \& \, \ldots x \ldots).^{25}$$

Russell's view raises the question whether

$$G(\imath x) \, F(x))$$
$$(\exists x) \, ((y) \, (F(y) \equiv (x = y)) \, \& \, G(x))$$

is supposed to be *equivalent* to

or an *abbreviation* of it. Of course, Russell claims that he is "defining" the incomplete symbol as it occurs in the context *G*. But we have learned from Frege's case to be rather wary of the claim that something is a matter of definition. As to the question, I am not sure that it has a clear-cut answer. Russell, I would venture to claim, was not always too clear about the nature of "philosophical analysis." In my view, the two sentences do not express the same thought; they do not represent the same state of affairs. Hence the one cannot be a mere abbreviation of the other. However, I do believe that the two sentences are equivalent to each other. It seems to me that the following sentence is a *logical truth*: 'For all properties *f* and *g*: the individual thing *x* which is *f* has the property *g* if and only if there is an individual thing *x* such that any individual *y* is *f* if and only if it is the same as *x* and, furthermore, *x* has the property *g*.' I consider this a logical truth, rather than, say, an arithmetical or set-theoretical one, because it is about entities and their *properties* in general. I think of the description quantifier as another quantifier in addition to *all* and *some*.

This, then, is my answer; but I hasten to add that I do not know how to "prove" that it is the correct one. If someone claims that the two sentences under discussion express the very same thought, that they represent the very same state of affairs, then I do not know how to persuade him that he is wrong. Obviously, he will also insist that he clearly intuits this fact, and how am I to show that he has in reality no such intuition? This kind of difficulty arises from the very nature of the case. Our ordinary intuitions do not allow us to decide the matter at a glance; it usually takes a rather complicated argument to convince us. That our ordinary intuitions often fail us is not due to any particular insurmountable difficulty but simply to the fact that we are, in ordinary life, not often called upon to distinguish sharply between saying the same thing in different words and say-

25. In the following discussion, I shall take considerations of scope for granted. I shall assume, with Russell, that we must distinguish between a primary and a secondary scope of descriptions. But I shall not explicitly mention this distinction unless it becomes important.

ing different things in logically equivalent ways. Another case in point is the "definition" of the so-called existential quantifier in terms of the universal one. In this case, too, we have, in my opinion, a logical equivalence. It is a matter of the logical structure of the world rather than a matter of the grammatical structure of our language that whenever some F are G, it is not the case that all things are not F and G.[26]

Consider next Russell's claim that '$(\imath x)\ F(x)$' is an incomplete symbol. If it is, then my view must be false. The two sentences cannot simply be equivalent to each other; rather, the shorter sentence must be an abbreviation of the longer one. If they were merely equivalent, then the sentence with the description would have a meaning of its own; it would not simply express the same thought and represent the same state of affairs as the longer "existential" sentence. But if it has a meaning of its own, then it is difficult to see how the expression '$(\imath x)\ F(x)$' could fail to have a meaning of its own. After all, the expression '$G((\imath x)\ F(x))$' consists of the predicate 'G' and the subject '$(\imath x)\ F(x)$' just like an expression of the form '$G(a)$.'[27] But it is the assertion that '$(\imath x)\ F(x)$' has a meaning by itself which Russell denies when he calls it an incomplete symbol. Hence it follows from Russell's contention that the two sentences are not merely equivalent but that the one is an abbreviation of the other. We seem to be faced with the following dilemma. Either '$(\imath x)\ F(x)$' is an incomplete symbol or it is not. If it is, then the sentence which contains it must be an abbreviation of the "existential" sentence. But it is not an abbreviation of that sentence. On the other hand, if '$(\imath x)\ F(x)$' is not an incomplete symbol, then it has an "independent" meaning. But this means that it must represent something. Yet, there are descriptions which do not represent anything.

The second horn of this dilemma reveals Russell's reason for calling '$(\imath x)\ F(x)$' an incomplete symbol. He argues as follows.[28] Consider the

---

26. It may be objected that *in a certain system*, like *PM*, one quantifier may indeed be used as a mere abbreviation for another. My answer is that inasmuch as '(x)' is used as a mere abbreviation of 'not $(\exists x)$ not,' the former expression does not represent the notion *all individuals* (are such that); if it does, then it is not really an abbreviation of the latter expression.

27. Russell must be wrong in denying an "independent" meaning to definite descriptions. We all understand expressions like 'the pen on my desk' or 'the present king of France' perfectly well even without a context.

28. Compare, for example, *PM*, I, 66. Notice how Russell at this point compresses the problem of equivalence versus abbreviation into the expression 'i.e.' when he says that the sentence 'The round square does not exist' is of the form

$$\text{`} {\sim} E!\ (\imath x)\ f(x) \text{' i.e., `} {\sim} (\exists x)\ ((y)\ (f(y) \equiv (x = y))).\text{'}$$

sentence 'The round square does not exist.' This is a true sentence. But we cannot assume that this sentence denies the existence of a certain entity called 'the round square.' Hence we seem to be forced to assume that 'the round square' does not represent anything. Obviously, though, we cannot formulate true sentences of nothing. If we assume that '$(\imath x) \ F(x)$' has a referent, we are forced to say that 'the round square' represents an entity, namely, the round square.[29] On the other hand, if we deny that this expression has a referent, then we seem to be unable to explain what the sentence 'The round square does not exist' is about and how it could possibly be true. Russell concludes from these considerations that we must reject the implicit assumption that '$(\imath x) \ F(x)$' functions like a singular term. His rejection leads him to hold that '$(\imath x) \ F(x)$' is not an independent expression with a separate meaning. For my purpose, it is extremely important to distinguish between the two quite different claims, (a) that a description is not a term, and (b) that it has no meaning outside of a context. I shall argue that (a) is indeed true, while (b) is false. Of course, it is very likely that Russell saw no way of denying that descriptions are terms other than by asserting that they have no meaning outside of contexts. If so, then he overlooked the most obvious alternative. At any rate, if I can show that descriptions have an independent meaning, then we may reject the view that sentences in which they occur are abbreviations of longer sentences in which they do not occur. In particular, we shall be able to hold that Russell's so-called definition of descriptions is in reality an equivalence statement.

Compare the three expressions 'All things are round squares,' 'Some things are round squares,' and 'The thing is a round square.' The last sentence is not very common, but we must not be too squeamish about matters of usage. I shall treat all three sentences alike and propose the following three abbreviations: '(Ax) round-square(x),' '(Sx) round-square(x),'

29. Meinong's view may be explicated as follows. He objects — correctly, I think — to Russell's claim that a definite description has no meaning outside of a context. Thus he objects also to the implicit claim that the definiens and the definiendum of Russell's crucial "definition" have the same meaning. In short, Meinong sees no other possibility but to treat a description as a term. Since he agrees with Russell that 'the round square' must have a referent if it is a term, he holds that some terms have referents which do not exist. I find Russell's view that descriptions are incomplete symbols as unsatisfactory as Meinong's view that they are terms which represent nonexistent entities. On the other hand, I do not see how one can avoid these views, unless one realizes from the very beginning of the analysis that descriptions are not terms.

and '(Tx) round-square(x).'[30] These three abbreviations correspond nicely to Russell's three expressions: '(x) round-square(x),' '$(\exists x)$ round-square(x),' and '$(\imath x)$ round-square(x).' But Russell does not even seem to notice how very much alike his three expressions are. He maintains that the first two are sentences while the third behaves like a term.[31] I, on the other hand, shall take their obvious likeness seriously and treat all three expressions as sentences. This is only the first step.

I conceded that expressions of the kind 'The thing is a round square' may not be frequent. The phrase that is common is 'The thing which is a round square.' But this group of words always occurs in a context like 'The thing which is a round square is green.' Compare therefore the sentence (1) 'The thing which is a round square is green' with the two sentences (2) 'All things which are round squares are green' and (3) 'Some things which are round squares are green.' If it is true, that these three sentences are expanded versions of the three sentences 'The round square is green,' 'All round squares are green,' and 'Some round squares are green,' then it is also true that the three grammatical terms 'the round square,' 'all round squares,' and 'some round squares' are merely short for three peculiar *predicative* expressions. They contain, if I may put it so, a hidden predication. In this respect, the states of affairs represented by (1), (2), and (3) differ essentially from the states of affairs represented by such sentences as 'This is green' and 'Berlin is an exciting city.' While the sentence 'This is green' predicates the color green of something, the sentence 'The round square is green' not only predicates a color of something but also predicates the property of being a round square of something. Frege, it is usually acknowledged, was the first who clearly realized that such sentences as 'All round squares are green' and 'Some round squares are green' conceal a double predication. But neither he nor Russell applied this important insight to sentences like 'The round square is green.' I shall do so. This is the second step.

Although the sentences (1), (2), and (3) resemble one another in that all three contain a double predication, nevertheless they represent quite different states of affairs. Their similar grammatical construction hides a profound difference among the states of affairs which they represent. For example, the sentences (2) and (3) differ only in the first word: (2) starts with the word 'all,' while (3) starts with 'some.' Yet, what they represent

30. The expression 'round-square(x)' is itself an abbreviation of 'round(x) and square(x).'
31. Russell, of course, in this respect follows in the footsteps of Frege.

is quite different in still another respect. We can change (3) into the sentence 'Some things are round squares and green,' but we cannot replace (2) by the sentence 'All things are round squares and green.' What we wish to say by means of (2) is not that all things in the world are round squares and green but merely that those things which are round squares are green. I am calling attention to this well-known difference between (2) and (3) because I maintain that there is a similar difference between (1) on the one hand and (2) and (3) on the other. A moment's reflection reveals that (1) 'The thing which is a round square is green' can neither be changed into 'The thing is a round square and green,' nor can it be replaced by 'The thing, if it is a round square, is green.' We can at best reformulate (1) as 'The thing is a round square and that thing is green.' This means that we cannot translate (1) into either '(Tx) (round-square(x) & green(x))' or '(Tx) (round-square$(x) \supset$ green(x)).' Russell, we know, replaces (1) by 'green $((\imath x)$ round-square$(x))$.' This translation reflects his conviction that '$(\imath x)$ round-square(x)' is a term. Since I do not share this opinion, I have to propose a different translation. Within the framework of *PM*, the best translation of (1) seems to me to be the sentence '(Tx) round-square(x) & (Sx) (round-square(x) & green(x)).' This is the third and final step.[32] However, if *PM* would allow for a simpler or more idiomatic formulation, I would be glad to accept it. I insist on only one point: Definite descriptions, since they contain a hidden predication, must be treated as representing states of affairs.

Russell is wrong when he holds that descriptions are incomplete symbols, but he is right when he claims that they are not "*ordinary* terms." Descriptions are not terms, because they abbreviate sentences. '(Tx) $F(x)$' has the form of a sentence, just like '(Sx) $F(x)$' and '(Ax) $F(x)$.' But descriptions are not incomplete symbols either. They have a meaning by themselves. Since they are sentences in disguise, they express whole thoughts and represent states of affairs. The expression '(Tx) $F(x)$' is as "complete" as the expressions '(Sx) $F(x)$' and '(Ax) $F(x)$.' Finally, just as we know that the sentence

$$(Af) ((Ax) f(x) \equiv \sim(Sx) \sim f(x))$$

is true, so we know that the sentence

$$(Af) ((Tx) f(x) \equiv (Sx) ((y)(f(y) \equiv (x=y))))$$

32. See Schröter, "Theorie des bestimmten Artikels," for an axiomatic treatment of this translation.

is true.[33] This means that '$(Tx)\ F(x)$' is logically equivalent to

$$(Sx)\ ((y)\ (F(y) \equiv (x = y))).$$

How do we analyze the sentence 'The round square does not exist'? We can express the same thought by '$\sim(Tx)$ round-square(x).' This is analogous to the sentence '$\sim(Sx)$ round-square(x).' The sentence '$\sim(Tx)$ round-square(x)' does not contain a singular term which may refer to a "subsistent" round square. It contains merely the predicate 'round-square.' Russell achieves the same result by holding that the relevant description is an incomplete symbol, and that the meaning of every sentence which contains this incomplete symbol is given by the familiar definiens in terms of the existential quantifier. However, this view forces him to introduce the peculiar symbol 'E!' Since he holds that a description is an incomplete symbol, he "defines" it only within a context. Under ordinary circumstances, the context is a predicative one. For example, if we say that the round square is green, then we have the predicative context represented by '. . . is green.' But when we say that the round square does not exist, then we no longer have an ordinary predicative context. Yet, according to Russell's view, there must be some kind of context if the sentence is to have any meaning at all. Hence Russell is forced to introduce the extraordinary context of existence through the symbol 'E!' This is analogous to writing the sentence 'It is not the case that there are some men' as '$\sim$E!$(Sx)\ F(x)$.' [34]

It follows from my view that every description has a referent, in Frege's sense of this term, for every description, since it is a disguised sentence, is either true or false. If we assume for the moment that Frege's view is correct and that there are such objects as the True and the False, then we need not cast about for artificial referents for "empty" descriptions. If the description is fulfilled, then it refers to the True; otherwise, it refers to the False. Of course, I do not agree with Frege that there are such objects as the True and the False. I hold that true sentences refer to actual states of

33. '$(Tx)\ F(x)$' is also equivalent, of course, to the arithmetical sentence '$(1x)\ F(x)$.'

34. Just as we have to distinguish between '$\sim(Sx)\ F(x)$' and '$(Sx)\ \frown\ F(x)$,' so we must distinguish between '$\sim(Tx)\ F(x)$' and '$(Tx)\ \sim F(x)$.' Furthermore, consider the sentence 'George IV wished to know whether some men are mortal.' The context in which it occurs may tell us whether what is meant is (1) 'George IV wished to know whether some individuals are men and are mortal' or (2) 'Some individuals are men and George IV wished to know whether these individuals are mortal.' Similarly, we must distinguish between (3) 'George IV wished to know whether the individual who wrote *Waverley* is Scott' and (4) 'The individual who wrote *Waverley* is such that George IV wished to know whether he is Scott.' This is, of course, Russell's distinction between secondary and primary scope.

affairs (facts), while false sentences represent possible states of affairs. Descriptions which are fulfilled represent actual states of affairs, while descriptions which are not fulfilled represent possible states of affairs. This general view seems to commit me to possible states of affairs, but actually it does not. I shall discuss this matter in the next section on truth.[35] Let me merely point out now that, according to my view, the problem of "empty" descriptions becomes the problem of false sentences.

Let us now turn to Frege's discussion of descriptions as they occur in ordinary discourse.[36] Frege's example is the sentence 'Whoever discovered the elliptic form of the planetary orbits died in misery.' Call this sentence *A* and the description in it *B*.[37] Frege claims that *B* does not express a Thought. He thus implies that *B* is not short for a whole sentence which would express a Thought and refer to a truth-value. Obviously, this runs counter to my explication of descriptions. How does Frege argue for his contention? He claims that it is impossible to reformulate the description in such a way that it becomes a sentence which expresses a Thought. According to Frege, *B* is not a disguised sentence, because the grammatical subject 'whoever' has no independent sense but merely establishes a relation to the clause 'died in misery.'

Frege's argument is not convincing. Consider the sentence 'Whatever is a whale is a mammal.' We may then argue in the Fregean fashion that the expression 'whatever is a whale' cannot represent a Thought, that it cannot be a sentence in disguise; for, otherwise, it would have to be possible to change this expression into a sentence. But this is impossible, because the grammatical subject 'whatever' has no independent sense but merely establishes a relation to the clause 'is a mammal.' However, we know that Frege would not argue like this in regard to the sentence 'Whatever is a whale is a mammal.' We know that he treats 'whatever is a whale' as a predicative expression of the form 'all objects are such that if they are whales.' The word 'whatever' has the same sense as the expression 'Every (all) object(s) which.' There is no reason why a similar analysis

35. See *SM*.

36. Compare *T*, pp. 68–70.

37. We take it, of course, that the meaning of 'whoever' is roughly that of 'the man' in this context, and that a definite description is intended.

must be rejected for descriptions. I believe that in this context 'whoever' means the same as 'the individual who' ('the individual thing which').

Frege does not consider this objection to his claim. Instead, he discusses a different criticism. Someone may object that *A* must contain the Thought that there was somebody who discovered the elliptic form of the planetary orbits, because whoever takes *A* to be true cannot deny this Thought. Frege agrees that whoever accepts *A* cannot deny the Thought mentioned, but he rejects the idea that this is because *A contains* the Thought. Rather, it is due to the fact that *A* could not be true unless the description *B* had a referent, and *B* could not have a referent unless there was somebody who discovered the elliptic form of the planetary orbits. Frege contends that the truth of *A presupposes* the existence of a referent of the description *B* and hence presupposes the truth of the Thought mentioned earlier. Frege argues that if *A* is true, then the Thought must be true — not because *A* contains the Thought, but rather because the truth of *A* presupposes the truth of the Thought. Before we discuss the notion of presupposition, let us see why Frege rejects the view that *A* contains the Thought rather than presupposes it.[38]

Since Frege complicates matters at this point by switching to the sentence 'Kepler died in misery,' I shall try to make his point in regard to *A*. Frege argues that if the Thought expressed by *A* contained the Thought that there was somebody who discovered the elliptic form of the planetary orbits, then the negation of *A* would have to be: "Whoever discovered the elliptic form of the planetary orbits did not die in misery, or the expression 'whoever discovered the elliptic form of the planetary orbits' has no reference." But, so Frege contends, the negation of *A* is not this sentence, but rather : "Whoever discovered the elliptic form of the planetary orbits did not die in misery." Hence, Frege concludes, *A* cannot contain the Thought that there was somebody who discovered the elliptic form of the planetary orbits.

Let us once more change Frege's example slightly. We shall assume that the negation of *A*, if it contained the Thought mentioned earlier, would have to read: 'Whoever discovered the elliptic form of the planetary orbits did not die in misery, or it is not the case that there was somebody who discovered the elliptic form of the planetary orbits.' Frege holds that this sentence is not the negation of *A*. How does he know that it is

38. It should be clear that I do not mean that the sentence *A* contains a Thought as a linguistic part.

not? Surely, whether we think of this complex sentence as the negation of A will depend on what we take A to mean. If we believe that A contains the Thought that somebody discovered the elliptic form of the planetary orbits, then we must take the disjunctive sentence as the negation of A. On the other hand, if we do not believe that A contains that Thought, then we may hold, as Frege does, that the negation of A is the sentence 'Whoever discovered the elliptic form of the planetary orbits did not die in misery.' Hence we cannot very well decide what A means by arguing that a certain sentence is or is not the negation of A.

According to my view, A can be reformulated as 'The individual thing which discovered the elliptic form of the planetary orbits died in misery.'[39] A is thus essentially a conjunction of two sentences, whose negation would read: 'It is not the case that the individual thing which discovered the elliptic form of the planetary orbits died in misery.' This sentence is *logically equivalent* to the sentence 'It is not the case that precisely one individual discovered the elliptic form of the planetary orbits or it is not the case that that individual died in misery.' Ordinarily, we would say that either nobody or more than one person discovered the elliptic form of the planetary orbits, or that the person who discovered the elliptic form of the planetary orbits did not die in misery. Hence we may think that A is false, because either we think that there was not precisely one person who discovered the elliptic form of the planetary orbits, or we believe that there was precisely one such person but that he did not die in misery. The context will have to make clear what we have in mind. For example, if someone says seriously 'The present king of France is bald,' we may object, 'But there is no present king of France,' thereby indicating that the first part of the conjunctive thought expressed by the sentence 'The present king of France is bald' is false. Since the first part is false, namely, the thought that just one thing is the present king of France, the whole sentence is false. On the other hand, if someone says 'The present president of the United States is bald,' we may object by saying, 'But he isn't bald,' thereby claiming that the second part of the conjunction is false.

I shall therefore assume that Frege did not refute the view that A is in reality an abbreviation of a conjunction of two sentences. He holds, as I mentioned earlier, that the truth of A *presupposes* that the description B

39. Of course, in English conversation we would instead say some such thing as 'The *person who* discovered the elliptic form of the planetary orbits died in misery.'

has a referent. He holds that if anything is asserted, then there is always the presupposition that the simple or compound proper names used have a reference.[40] On the face of it, Frege's view does not seem to differ from Russell's view or my view. We all agree that the truth of *A* presupposes the truth of *B*; that is, we agree that *A* could not be true unless there were precisely one individual of a certain kind. But this is not what Frege has in mind. A difference of opinion appears as soon as we consider a description which is not fulfilled, or, in other words, is false. In this case, it follows from both Russell's view and my view that *A* is false. According to Frege, however, *A* lacks a truth-value if the description *B* is not fulfilled. Thus, in both Russell's view and my own, *A* is false if the description is not fulfilled, while on Frege's view *A* is then neither true nor false. According to Frege's view, there are therefore declarative sentences which are neither true nor false.

I do not wish to give the impression that one cannot or must not speak about the *presupposition* that a certain term represents something. Quite to the contrary, not only may we talk that way but we often do. The question is, when we talk this way do we mean something that is perfectly compatible with, say, Russell's view, or are we committing ourselves to the Fregean view that certain (declarative) sentences are neither true nor false? Furthermore if we are committing ourselves to this latter view, can we successfully defend it or is it false?

Consider the expression 'the man who discovered the elliptic form of the planetary orbits' and assume that there is no such man. It is a fact that we understand this description, regardless of whether there is a man so described, regardless of whether or not it is fulfilled. How is this possible if descriptions which are not fulfilled are empty signs? How could we possibly know what kind of entity a given description describes, even though there may be no such entity, if all we have to go on is the linguistic expression as such and the grammatical rules for its use? Clearly, something else must be involved. What is involved, I submit, are the existing referents of the elements of the description. Just as we understand what a false sentence asserts because we know what the words in it represent, so we understand what an empty description describes because we know what the words in it represent. Since we know what such words as 'the,' 'individual,' 'man,' and so forth, represent, and since we know that a

40. For a painstaking discussion of "presupposition interpretations" of definite descriptions, see G. Nerlich, "Presupposition and Entailment," *American Philosophical Quarterly*, II (1965), 33–42.

certain combination of these words represents a state of affairs, we also know what state of affairs is represented by the description 'the individual thing which is a man who discovered the elliptic form of the planetary orbits.'

Frege cannot give this kind of explanation. He does not see that descriptions are disguised sentences. If they are terms, as he believes, then they should be indistinguishable from uninterpreted signs of a calculus as long as they have no reference. But, of course, they are not. We know what 'the present king of France' represents in a sense in which we do not know what the expression 'A§B' of an uninterpreted calculus means, even if we are acquainted with all the syntactical rules of the calculus. It may be objected that this analogy between descriptions and uninterpreted expressions does not hold. The correct parallel could be drawn by making a comparison of *complex interpreted* signs without reference and descriptions without reference. However, this objection overlooks the fact that, according to Frege, descriptions do not have complex referents. For example, the referent of 'the man who discovered the elliptic form of the planetary orbits' is, according to Frege, the simple object named by 'Kepler.' Hence, he cannot explain the "meaning" of a description in terms of the referents of the words in the description.

Frege, as we know, has another way out. Descriptions, he claims, always have a sense, even if they do not have a referent. Hence they are not just empty signs, governed by grammatical rules, if they have no reference. Assume now that there really are no such entities as Fregean senses. Then the problem remains of how we could possibly know what "empty" descriptions describe if they are conceived of as terms. This, I submit, is as close as one can come, along this line of reasoning, to showing on philosophical grounds that Frege's view is unacceptable.

Since Frege introduced senses in order to explain why certain identity statements are synthetic, he did not have to cast around for "meanings" of "empty" descriptions. And since senses were at hand, he did not have to weigh more carefully some of the implications of the presupposition view. In other words, one may speculate that Frege found the presupposition view plausible because he had already convinced himself that all descriptions have a sense. Be that as it may, I want to return to the notion of identity since it occupies the center of Frege's doctrine of sense and reference.

The problem of identity, we recall, arises from the fact that some identity statements seem to be synthetic. We have seen how Frege solves this problem. Briefly, he holds that synthetic identity statements do not merely state that something is identical with itself, but assert that two different senses are connected with the same referent. Since I have already disclaimed the existence of senses, how, then, do I propose to solve the problem of identity?

Consider the sentence 'The man called Scott is the author of *Waverley*.' In my view, this sentence expresses the same thought (and represents the same state of affairs) as the sentence 'The individual thing x is a man called Scott and the individual thing y is an author of *Waverley* and x is the same as y.'[41] Hence, this identity statement does not just assert that something is identical with itself. Rather, it states that precisely one thing is a man with a certain name and that only one thing wrote a certain book and that the former thing is the same as the latter. Surely, this is a synthetic statement. It is certainly not a logical or linguistic truth. In my view, as well as in Frege's, one can explain why it is that certain identity statements "extend our knowledge" about the world.

In the light of this solution, the importance of the sign of identity appears in the proper perspective. Let us assume that we have a language in which there is only one label for a given entity and in which no two entities have the same label. Then there is no need for the sign of identity in regard to labels. We do not have to *state* that a and b are not the same; this follows from the fact that we have two different labels 'a' and 'b.' Similarly, we do not have to *assert* that a is the same as a; this follows from the fact that 'a' is the same label as 'a.' Of course, this does not mean that we can get along without the *notion* of identity when we construct the language. We must use that notion in order to determine whether a given entity already has a label. But an identity *sign* between labels is superfluous in the language. According to my view, moreover, it does not occur between descriptions, either, for descriptions are abbreviated sentences. Hence, the identity sign need not occur between labels and cannot occur between descriptions. However, if we look back at the analysis of the identity statement about the author of *Waverley*, we see that the identity

41. I take for granted, for the moment, that only one person is called Scott. The expanded version of the identity statement is of course *equivalent* to Russell's sentence

$$(\exists x) \, (\exists z) \, ((F(y) \equiv_y (y = x)) \, \& \, (G(y) \equiv_y (y = z)) \, \& \, (x = z)).$$

Compare *PM*, I, 174.

sign does not entirely disappear from the language. It occurs between the variables 'x' and 'y.' It is in connection with variables, then, that a sign of identity is indispensable, as long as there are descriptions in the language.[42]

In an earlier chapter I defended the view that the pen on my desk is an individual thing and not a state of affairs which contains a so-called particular. Now we see that this was not intended to mean that the description 'the pen on my desk' *represents* an individual thing rather than a state of affairs. This description does indeed *represent* a state of affairs, but the state of affairs *describes* a certain individual, and this individual is not a state of affairs. Perhaps the matter becomes clearer when we consider the sentence 'The pen on my desk is an individual thing and not a state of affairs.' According to my view, this sentence represents the same state of affairs as the sentence 'The individual thing which is a pen on my desk is an individual thing and not a state of affairs.' And this latter sentence is obviously true.

In conclusion, I would like to draw a sweeping comparison between Frege's and my own solutions of the problem of identity. Consider the two descriptions 'the x which is F' and 'the x which is G.' According to Frege, they express different senses. In my view, they represent different states of affairs. Why are the states of affairs different? The answer is obvious. The first state of affairs contains the property F, while the second contains the different property G. Put in Frege's terms, we could say that the first description mentions the concept F, while the second mentions the concept G. It is clear that a difference in properties (concepts) always corresponds to a difference in sense.[43] Hence we can explain the difference between different descriptions of the same entity, without having to assume that there are senses. We can explain this difference in terms of the referents of certain concept words. Compare the case of descriptions with the following example. Consider the two expressions 'all F' and 'all G' and assume that F and G are coextensive. Someone may argue, in the Fregean spirit, that these two expressions represent the same class of things but differ in the way in which they present that class. Hence he may say that the two expressions have the same referent but differ in their senses.

---

42. I take it for granted that the notion (relation) of identity cannot be "defined" in the Russell-Leibniz fashion. Compare my earlier remarks about this point.

43. I assume that descriptions, but not labels, have a sense.

We would of course reply that there are no such entities as senses and that the difference between 'all *F*' and 'all *G*' consists in the fact that the former mentions the property *F*, while the latter mentions the property *G*. Considerations of this nature lead us to expect that Fregean senses must closely resemble concepts (properties) if they are to fulfill their purpose in Frege's system. We would expect that senses could be identified with concepts now and then in Frege's philosophy, even though Frege himself does not identify them. We would further expect a number of problems to arise for this philosophy, because even though senses cannot be anything but concepts, Frege denies that they are. All these expectations, I believe, are fulfilled by a careful reading of Frege's later works.

TRUTH

ONE PROBLEM REMAINS from the difficulties that arose in the *Begriffsschrift*: Frege must in some way account for the objectivity of truth. Since all sentences are said to express contents, it cannot be the existence of a content that distinguishes a true from a false sentence. Nor can the difference lie on the side of the mental act of judging, if I may so put it, for false as well as true sentences may be affirmed. What, then, accounts for the difference?

In "Über Sinn und Bedeutung," Frege approaches this problem from a different direction. He asks whether sentences, too, have a sense and a reference. This step from names to sentences is an obvious one. At least two features of Frege's earlier system suggest it. First, there is the view that sentences as well as names represent complex "things" rather than states of affairs.[44] In the *Begriffsschrift*, as we noted, all complex expressions represent complex concepts. In the *Grundlagen*, the situation is not quite so obvious, but there seems to be no clear distinction between a complex "thing" and a state of affairs. Second, in Frege's philosophy the stress is put on the distinction between saturated and unsaturated entities. Both names and sentences are saturated and hence are treated alike. In Frege's system, the distinction between states of affairs and other kinds of entities is simply supplanted by the distinction between objects and concepts.

After having discussed the sense-reference distinction for proper names,

---

44. By a "thing" in quotation marks I mean here an entity that is not a state of affairs (fact).

Frege turns next to whole sentences. He holds that a sentence contains a *Thought*. At this point, one could probably substitute a word like 'content' or 'proposition' for Frege's 'Thought,' because it is quite clear that such Thoughts are supposed to be nonmental entities. However, I shall try to be as faithful as possible to Frege's terminology in the following discussion. Granted, then, that every sentence expresses a Thought, is this Thought its sense or its reference? Frege argues that it is a sense. He assumes that a sentence has a reference. If so, and if we replace part of a sentence by another expression with the same reference but a different sense, then the Thought of the sentence changes. Hence it is the Thought that varies with the substitution of different senses for each other, the Thought that is made up of the senses of different parts of the sentence.

Consider Frege's example. The Thought expressed by 'The morning star is a body illuminated by the sun' is claimed to be different from the Thought expressed by 'The evening star is a body illuminated by the sun.' This can be shown by the fact that someone may believe one of these two sentences but not the other. Therefore, he must be able to grasp the Thought expressed by one of these two sentences without at the same time grasping the Thought expressed by the other. Now, the only difference between the two sentences is that they contain different descriptions of the same planet. The two descriptions 'the morning star' and 'the evening star' refer to the same object, but they have different senses. This shows that we get a different Thought if we replace part of a sentence by an expression with a different sense. Hence Thoughts must be senses.

We can easily apply Frege's reasoning to our view of descriptions. According to that view, two descriptions differ in the properties which they mention. They represent two different states of affairs, because they mention different properties. Let us assume, for the sake of the argument, that 'the morning star' and 'the evening star' are short for 'the individual thing which is the brightest star visible in the morning' and 'the individual thing which is the brightest star visible in the evening,' respectively. The sentence 'The evening star is a body illuminated by the sun' is an abbreviation of a complex sentence of the form 'The x which is F is also H.' It represents a certain state of affairs. Now, if we replace the description 'the x (which) is F' by the different description 'the x (which) is G,' then we get the sentence 'The x which is G is also H.' This sentence expresses a state of affairs which is different from the earlier one. In general, in a complex sentence, if we replace a constituent sentence by a different one, then the result of this substitution will no longer represent the same complex state of affairs as the original complex sentence. Just as we saw earlier that the so-called sense of a description is in reality the state of affairs represented by the description, so we see now that the so-called Thought expressed by a sentence is nothing but the (complex) state of affairs represented by the (complex) sentence.

Frege asks whether sentences have a reference in addition to having a sense. He argues that as soon as we are interested not only in the Thought of a sentence, but also in whether it is true, we must turn our attention to the reference of the proper names in the sentence. This fact, he claims, indicates that we "generally recognize and expect a reference for the sentence itself." [45] Moreover, since it is only in connection with inquiries after the truth-value of a sentence that the question of the reference of names becomes relevant, we are "driven into accepting the *truth-value* of a sentence as constituting its reference." [46]

Frege assumes that false as well as true sentences express Thoughts. He also believes that one cannot turn to questions about truth-values without leaving the level of Thoughts and considering the referents of names. But, if true, this merely shows that questions of truth are intimately connected with questions about referents of proper names. Indeed, the same conclusion follows from Frege's view that the truth-value of a sentence presupposes a referent for the proper name in the sentence. Without such a referent, Frege claimed earlier, the sentence is neither true nor false. Thus he really gives no new argument for his contention that truth-values are referents of sentences.

According to our view, it makes sense to ask whether a description is true, but not whether it refers, in Frege's sense of the term. Consider now a sentence which contains a description. If we are interested in the truth-value of the complex sentence, we shall have to ask whether the description in the sentence is true or false, for the truth of the whole sentence depends on the truth-value of the description. Hence, whenever we are interested in whether a complex sentence with a description is true or false, we have to pay attention not to whether the description refers, but rather to whether it is true or false. However, even though the truth-value of

45. *SB*, p. 33; *T*, p. 63.
46. *SB*, p. 34; *T*, p. 63.

such a complex sentence depends on the truth-value of a description, it does not follow that truth-values are referents of complex sentences or of descriptions.

Frege seems to realize that he has not as yet shown that truth-values are referents of sentences, for he argues next that they must be objects and cannot possibly be properties of Thoughts. This argument is very interesting because it reveals another important tension in Frege's philosophy.

First, Frege asserts that the sentence '*P* is true' does not say any more than the sentence '*P*.' Second, he maintains that the truth claim arises for either '*P*' or '*P* is true' from the assertive force with which these sentences are uttered.[47] What is the connection between these two assertions? And what is the connection between these assertions and Frege's desired conclusion that truth-values must be objects? If we assume that his first statement is true, then we may perhaps conclude that 'is true' cannot be a predicate, for we may wish to defend the principle that a predicate adds something to the meaning of an expression. But it seems that Frege's second statement is supposed to back up his first assertion; and it is not at all clear how it could do so. Mere thinking is not, as yet, judging or affirming. Hence we may think the Thoughts expressed by '*P*' and '*P* is true' without affirming anything. Even if this is true, how does it follow that '*P*' expresses the same Thought as '*P* is true'? As a matter of fact, it seems that, according to Frege's own position, '*P*' and '*P* is true' cannot have the same sense, for if they have both the same truth-value and the same sense, then it is difficult to see how the expressions 'is true' and 'truth' could have any meaning whatsoever. Frege's argument that truth-values cannot be properties of Thoughts because '*P*' and '*P* is true' have the same sense also seems to show that truth-values cannot be objects. It seems to follow that they are nothing at all. On the other hand, if we accept the notion that truth-values are objects, then it seems to follow that '*P*' and '*P* is true' cannot have the same sense. This conclusion can also be reached through a different consideration. Assuming that '*P*' and 'true' refer to objects, '*P* is true' would have to be an identity statement of the form '*P* = true.' Is this identity statement, assuming that it is true, analytic or does it convey valuable information? The answer is obvious; if anything conveys valuable new information, it is a statement of this kind. That a certain sentence '*P*' is true or false, as the case may be, is certainly not as uninform-

47. These two assertions occur time and again in Frege's later writings, for example, in his unpublished manuscripts and in his paper on the Thought.

ative a statement as *a* is *a* or *P* is *P*. But if '*P* is true' is a synthetic truth, in Frege's sense of the term, then '*P*' and 'true' must express different senses. From this one may conclude that '*P*' and '*P* is true' cannot have the same sense.

Frege seems to have become aware of this difficulty several years later.[48] He still insists that '*P*' and '*P* is true' have the same sense, but he also holds now that 'true' has a sense. He argues that 'true' must have a sense, because otherwise the sentence '*P* is true' could not have a sense. Be that as it may, he now takes the view that even though 'true' has a sense, '*P*' and '*P* is true' have the same sense. He avoids an apparent contradiction by claiming that we simply have to accept as a fact that 'true' has a sense which does not contribute to the sense of the sentence in which it occurs. In effect, what he asks us to do is to accept as a fact something that makes no sense against the background of his theory of sense and reference. Frege's way out, such as it is, merely shows that his system contains two quite different views on truth. According to one, truth somehow resides in acts of affirmation; according to the other, there are such entities as the True and the False. To Frege's mind, the first view somehow implies that '*P*' and '*P* is true' must have the same sense, while the second view implies that 'true' has a sense. From the open clash of these two implications, Frege should have concluded that truth cannot reside in mental acts and at the same time be an independent object.

This tension becomes even more visible when we consider Frege's further deliberations in "Über Sinn und Bedeutung" about the relation between Thoughts and truth-values. According to Frege, the connection between a Thought and its truth-value, say, the True, must not be compared with the relation of subject to predicate, for the former connects a sense with an object while the latter connects two senses. If the relation between a Thought and the True were the relation between subject and predicate, then, according to Frege, we could never break out of the circle of senses. Let me try to explain what Frege may have had in mind.

He seems to argue as follows: (1) Whenever we predicate a concept of something, we merely grasp a certain Thought. What we do in effect, is to combine the sense of a proper name with a concept, so that they form a

48. In "Meine grundlegenden logischen Einsichten," *FN*, no. 18.

Thought. (2) Now, if truth-values were concepts, then to predicate a truth-value of a Thought would be nothing more than to grasp another Thought. For example, to predicate truth of the Thought *P* would be to grasp the Thought that *P* is true. (3) But merely having the Thought that *P* is true is not essentially different from having any other Thought, be that Thought true or false. Hence, by grasping the Thought that *P* is true, we remain within the circle of Thoughts where there is as yet no distinction between truth and falsehood. (4) But when we judge that *P* is true, we break out of that circle of Thoughts; we no longer just have a Thought. (5) Therefore, truth-values cannot be predicated of Thoughts, and the judgment that *P* is true does not involve predication. Judgment, in distinction to predication or thinking, transcends the circle of Thoughts.

This formulation shows that Frege thinks of judgment as uniquely concerned with truth. Only through judgments do we have access to truth-values. Or, as Frege puts it, judgment can be regarded as an advancement from a Thought to a truth-value.[49]

My rendition of Frege's argument also shows that he is faced with several dilemmas. First, if he holds that thinking can break out of the realm of Thoughts, then it is not so plausible to assume that truth-values are referents of sentences. On the other hand, if he holds that thinking cannot break out of the realm of Thoughts, then it becomes implausible that the parts of sentences have referents. In the latter case, there is an added difficulty; Frege must now explain how the mind can at all transcend the circle of Thoughts. He must provide some reason why judgment should be able to achieve what just plain thought cannot accomplish. Second, if he insists that truth is not a concept, then it becomes implausible that concept words have referents. But if concept words in sentences have referents, then it is unlikely that truth-values are referents of sentences. Let me fill in the details.

I shall distinguish between thinking a thought and thinking of a state of affairs. By thinking the thought *that P*, one thinks of the state of affairs *P*. For example, by thinking the thought that 5 is a prime number, one is thinking of the state of affairs that 5 is a prime number. Recall now that, according to Frege, objects are presented to us through their senses. Hence, in thinking the sense of 'the pupil of Plato and teacher of Alexander the Great,' one presumably thinks of Aristotle. This part of Frege's

49. *SB*, p. 35; *T*, p. 65.

view agrees with the distinction I just made. But it does not agree at all with his own argument that truth-values cannot be predicated of Thoughts. It is one of the premises of this argument that thinking does not aim through a Thought at a reference, but rather aims at the Thought itself. He assumes that when one thinks a Thought, one is thinking of the Thought. Otherwise, why would there have to be judging, in addition to thinking, in order to allow us to break out of the circle of Thoughts? If thinking a Thought were not the same as thinking of a Thought but would amount to thinking of a referent, then thinking itself could transcend the realm of Thoughts. Just as we think of Aristotle when we think the sense of 'the pupil of Plato and teacher of Alexander the Great,' so we would be thinking of some referent, be it a truth-value or a state of affairs, when we think the Thought that 5 is a prime number.

To return to the undesirable alternatives mentioned earlier, if Frege holds that in thinking a Thought one thinks of something other than that Thought, then he cannot plausibly hold that sentences refer to truth-values. For if it is true that we think of Aristotle when we think the sense of 'the pupil of Plato and teacher of Alexander the Great,' then it appears equally true that to think the Thought that 5 is a prime number is to think of the (arithmetical) state of affairs that 5 is a prime number. To think this Thought, one might suggest, is to think of the circumstance that the number 5 has a certain property; it is to think, in Frege's terms, of an object as falling under a certain concept.[50] On the other hand, since Frege holds that thinking does not break out of the circle of Thoughts, it may or may not be plausible that truth-values are referents of sentences, but it is certainly implausible that the parts of sentences have referents in addition to having senses. If, in thinking the Thought that 5 is a prime number, one thinks of the Thought that 5 is a prime number, then there is no reason why in thinking the sense of 'the pupil of Plato and teacher of Alexander the Great,' one should be thinking of Aristotle rather than of a certain sense. Hence there might be no good reason left for distinguishing between Aristotle and a certain sense. The sense-reference distinction for names could be dispensed with. In a nutshell, if Frege believes that he does not have to mention the referents of sentence parts when he explains what we think of when we think a Thought, then it seems that he does not have to mention such referents at all.

Further, since he holds that thinking remains confined to the realm of

50. I assume for the moment that concepts are referents of concept words.

Thoughts, he must either admit that we cannot transcend that realm at all, or he must explain what it is that makes judging so different from thinking that the former — but not the latter — breaks through the circle of Thoughts. Frege, as we saw, claims that in judging we step from a Thought to a truth-value. But this explanation is of little help, as I shall try to show. Let us distinguish between two different kinds of mental acts, namely, assumptions and affirmations. For example, you may either assume that Aristotle was born in Stagira or you may affirm it. What you assume or affirm is always a certain state of affairs, or, perhaps more accurately, *that* a certain state of affairs *obtains*. Neither one of these two kinds of acts advances any further than the other; both terminate in states of affairs, if I may so put it. Hence, Frege's distinction between thinking and judging cannot possibly be the same as this new distinction between assuming and affirming. Judgments, in his view, reach further than mere thinking. But what precisely is it that is reached by judgments but not by thinking? It cannot be states of affairs, as we know. In particular, it cannot be the state of affairs that a certain Thought is connected with a certain truth-value. This leaves truth-values as the only possibility. Does judgment then aim at a truth-value? How could it? Thinking *of* the True, even though this may be accomplished through a Thought, is not the same as thinking *that* something or the other is true. Since the True is an object, an entity of the same kind as Aristotle, it is hard to see how it could be reached through a judgment. Objects, according to the tradition, are presented through ideas rather than through judgments.

We touch here a familiar point. Frege's ontology does not comprise states of affairs. This is probably its most serious fault. On the linguistic level, this shortcoming appears as the doctrine that sentences are names. However, if thinking a Thought amounts to nothing more than thinking of a truth-value, then there must be something else that is not a thinking *of*, but a thinking *that*. There must also be something else that is not a name of an object or concept but is an expression of an entirely different sort. This, I take it, is the judgment stroke '⊢.' The expression '⊢2 + 3 = 5' does not refer to an object, according to Frege, but asserts something.[51] Expressions of this sort are Frege's substitutes for sentences (as ordinarily conceived of). Like sentences, they do not name entities but represent how things are. However, Frege does not explain how the mind

51. *FB*, p. 22n; *T*, p. 34n.

gets to these queer states of affairs. The step from a Thought to a truth-value remains shrouded in mystery.

As to the second dilemma on page 186 above, since Frege holds that if truth were a concept, thinking that P is true would be thinking of the Thought that P is true, he seems to imply that concept words do not have referents but only express senses. Assume that concept words have a reference as well as a sense. Then in thinking the sense of '(is) green,' one would be thinking of the referent of 'green' just as in thinking the sense of 'the pupil of Plato and teacher of Alexander the Great,' one thinks of a certain person. Hence one could not maintain, as Frege does, that through predication one merely reaches another Thought. One would have to hold instead that, in thinking the Thought that P is true, one predicates of a Thought the referent of the concept word 'true.' Since this referent is not a part of a Thought, in thinking that P is true one would automatically have transcended the circle of Thoughts. But if we agree that in thinking the sense of a concept word we think of a given referent, then it would hardly occur to us that the referent of a sentence could be a truth-value; for then we would most naturally conclude that, in thinking the Thought that P is true, one thinks of the *circumstance* that a certain Thought is true.

I am inclined to believe that Frege maintained, at the time of the paper on sense and reference, that concept words do not have both a sense and a reference. He held, I think, that they represent concepts and that such concepts are parts of Thoughts. I do not mean to say, though, that he had first contemplated at great length an extension of the sense-reference distinction to concept words and had then rejected it. Rather, it seems to me that he introduced the distinction for proper names in order to solve certain urgent problems, but that he saw no problems which would necessitate a similar distinction for concept words. His system seemed to work without such an extension of the distinction. If this interpretation is correct, then we get the following picture of Frege's ontology at the time of his argument against truth-values as concepts. On the side of senses, there are two kinds, namely, senses of proper names and senses of sentences. On the side of referents, there are, correspondingly, (ordinary) objects and truth-values. The only complex entities of this ontology are located on the side of the senses; all referents are simple.[52] If it were not for the existence of Thoughts, concepts would be homeless, so to speak, since they occur only as constituents of Thoughts.

Frege introduces the sense-reference distinction in order to solve the problem of identity. However, he holds that identity cannot obtain between concepts. If so, then the problem of identity cannot arise for concepts. Hence the most powerful reason for the sense-reference distinction does not apply to concepts. Moreover, even if identity could hold between concepts, there is still another reason why the problem of identity cannot arise for concepts. We saw earlier that the problem arises for objects, because there are descriptions of objects. But Frege holds that there are no descriptions of concepts. 'The concept horse,' as we have seen, does not, according to Frege, represent a concept. He holds, in general, that every description represents an object. This means that there simply are no descriptions of concepts. If we assume that Frege is right, and if we consider a language in which there is at most one label for every concept, then all true identity statements for concepts would be of the unproblematic form '$F = F$,' and all false ones would be of the form '$F = G$.'

On the other hand, had Frege acknowledged the existence of descriptions of concepts, there would then be an excellent reason for adopting a sense-reference distinction for concept words. Assuming that the referent of a concept word is a certain concept, what would its sense be? Two descriptions of the same individual thing differ, in my view, in that they mention different properties of the individual. From this point of view, the "sense" of a description is simply the property mentioned by the description, that is, the property which is used to describe. If we now consider two descriptions of the same concept, we find that they, too, differ in that they mention different (higher) concepts. For example, the two descriptions 'the color of my shirt' and 'the color of this wall' describe the same property, namely, the color white, but they do so by means of different (relational) properties. Hence we may suggest that descriptions of concepts refer to concepts, and express as their senses certain higher-level concepts. However, we must keep in mind that Frege neither admits descriptions of concepts nor holds that senses expressed by names are (ordinary) concepts.

Nevertheless, we would expect him to consider an extension of the sense-reference distinction to concept words; after all, such an extension is

52. I am neglecting the fact that senses themselves can be referents of expressions.

a most natural move. And we shall see in the next chapter that Frege indeed considered this possibility. What should be clear from our discussion up to this point is that an extension of the distinction will clash with Frege's view on truth, for it leads to the view that, although the parts of a sentence have certain referents, the referent of the sentence as a whole does not consist of these individual referents. According to my view, there are no senses. Sentences represent states of affairs; they do not represent truth-values. Nor do I think that there are such objects or things as truth-values. What, then, is the nature of truth?

A sentence, I said, represents a state of affairs. But it may also be said to express a certain thought, that is, a certain mental, subjective entity. In order to distinguish this kind of entity from Frege's so-called Thought, I shall continue to call it a thought and spell it with a small 't.' When we think a certain thought, we think of a certain state of affairs. We usually say that sentences may be either true or false. I shall assume that what we mean is not that certain written marks or spoken noises are true or false, but rather that the thoughts expressed by these marks and noises are true or false. When we think that a certain thought is true, we think a thought, but we do not think of the thought that that thought is true. Rather, we think of a state of affairs, namely, the state of affairs that the given thought is true. One may be tempted to say that truth and falsehood are properties of thoughts, but this would be a mistake. They are not properties in any straightforward sense of the term. To see this clearly, let us ask when a thought is true. The answer is obvious. A thought is true if and only if it intends an actual state of affairs (a fact); it is false if it intends not an actual but a possible state of affairs. However, I do not think that the two statements 'P is true' and 'P intends an actual state of affairs' are merely equivalent. I am inclined to believe that the first sentence is just an abbreviation of the second. I am inclined to believe that thoughts do not have (nonrelational) properties called 'true' and 'false.' Instead, they are related to actual and possible states of affairs, and to say that a given thought is true is to say nothing else but that it intends an actual state of affairs. If truth and falsehood were genuine properties of thoughts, then it should be possible to determine whether a given thought is true merely by inspecting the thought. If the thought has the property true, then it intends an actual state of affairs; otherwise it intends a possible state of affairs. But it seems to me that this is impossible. The only way in which we can discover whether a given thought is true is to inspect the relevant state of affairs. If the state of affairs obtains, then the thought is true; otherwise it is false. In brief, if truth and falsehood were genuine properties of thoughts, then we should be able to tell what the world is like merely by inspecting our thoughts. In one sense, all knowledge would then be "*a priori.*" But I mentioned earlier that in my opinion all knowledge is based on "experience," even our knowledge of the ontological and logical features of the world.

In contrast to Frege, I thus hold a "correspondence theory" of truth. To say that a thought (or a sentence) is true is to say that it "corresponds" to an actual state of affairs. This kind of view was later criticized by Frege.[53] I shall at this point jump ahead in my chronological exposition and consider Frege's arguments.

Frege opens the discussion with the following question: "Can it not be laid down that truth exists when there is a correspondence in a certain respect?" But he rejects this possibility. If the correspondence theory were true, he argues, then we would have to know whether a certain correspondence holds in order to know whether a certain thought is true. This would merely lead back to the original question, for we would have to ask next whether it is true that the correspondence obtains. In order to determine whether a given thought P is true, we would have to find out whether the thought that P corresponds to something is true. The correspondence theory leads in this manner to an infinite regress. Thus Frege concludes that any attempt to explain truth as correspondence must collapse.

But Frege's argument is not directed only against the correspondence theory of truth. He claims that it applies to every attempt to "define" truth. He says:

And every other attempt to define truth collapses too. For in a definition certain characteristics would have to be stated. And in application to any particular case the question would always arise whether it were true that the characteristics were present. So one goes around in a circle. Consequently, it is probable that the content of the word 'true' is unique and indefinable.

Let us evaluate this argument. Assume that truth is a property of thoughts. Now consider the following formulation of the condition under

53. See *G.*

which a thought is true: A thought P is true if and only if it intends an actual state of affairs. Frege would no doubt apply the argument mentioned in the last paragraph. He would argue that in order to find out whether a given thought P is true, we would have to find out, according to our condition, whether it is true that P intends an actual state of affairs. In this manner, one presumably goes around in circles.

In reality, though, there is no circle, no infinite regress. In order to find out whether the thought P is true, I must find out whether a certain state of affairs, call it S, obtains. But in order to find out whether S is actual, I do not have to consider another thought, the thought that S is actual, and then ask myself whether this thought now is true. Whether S is actual is not to be decided in terms of whether a certain thought is true. Frege, it appears, has quite a different kind of "definition" in mind: A thought P is true if and only if the thought that S is actual is true. He seems to be thinking of "definitions" according to which a thought is true if and only if it is true that the thought has certain characteristics. If so, then he is of course correct in his criticism; "definitions" of this kind do indeed confine us to the circle of our thoughts. But not every "definition" of truth has to be of this kind, as we saw. Why did Frege overlook other possibilities? Why did he believe that his argument applies to all attempts to "define" truth?

Frege could not possibly have proposed the "definition" which I introduced, for truth is "defined" in terms of states of affairs, and Frege's ontology does not comprise such entities.[54] But if we assume, as Frege does, that there are only Thoughts and truth-values but no states of affairs, then it immediately follows that truth cannot be "defined" in terms of certain characteristics. There could be no such state of affairs as, say, that a certain Thought P has the characteristic F. Instead, there would be another Thought, namely, the Thought that the Thought P has characteristic F. Within the range of Frege's ontology, a "definition" of truth of Thoughts can only be formulated in terms of truth of other Thoughts. Hence any such "definition" must lead to a regress. Frege's argument that truth is "indefinable" is sound if we restrict ourselves to his ontology, but it breaks down as soon as we admit the existence of states of affairs.

Up to now, we have assumed that truth is a property of thoughts (or of Thoughts). I mentioned earlier, though, that I think that this assumption

---

54. I mean, of course, that it does not comprise states of affairs in addition to Thoughts. At one point in "Über Sinn und Bedeutung" Frege identifies a fact with a true Thought.

is false. It seems to me that saying that a thought is true is short for say-ing that it intends an actual state of affairs, so there can be no question of "defining" truth in Frege's sense. It cannot be a matter of specifying a characteristic of all and only true thoughts. Or, rather, it is then obvious what that characteristic must be. We are not forced into an infinite re-gress. Since to say that a thought is true is to say that it intends an actual state of affairs, we can only find out whether a given thought is true by finding out whether it intends an actual state of affairs. How do we find out whether a given state of affairs obtains? We do not turn to our thoughts, nor do we have to decide first whether it is a fact that the given state of affairs is actual. Rather, we consider the state of affairs itself. If I want to know whether the pen on my desk is black, I neither consult my thoughts about the pen nor do I concentrate on the state of affairs that it is a fact that the pen is black; I simply turn my head and look at the pen.

Frege's view that sentences are names of truth-values encounters quite a number of serious problems. Most of these, as I have tried to show, arise because Frege's view leaves no room for states of affairs. Now, if the ledger showed nothing but difficulties on the side of Frege's view, then this view would hardly deserve the attention which philosophers have paid to it. Philosophers seriously consider Frege's theory because it seems to give satisfactory answers to two important problems. I shall call these the *problem of nonexistent objects* and the *problem of substitutivity*.

When one sees a hallucinatory dagger, thinks of the golden mountain, or believes that the earth is flat, there occur certain mental acts which in-tend certain "objects." One may hold that, in these and similar cases, men-tal acts somehow connect with their "objects." One may hold, in other words, that mental acts are in some sense relational, that they are some-how related to their objects. Or one may reject this view. One may attempt to give an ontological assay of, say, perceiving, which does not involve a relation between the perceiver and the perceived. I am convinced that any such attempt must fail, but I shall not argue for this conclusion.[55] I shall simply assume that there is some kind of connection between "the knower" and "the known."

If, in order to avoid idealism, we have to hold that mental acts are re-

55. Compare the discussion of Brentano's view in *SM*.

lated to what they intend, then we have to face the problem of nonexistent objects. For example, when one sees a hallucinatory dagger, the
mental act of seeing intends something; yet it cannot intend a dagger, for
there is no such thing present. When one thinks of the golden mountain,
this thought relates to something; yet there is no such thing as the golden
mountain. Finally, when one believes that the earth is flat, one's belief concerns the circumstance that the earth is flat; yet there is no such circumstance, for the earth is not flat but round. The "objects" of these three
mental acts do not exist. Hence the question arises of what their real
"objects" are.[56]

Since the earth is not flat, there is no such fact as that the earth is flat.
The thought that the earth is flat therefore cannot intend the fact that the
earth is flat. If one could only believe what is true, then one could hold
that all beliefs intend facts. But many of our beliefs are false. Similarly, if
all sentences were true, then one could maintain that they represent facts.
But since many sentences are false, this view is unacceptable. That even
false sentences represent something is obvious; we cannot possibly decide
whether a sentence is true unless we know what it represent before we
make our decision. A sentence is false because what it represents is not the
case. It is clear that the problem of false beliefs is also the problem of false
sentences.

Next, consider the thought of the golden mountain. As Meinong origi-
nally formulated the problem, it involves the definite description 'the
golden mountain.' Since there is no such individual thing as a golden
mountain, the thought of the golden mountain seems to have no "object."
Nor does the description seem to have a referent. We can again approach
the problem from either of two directions. Let us ask what the description
'the golden mountain' represents. According to my view, this (grammatical) term really expresses a propositional thought; it is a sentence in disguise. As it happens, the sentence is false; there is no such individual
thing as a golden mountain. Thus the problem of "empty" descriptions
reduces to the problem of false sentences. However, we must take note of
the following point. A singular sentence may be false because a certain
existing individual does not happen to have a certain property, even
though there are other individuals which have that property. In the case
of the description 'the golden mountain,' though, the relevant sentence is

56. For a detailed discussion of the problem of nonexistent objects, see *ibid.*

false because no individual whatsoever (and hence not precisely one) is a golden mountain. We have here a case of an "empty" predicate, as it were. This raises the question of what the expression 'golden mountain' represents, since there is no such property as being a golden mountain.[57] That this predicate represents something is again clear, for unless we know what it represents, we cannot look out for things which have or are what it represents. Unless we know what the expression means, we cannot know whether there are golden mountains. Just as we understand what a sentence represents before we know whether it is true or false, so we understand what a (complex) predicate represents before we know whether there are things of that sort.

I have to be even more concise about the hallucinatory dagger. I have argued elsewhere that what one *sees*, when one sees a hallucinatory dagger, is not a sense-impression or a bundle of sense-impressions.[58] This does not mean that one does not *have* sense-impressions while one hallucinates. To the contrary, while hallucinating one both sees a hallucinatory dagger and has sense-impressions. But one cannot see sense-impressions, one can only have them; and one cannot "have" perceptual objects like daggers, one can only perceive them.[59] Let us therefore turn to the mental act of seeing a hallucinatory dagger, leaving sense-impressions completely out of the picture. I have also argued elsewhere that this mental act, as all acts of perception, is propositional.[60] This means that its "object" is not an individual thing, but rather is a state of affairs. In our case, it could be the state of affairs represented by the sentence 'This is a dagger.' Acts of perception, if I may so put it, are not perceptions *of* things, but are perceptions *that* something or the other is the case. If this view is correct, then it immediately follows that the problem of nonexistent objects, as it arises for illusion and hallucination, reduces to the problem of false sentences. This means that the problem of nonexistent objects for all of our three paradigm cases comes down to the problem of false sentences.

57. Frege, remember, holds that the concept represented by 'golden mountain' exists, even though there are no objects which fall under the concept. I shall argue presently for my view.

58. In *SM*. Compare also Bergmann's "Realistic Postscript" in *LR*.

59. In *G* Frege makes the same distinction. He contrasts subjective ideas with things of the outer world: (1) Ideas cannot be seen, touched, smelled, tasted, or heard. They cannot be perceived. But things of the outside world can be perceived. (2) However, ideas are had, while perceptual objects are not. I think that these two points amount to saying that to the two kinds of entities, ideas and perceptual objects, there correspond two kinds of mental acts. (3) Ideas, according to Frege, need a bearer, while perceptual objects are independent of a bearer. (4) Every idea has only one bearer, while perceptual objects are perceived by many.

60. In *SM*.

What, then, does a false sentence represent? Frege's system, as we know, contains an answer. According to Frege, all sentences, even false ones, express Thoughts; hence there is an "object" for every propositional mental act. For example, if one believes or thinks that the earth is flat, then there is a Thought which is intended by a mental act. However, the Thought that the earth is flat is not a state of affairs. There are at least two reasons for this. First, if it were a state of affairs, then the earth would be a constituent of it; however, it is not the earth that is part of the Thought that the earth is flat, but rather the sense of 'the earth.' Second, assuming that there exists in fact such a Fregean Thought, this Thought cannot be a state of affairs because there is no such state of affairs as that the earth is flat. So much for a false belief or thought. In the case of hallucination, the situation is similar if we assume that perceptual acts are propositional. For every hallucinatory perceptual act there presumably exists a Fregean Thought as its "object." Hence there is an answer to the question of what these mental acts intend. Finally, in regard to empty predicates, Frege simply holds that there are no such things. He would say, for example, that the predicate 'golden mountain' represents a concept, even though there is no object that falls under this concept.[61]

Is Frege's answer satisfactory? Are there Fregean Thoughts? Do these complex entities, which are neither ordinary thoughts nor states of affairs, exist? I do not think so. There are, to be sure, thoughts and other kinds of mental acts. There are also actual states of affairs, or facts. But there are no such intermediate entities between mind and world as Thoughts, and therefore we cannot accept Frege's solution to the problem of nonexistent objects.

Of course, this is not an argument against Frege's view. Insofar as one can ever hope to argue that a certain ontological kind does not exist, my argument against senses in general and Thoughts in particular started with the discussion of identity and continues into the next chapter. What I wish to do now is to show that the problem of nonexistent objects can be solved without Thoughts, and hence that it does not compel us, or even nudge us, to subscribe to Frege's ontology of senses. However, I shall merely indicate the kind of solution which I find acceptable. For a detailed description of it, refer to *The Structure of Mind*.

61. For Frege, there remains the question of what an empty description refers to.

First, let us dispose of the problem of empty predicates. Frege holds that all concept words represent concepts. Even if nothing falls under a given concept, the concept itself is said to exist.[62] This view is shared by many contemporary philosophers. For example, Carnap has argued that there is an objective interpretation of the term 'proposition' which applies both to false and to true sentences, and he based his argument on the assumption that properties can exist even if they are not exemplified.[63] In discussing Carnap's view, we can kill two birds with one stone. We shall consider yet another attempt to defend the existence of a kind of entity which is essentially similar to Frege's Thought, and we shall also look more closely into the matter of empty predicates.

Carnap assumes that true propositions are *exemplified* by facts, while false propositions are not exemplified by anything. Propositions, therefore, are conceived of as properties of facts. Carnap now asks: Are there entities of which we can say that they are expressed by false sentences, but which are not exemplified by any fact? He answers that there are, and he argues for his answer as follows.

A proposition, according to Carnap, is a complex entity. Now, even if we assume that the ultimate components of a proposition must be exemplified, the whole complex — that is, the complex proposition itself — need not be. I shall take it that what Carnap means to say here is that the complex proposition need not be exemplified *in order to exist*. If so, then we are not forced to conclude that propositions cannot possibly exist unless they are exemplified by facts. In order to shed more light on his viewpoint, Carnap draws an analogy between complex properties of the ordinary kind and complex propositions. He maintains that a complex property, say, the property of being both *F and G*, exists even though it may not be exemplified — for this property consists of the two simple exemplified properties *F* and *G* which stand in a certain logical relation to each other. Carnap seems to be saying that just as there are *quite obviously* such complex properties, so there are, by analogy, false propositions. Or, perhaps, he merely wishes to argue that the two cases are sufficiently simi-

---

62. One might argue that, according to Frege, concepts and senses do not really exist but participate in a lesser mode of being. Frege holds that such entities as concepts and senses are not real, that is, localized in space and/or time. Yet, he also insists that these entities have existential status, that they are not just nothing, for the mind can make contact with them. Compare *F*, p. 35; also *G*.

63. See R. Carnap, *Meaning and Necessity*, 2nd ed. (Chicago, 1956), pp. 29–31.

lar that someone who accepts unexemplified properties may as well accept false propositions.

However, the admitted analogy between complex properties and false propositions does not solve the problem. Carnap's argument for false propositions is only convincing if we are willing to grant that there are unexemplified complex properties. But to me it is as certain that there are no unexemplified properties as it is that there are no propositions or Fregean Thoughts.[64] I therefore agree with Carnap that the case of false propositions may offer no greater difficulties than the case of unexemplified properties. But it does not offer any fewer difficulties either. In fact, the case of complex properties reduces to the case of propositions. The sentence 'The pen on my desk is black and round' is merely an abbreviation of the sentence 'The pen on my desk is black and it is round.' Instead of saying that nothing has the property of being F *and* G, we can say that nothing has the property F and at the same time the property G. And if there is nothing that has the property F and and also the property G, then the sentence 'There is something which is F and which is G' is false. Hence to claim that an empty complex predicate represents something amounts to claiming that a false sentence represents something. A solution to the problem of false sentences automatically yields a solution to the problem of empty complex predicates. In other words, there is only one problem, the problem of false sentences.

Carnap's attempt to make the existence of false propositions plausible thus fails. But perhaps he had more in mind than a simple appeal to the similarity between ordinary complex properties and his so-called proposition. It may be, for example, that Carnap wants to call our attention to the fact that we can form in our minds ideas of complex properties, even if these properties are not exemplified. He may be saying that we can form complex ideas of nonexistent properties from simple ideas of existing properties. If so, then we cannot disagree with him. It is undoubtedly true that we can conceive of properties which are not found in the world. No doubt we can think of states of affairs which do not exist. But it does not follow from these facts that there are unexemplified properties or propositions. That we can think of states of affairs which do not exist does not prove that therefore we must be thinking of something that does exist, namely, propositions.

---

64. Strictly speaking, there is not even such an entity as the (exemplified) *property* of being green and round, even though there are, of course, things that are are green and round.

Carnap may also be saying that we understand what a sentence repre-sents, even though it does not represent a fact, if we understand what the parts of the sentence represent. He points out, in other words, that we grasp what a false sentence represents because this is determined by the words in it. But this fact is not at issue. I agree that the words in a sen-tence (and their combination) determine what the sentence says.[65] But the question is whether a proposition or a Fregean Thought is determined in this manner. I do not think so.

In summary, I have tried to show that Carnap's attempt to defend propo-sitions fails. I have also tried to argue that there are no such things as unexemplified properties. Let us now return to our main concern, the general problem of false sentences.

Frege's solution in terms of Thoughts has a rival, proposed by another great ontologist. I am talking about Meinong's theory of objectives.[66] Ac-cording to Meinong, propositional mental acts intend so-called objectives. Every thought, for example, be it true or false, intends an objective. Up to this point, Meinong's solution runs parallel to Frege's. A difference ap-pears as soon as we consider the ontological status of objectives. Frege holds, as we saw, that false Thoughts have the same existential status as true ones.[67] Meinong, on the other hand, thinks that some objectives have a lesser mode of being than others. He distinguishes between factual and unfactual objectives. Factual objectives are said to subsist. Unfactual objec-tives do not subsist; they merely have what Meinong calls *Aussersein*.[68] According to him, they dwell beyond being and nonbeing. Yet they are not just nothing; they have some kind of ontological status. Factual objec-

65. Compare the following remark by Wittgenstein: "We understand a proposition when we understand its constituents and form. If we know the meaning of '*a*' and '*b*' and if we know what '*xRy*' means for all *x*'s and *y*'s, then we also understand '*aRb*' " (*Notebooks 1914–1916* [New York, 1961], p. 94).

66. See, among other works, A. Meinong, *Über Annahmen*, 2d ed. (Leipzig, 1910); *Untersuchungen zur Gegenstandstheorie und Psychologie* (Leipzig, 1904); and *Über Möglich-keit und Wahrscheinlichkeit* (Leipzig, 1915). A similar view can be found in K. Twardowski, *Zur Lehre vom Inhalt und Gegenstand der Vorstellungen* (Vienna, 1894). For a contem-porary version of Meinong's view, see *LR*.

67. Recall, however, that Frege holds that Thoughts are not real in the same way as the earth is real.

68. This is one of Meinong's later views, although I am not too sure that it really differs from his earlier view. Compare the excellent account by J. N. Findlay, *Meinong's Theory of Objects* (London, 1933).

tives thus have a much more exalted ontological status than unfactual ones, but even unfactual objectives participate in a shadowy kind of being. True sentences represent factual objectives, while false sentences represent unfactual objectives. Meinong's solution of the problem of false sentences is that such sentences represent entities which are very much like actual states of affairs, except that they have a lower degree of being.

Frege solves the problem by introducing extraordinary *entities* in the form of *Thoughts*, while Meinong solves it by introducing an extraordinary *mode of being* in the form of *Aussersein*. Frege, if I may put it so, assumes the ordinary existence of extraordinary entities, while Meinong assumes the extraordinary existence of ordinary entities. But I am as convinced that there are no modes of being as I am that there are no Fregean Thoughts or propositions. It is not true that some entities exist while others subsist and still others have *Aussersein*. What there is, exists; and what there is not, does not exist. Something exists or it does not exist; there is no third alternative.

Yet, that there are modes of being is almost a dogma among ontologists. How could so many philosophers go wrong so often? My impression is that they have confused differences among kinds of entities with differences among kinds of being. The kinds of entities which constitute a philosopher's ontology differ from each other in the most fundamental respects. Since these differences are so basic, it seems to me that they are often taken to be modes of being. For example, assume that a philosopher arrives at the view that there are entities which are in space and/or time and also entities which are not so localized. He may then become so overwhelmed by the difference between these two realms of being that he thinks of it explicitly or implicitly as a difference in being. He may even begin to argue, for example, that only individuals exist, because only individuals are localized in space and time, while universals can at most be said to subsist. Or he may insist that only universals really exist because they alone are timeless and unchangeable. To take a different example, a philosopher may argue that substances exist while accidents merely subsist, because substances, but not accidents, are independent entities. In each of these cases, a difference between two kinds of entities is turned into a difference between two modes of being. But there are no modes of being. There are only different kinds of entities.[69]

69. I cannot resist citing Russell's well-known words about the existence of fictional characters, since they apply to a currently fashionable view: "To say that unicorns have an

Let us lay aside this decisive objection against Meinong's ontology and take a closer look at his theory of objectives. Assume that O is a certain objective, and let P be the objective represented by the sentence 'O is factual.' Meinong argues that O cannot get its factuality simply by being the material of a higher objective. If it could, then O would have to be factual, since it serves as the material for P. What holds for O holds for all objectives: there is always a higher objective that would confer factuality on the lower one. Hence, all objectives would be factual. On the other hand, if one holds that O is factual because P is factual, then one invites an infinite regress. P confers factuality on O; but P must get its factuality from a higher objective Q, and Q in turn must receive its factuality from a higher objective R, and so on. Meinong concludes, therefore, that factuality cannot be given to an objective by a higher objective; factuality must reside in O itself. If it does, then P will be factual, and so will be the objective represented by 'P is factual,' and so on. Meinong holds that factuality is an indefinable property which certain objectives have and others lack. The presence or absence of this property distinguishes factual from unfactual objectives. Since this property is not attached to an objective by us, Meinong's view accounts for the difference between true and false thoughts and sentences in objective terms.

However, a moment's reflection shows that Meinong is still faced with an infinite regress. Factuality is conceived of as a property of objectives. We must therefore distinguish, according to Meinong's view, between a given objective and its factuality; there are two entities and not just one. Meinong cannot really hold anything else. If factuality were so intimately fused with the objective that we could not distinguish between them, then, it seems, no factual objective could ever be presented to us without our knowing that it is factual. The very "content" of a factual objective would then be different from the "content" of an unfactual objective, and

---

existence in heraldry, or in literature, or in imagination, is a most pitiful and paltry evasion. What exists in heraldry is not an animal, made of flesh and blood, moving and breathing of its own initiative. What exists is a picture, or a description in words. Similarly, to maintain that Hamlet for example, exists in his own world, namely, in the world of Shakespeare's imagination, just as truly as (say) Napoleon existed in the ordinary world, is to say something deliberately confusing, or else confused to a degree which is scarcely credible. There is only one world, the "real" world: Shakespeare's imagination is part of it, and the thoughts that he had in writing Hamlet are real. So are the thoughts that we have in reading the play. But it is of the very essence of fiction that only the thoughts, feelings, etc., in Shakespeare and his readers are real, and that there is not, in addition to them, an objective Hamlet" (*Introduction to Mathematical Philosophy* [London, 1919], p. 169).

by merely considering the "content" we could decide whether a given objective is factual. But it is clear that this is in fact impossible. Hence we must assume that we can and must distinguish between factuality on the one hand and the objective on the other. Yet, according to Meinong's theory, we are supposed to think that the objective itself contains factuality. Assume that *O* is the objective *that the earth is round.* This is the "pure" objective. As such, it cannot contain factuality, because the pure objective must be distinguished, as we just saw, from the property of factuality. When we add this property to the pure objective *O*, we get the objective *that O is factual.* But this is the objective *P*. Hence we are driven to the conclusion that it is the higher objective *P* that confers factuality upon the objective *O*. This conclusion, moreover, raises the question that leads to the infinite regress: What now confers factuality upon the higher objective *P*? Meinong cannot avoid this regress by holding that factuality somehow belongs to *O* as long as he admits that factuality is a property of objectives.

A thorough diagnosis of Meinong's quandary throws some new light on Frege's obscure argument against the predicative nature of truth. What lies at the root of Meinong's predicament? [70] I think that it is the assumption that to every sentence, be it true or false, there corresponds a certain complex entity, an objective. If '*O*' is true, then there corresponds to '*O*' the objective *O*; to '*P*', the objective *P*; and so on. Even if '*O*' is false, then "there is" some objective *O*; "there is" also the objective *that O is factual*; and so on. Hence there "exists" a whole hierarchy of objectives, some of which are factual and some of which are unfactual. Furthermore, it is assumed that there is no "internal" difference that distinguishes factual from unfactual objectives. Nothing *in* the objective *O* can possibly tell us whether it is factual. What, then, can make a difference? There is only one possible answer, and this answer will not do. Whether *O* is factual must somehow depend on the next higher objective. But, of course, what holds for *O* holds also for *P*; no internal difference indicates whether *P* is factual or not. Looked at from this point of view, it becomes clear that Meinong's theory is incapable of differentiating between factual and unfactual objectives.

70. Compare also Findlay's analysis of this in *Meinong's Theory of Objects*, pp. 102–12.

Consider the similar case for objects. According to Meinong, the earth, for example, exists, because it is part of the factual objective *that the earth exists*. The existence of objects is thus explained in terms of the difference between factual and unfactual objects and, therefore, stands or falls with the soundness of this distinction. Be that as it may, consider the sentence '*A* exists.' If we treat existence as if it were a property, then we are forced to hold that this sentence represents an objective, even if *A* does not exist, for a sentence like '*A* is green' is said to represent an objective, even if *A* is not green. But if '*A* exists' represents an objective, regardless of whether *A* exists, how are we to distinguish between fact and fiction? Since there is nothing in or about the objective that could make a difference, and since the objective is the only entity associated with the sentence, we are unable to distinguish between true and false sentences. We saw a moment ago that the introduction of the notion of factuality merely leads to the same conclusion on the next higher level.

The dialectics of Meinong's situation revolves around the following three principles: (1) To every sentence, true or false, there corresponds a certain (complex) entity (an objective). (2) No other entity corresponds to a sentence. (3) No matter which pair of predicates we choose, true-false, factual-unfactual, exist-subsist, actual-possible, etc., any sentence that contains one of these predicates represents an entity, even if the sentence happens to be false. If these three principles are accepted, then it is impossible, as we have seen, to explain the distinction between fact and fiction. If the distinction must be made, as it surely must, then at least one of these three principles has to be rejected. Frege rejected the second principle: according to him, truth-values, as well as Thoughts, are associated with sentences. I shall venture to reconstruct the line of reasoning that led him to this view. First, he agrees with (1) that to every sentence corresponds a Thought; that every sentence, true or false, expresses a Thought. Second, he considers principle (3), quietly assuming (2), and concludes that if we accept (3), then we are caught in the circle of our Thoughts and hence are unable to distinguish between fact and fiction. Therefore he rejects principle (3); truth-values, he asserts, are not predicative entities. Third, he proposes the alternative view that truth-values are referents of sentences. In doing so, he implicitly rejects principle (2) as well. His crucial step is the second one, namely, his criticism of the view that truth-values (or such notions as existence) are properties of Thoughts.

But Frege runs into a difficulty of a different sort. He holds that some

Thoughts are connected with the True, while others are connected with the False. In other words, *P* is true, because of the *circumstance* that *P* is connected with the True rather than with the False. Yet there are no such circumstances, according to Frege's ontology. There are only Thoughts and truth-values. Frege's ontology has no room for the circumstance that *P* is true; there is only the Thought that *P* is true (as well as the Thought that *P* is false) and the True. But this means that, according to Frege's ontology, *P* cannot really be connected with the True. Hence he cannot really explain the difference between true and false sentences. There is only one way in which Frege can somehow connect Thoughts with truth-values, and that is by including relational states of affairs in his ontology.[71]

With these considerations in mind, recall once more the mysterious role which judgments play in Frege's philosophy. In thinking a certain Thought, according to Frege, we think of a certain truth-value, even though we may not know which truth-value it is. Judgment is not needed, then, to reach a truth-value; mere thinking suffices. Why do we need judgment? Well, to think *of* the True, say, while thinking the Thought that the earth is round, is not to think *that* this Thought is true. It is not to think of the state of affairs or circumstance that this Thought is true. I believe that it is the function of judgment in Frege's system to reach what, if one is to believe his ontology, is not there at all — the state of affairs that a certain Thought *P* is true or false. The role of judgment in Frege's philosophy is so mysterious because it cannot really be played on the stage provided by that philosophy.

Both Meinong's and Frege's accounts break down, because neither one acknowledges the existence of states of affairs. In Frege's case this is quite obvious. In Meinong's case there may still be some doubt, for it may seem that Meinong's objectives are nothing but states of affairs. Objectives are different from Fregean Thoughts; that much is clear. While the earth does not enter into the Thought that the earth is round, it enters into the objective that the earth is round. In this respect, Meinong's objectives are more nearly like states of affairs than like Thoughts. In another crucial

---

71. We shall see below that Frege contemplates the introduction of a sense-reference distinction for concept words in connection with a *relational* sentence.

respect, objectives differ from states of affairs; and it is this difference that leads to the breakdown of Meinong's view. Take the sentence '*A* is green' and assume that *A* is not green. According to Meinong, there is nevertheless such an objective as *that A is green*. But there is no such state of affairs, in my view. The individual thing *A*, we may assume, exists; and so does the color green. But these two entities do not form the state of affairs that *A* is green. *A* is not "connected" with green; it does not exemplify the color. In short, while false as well as true sentences are supposed to represent objectives, only true sentences can be said to represent states of affairs.[72]

It is this difference that is important. Consider the earlier sentence '*O*.' How does the world differ when '*O*' is true from when it is false? According to my view, if '*O*' is true, then there exists a certain state of affairs; that state of affairs does not exist when '*O*' is false. In the first case something exists which does not exist in the second case. I do not have to explain, as Meinong does, why *O* is factual in terms of the higher objective *P*. Hence I do not have to face, as Meinong does, an infinite regress. If '*O*' is true, then *O* is factual, as I will put it for the moment. However, if '*O*' is false, then there is nothing that could be either factual or unfactual, for there is no *O* whatsoever. In the case of existence, I do not have to explain the difference between an entity that exists and the same entity when it does not exist. An entity either exists or it does not exist, and if it does not exist, then it is neither like nor unlike anything that exists. To put the matter differently, if *A* exists, then it may or may not have the property *F*. But something that does not exist cannot be said either to have or not to have the *property* of existence. Existence simply is not a property which an entity may or may not have. It is not a property which may or may not belong to what is at any rate already there, in some sense of "is there." Meinong's objectives are supposed "to be there," whether they are factual or not. Hence their factuality cannot be explained in terms of whether they "are there," or in terms of the factuality of higher objectives.

Granting that there are states of affairs, do we not jump from the frying pan into the fire when we admit that false sentences do not represent states of affairs? Frege's and Meinong's views, no matter how unsatisfactory they may be in some respects, at least account for the fact that we understand false sentences quite as well as true ones. They do not deny

72. It would be more correct to say that only in the case of true sentences is there something that is represented. Compare the discussion below.

the obvious fact that false sentences represent something, and that we know what they represent, even before we know that they are false. In saying that false sentences do not represent states of affairs, do we not deny this fact? With this question we are back at our starting point, namely, the problem of nonexistent objects.

Allow me to speak for the moment about *actual* and *possible* states of affairs. A true sentence represents an actual state of affairs, while a false sentence represents a possible state of affairs. For example, if *a* has the property *F*, then the sentence '*a* is *F*' represents an actual state of affairs, namely, the state of affairs that *a* is *F*. On the other hand, if *a* does not have the property *F*, then I shall say that '*a* is *F*' represents a possible state of affairs, namely, the possible state of affairs that *a* is *F*. But I shall also hold that only actual states of affairs exist. Hence only true sentences represent existents. When I say that a false sentence represents a possible state of affairs, I do not mean to imply that there is something, namely, a certain state of affairs, which is represented by this sentence.

However, if there is nothing that a false sentence represents, does it not follow that it represents nothing? And how can we reconcile this conclusion with the fact mentioned earlier that we understand what false sentences represent? There seem to be only two possibilities. If we deny that false sentences represent possible states of affairs, we are in effect saying that they do not represent anything at all. On the other hand, if we hold that false sentences represent possible states of affairs, then we seem to be forced to say that there are such entities as possible states of affairs. In the first case, we are denying the obvious fact that we understand what false sentences represent. In the second case, we are forced to introduce a distinction between what there is and what exists. Hence we shall have to deny what I also consider to be a fact, namely, that there are no modes of being.

To see the way out, we must recall that the basic problem of nonexistent objects arises not with respect to false sentences but rather in regard to false thoughts. Sentences, strictly speaking, do not by themselves represent anything. We *use* sentences in order to represent the intentions of our mental acts. When I say that the pen on my desk is black, I use the sentence 'The pen on my desk is black' in order to convey what state of affairs I have been thinking of, or perceiving, or imagining, etc. To say that a certain sentence represents an actual state of affairs is to say, speaking more precisely, that it is used to represent the intention of certain mental acts, and that this intention happens to be an actual state of affairs.

Therefore, the two horns of the dilemma have the following form. If we deny that false thoughts intend possible states of affairs, we are in effect saying that they do not intend anything. On the other hand, if we insist that false thoughts intend possible states of affairs, we are forced to conclude that possible states of affairs belong to the furniture of the world.

We cannot deny that false thoughts intend states of affairs. We may not know whether the state of affairs we are thinking of is actual or possible, but we know that we are thinking of a certain state of affairs. However, it does not follow that we must therefore embrace either Frege's or Meinong's view. We are only forced to seek their ways out if we make one further assumption. Thoughts, we must assume, cannot intend entities without ontological status. We must assume, implicitly or explicitly, that the intentional nexus can only hold between a mental act and an entity which has some mode of being, be it existence, subsistence, or *Aussersein*. It is this assumption, I submit, that led Meinong to speak of different kinds of being. It may also have contributed to Frege's theory of Thoughts.

The problem of nonexistent objects, as we now see, arises from the assumption that a connection can only hold between two or more entities with some form of being. Specifically, the assumption is that both the thought and the intention must have some ontological status, whenever a thought intends an intention.[73] But possible states of affairs do not exist; nor do they subsist or have *Aussersein*. When I say that a thought intends a possible state of affairs, I mean to say that it intends a state of affairs which could exist but in fact does not exist. The intentional nexus, in my view, obtains not only between a thought and a fact but also between a thought and a state of affairs which is not a fact. In brief, I hold that the intentional nexus is a connection of a rather peculiar kind, in that it can connect mental acts with mere possibilities.[74]

73. Of those philosophers who discussed the problem of nonexistent objects, Twardowski and Brentano, at one time or another, questioned this assumption. See Twardowski, *Zur Lehre vom Inhalt und Gegenstand der Vorstellungen*, p. 27; and Brentano, *Psychologie*, reprinted (Hamburg, 1959), vol. II.

74. I have heard the objection that my view does not solve the problem of nonexistent objects but merely reformulates the fact that one can think of nonexistent states of affairs. I have the suspicion that this kind of objection rests not only on a misunderstanding of my view but also on a general misconception of the ontological enterprise. That one can think of nonexistent states of affairs is a fact equally accepted by Frege, Meinong, and me. But we propose quite different ontological assays of this fact. The differences between these

This view suggests a classification of kinds of relations or connections. Let me briefly indicate what I have in mind.[75] Ordinary (descriptive) relations, such as spatial and temporal ones, obtain only if their terms exist. The same holds for the nexus of exemplification. In this respect, the nexus of intentionality differs from both ordinary relations and the nexus of exemplification. But intentionality and exemplification are alike in another respect; both connections connect entities without having to be connected with the entities which they connect.[76] Furthermore, there is another kind of connection that can connect with possible as well as actual states of affairs — for example, the logical relations *if-then* and *or*. If we assume that the sentence '*a* is *F*' represents an actual state of affairs and that '*b* is *G*' represents a possible state of affairs, then the sentence '*a* is *F* or *b* is *G*' represents an actual state of affairs. So-called logical relations, as we see, may also hold between existent and nonexistent entities. But there is also a difference between these relations and the nexus of intentionality. The former obtain between states of affairs, while intentionality obtains between mental acts, that is, individual things and states of affairs.[77] These brief remarks must suffice to show that my ontology contains very different kinds of connections.

To sum up, one can think of nonexistent states of affairs, not because one really thinks of existent Fregean Thoughts, or because there really are such states of affairs in some peculiar sense of 'there are,' but because a thought's relation to what it is about need not connect two existents.

However, even though a false sentence does not represent an actual state of affairs, it could represent one. To talk about actual and possible states of affairs means, among other things, to talk about what there is and what

assays are far from being trivial or verbal. Frege holds that there are Thoughts; Meinong asserts that there are objectives with *Aussersein*; and I maintain that there are neither Fregean Thoughts nor Meinongian objectives, but that the nexus of intentionality is of a peculiar sort.

75. For details, see *SM*.

76. That there are such connections is the lesson of Bradley's regress argument. Bradley's regress only arises if one assumes that *all* connections need further connections in order to be connected with what they connect. This assumption is simply false.

77. This is not quite correct. According to my view, the intentional nexus holds between certain *properties* of mental acts on the one hand and states of affairs on the other. Still, they do not connect states of affairs with each other, as do logical connections. For details, see *SM*; also *ME* and *LR*.

there could be. In what sense of 'possible' are certain states of affairs merely possible states of affairs? [78]

Consider the two categories of individual things and properties of individual things. Individual things are the kind of entity that exemplify properties. On the other hand, properties never exemplify individual things. To take another example, the logical connection *and* connects states of affairs, but it never connects a state of affairs with an individual thing or a state of affairs with another logical connection. What these two examples are meant to show is that the categories of the world obey certain laws. It is a categorial law that individual things exemplify properties, while properties never exemplify individual things. It is another categorial law that logical connections obtain between states of affairs but never between entities of other categories.

Now when we say that there is no such state of affairs as a's being F, but that there could be, we call attention to certain categorial laws. What we mean is that the categorial laws allow for this particular combination of entities. On the other hand, when we say that there could be no such state of affairs as F's being a, we claim that the categorial laws exclude this combination. A possible state of affairs, according to this explication, is possible in the sense that it conforms to the categorial laws of the world.[79]

This explication implies, among other things, that we can conceive of something that, as a matter of actual fact, is not the case. It even implies that we can conceive of something that, as a matter of logic, is not the case. Even contradictions are possible states of affairs. We do know "what it would be like" for a contradictory sentence like '(a is F) and (a is not F)' to be true. We do know what state of affairs this sentence represents. For the sentence to be true, a would have to be F and also not F. Since we know that nothing could be both F and not F as long as the logical laws remain what they are, we also know that this sentence is false. More precisely, since we know that no individual both has the property F and does not have it, we know that the sentence '(a is F) and (a is not F)' cannot represent an actual state of affairs. A contradictory state of affairs might

78. What is possible is often contrasted with what is necessary. To say that '*P*' represents a possible state of affairs is not to deny, in this sense, that '*P*' represents a fact. I am now using the expression 'possible states of affairs' with quite a different meaning, but it is not difficult to see how my use hangs together with the other, perhaps more traditional, one.

79. What is possible depends of course on the categorial laws of *our* world. A different world with different categories and categorial laws would allow for different possibilities.

not be *imaginable*; we might not be able to "picture" it in our mind. But it is certainly *conceivable*. A contradictory sentence is a (logically) false sentence, but it is not a "meaningless" expression. It is neither "nonsense" nor in any way "unintelligible."

In the sense of 'possible' under discussion, even a contradictory sentence represents a possible state of affairs. What is possible, in this sense, is relative to the known laws of ontology which govern our world.[80] But this is by no means the end of the story. A whole series of further distinctions can and must be made. There are other kinds of possibilities which are relative to other kinds of known laws. For example, a state of affairs may be said to be possible if it is not actual and if it does not contradict known laws of nature, that is, laws of physics, chemistry, and so on. It is then possible with regard to laws of nature. Or a state of affairs may be called possible if it is not actual and if it does not contradict the principles of logic. It is then possible with regard to the laws of logic. And so on.

When Meinong first pondered such contradictory entities as the round square, he came to the conclusion that they participated in a certain mode of being called *Quasiesein*. However, he later changed his mind and claimed that such entities fall entirely outside of the dichotomy between being and nonbeing. He said that they have *Aussersein*. The main reason for his change of mind was his conviction that so-called *Quasiesein* would have to have some kind of opposite, if it were a true mode of being. Now, I have mentioned earlier that even *Aussersein* ultimately seems to be a form of being. Hence there is no escape for Meinong. Be that as it may, is it true, as Meinong claims, that *Aussersein* has no opposite?

Possible states of affairs which do not contradict known laws of nature can be contrasted with states of affairs which do contradict such laws. Hence one can speak of impossible as well as possible states of affairs with regard to the laws of nature. The same holds for possible states of affairs which do not violate the principles of logic; they can be contrasted with impossible states of affairs, that is, contradictions. In the "ontological"

80. The stress here is on the word 'known.' The modalities are not ontological constituents of the world. I cannot hope to be more concise than Frege at the beginning of the *Begriffsschrift*: "The apodictic judgment differs from the assertory in that it suggests the existence of universal judgments from which the proposition can be inferred, while in the case of the assertory one such a suggestion is lacking." In the next paragraph he states: "If a proposition is advanced as possible, either the speaker is suspending judgment by suggesting that he knows no laws from which the negation of the proposition would follow or he says that the generalization of this negation is false."

sense, though, even contradictions are possible. What are the corresponding impossible states of affairs? The answer is obvious; ontologically possible states of affairs can be contrasted with states of affairs which are impossible in that they would violate the ontological or categorial laws of our world. Again, it should be emphasized that I do not claim that we can imagine what these impossible states of affairs would look like. I do think that we can conceive of a world in which different categorial laws hold and which, therefore, consists of "states of affairs" quite different from anything we encounter in our world.[81]

This concludes our discussion of the problem of nonexistent objects. I turn, next, to the problem of substitutivity.

The following assertion constitutes the *principle* of substitutivity: The referent of a sentence does not change if we substitute for a component expression another expression with the same referent. Frege accepts this principle. Since he holds that the referents of sentences are truth-values, the principle of substitutivity takes the following form. A sentence does not change its truth-value if we replace a component expression by another with the same referent. In the special case of complex sentences, we get the *rule* that a complex sentence does not change its truth-value if we replace a component sentence by another with the same truth-value.[82] However, there seem to be a number of exceptions to this rule. It does not seem to hold for so-called modal contexts, nor does it seem to work for sentences about mental acts. Frege tries to show that this appearance is deceptive. He argues that there really are no exceptions to the rule.

Consider the two sentences (1) 'John believes that the earth is round,' and (2) 'John believes that the earth is a planet.' Assume that (1) is true, while (2) is false. In Frege's terminology, we would have to say that (1) refers to the True, while (2) refers to the False. Both the sentences (a) 'The earth is round' and (b) 'The earth is a planet' are true. Hence both refer to the True. We can get (2) from (1) by substituting (b) for (a) in (1). Hence (1) seems to constitute an exception to the rule mentioned above. Frege denies this. He claims, first, that although (1) refers to a

81. I put the expression 'states of affairs' in double quotation marks, because in a world with different categories and different categorial laws there would be no states of affairs as we know them.
82. *SB*, pp. 35–36; *T*, pp. 64–65.

truth-value, (a) — *as it occurs in (1)* — does not. By itself, however, and not as a part of (1), (a) refers to the True. He claims, second, that (a) in (1) refers to the Thought which (a) *expresses* when it occurs alone. If Frege is right, then there is no violation of the rule. A sentence like (1) would yield an exception only if the component sentence (a) could not be replaced in it *salva veritate* by another sentence with the same sense as (a). Third, Frege implies that, in contexts like (1), substitutivity *salva veritate* is possibile for different sentences which express the same Thought.

The principle of substitutivity, however, is not restricted to components of contexts which are sentences. It is supposed to hold for terms as well. For example, two sentences are supposed to have the same truth-value if they differ only in that the first sentence contains a different label or description for an entity which is also mentioned in the second sentence. Put differently, if we have a true identity statement, then one side of it can presumably be substituted for the other side in every sentence *salva veritate*, irrespective of whether we consider identity statements for individuals, for properties, for relations, and so on. But just as there seem to be exceptions for component sentences, so there seem to be exceptions for component terms. Consider the two sentences (3) 'John believes that the morning star is the morning star,' and (4) 'John believes that the morning star is the evening star.' Now (3) may be true, while (4) may be false. If so, then we cannot substitute 'evening star' for 'morning star' in (3) *salva veritate,* even though the evening star is the morning star. Frege would say that the sentence 'The morning star is the morning star' as it occurs in (3) does not refer to the same entity as the sentence 'The morning star is the evening star' as it occurs in (4). This follows from his assertion that these two sentences do not express the same Thought when they occur alone. Why do they not express the same Thought? Frege's answer is that 'the morning star' and 'the evening star' do not express the same sense. Our example seems to show that there are contexts in which we cannot substitute *salva veritate,* even though the relevant terms have the same referent. This result is much more surprising than our previous insight that we cannot substitute sentences with the same truth-value for each other in certain contexts. After all, it stands to reason that if someone believes a certain true sentence P, he does not have to believe any other conceivable true sentence as well. What the present example seems to show is that he does not even have to believe another true sentence *Q* which happens to say "the same thing" as *P*.

The problem of substitutivity is how to reconcile these and other exceptions with the general validity of the principle. Frege's solution rests on the assumption that there are contexts in which component expressions do not refer to their ordinary referents, but refer instead to the senses which they ordinarily express.

◪

This solution raises an interesting question: Granted that we can determine whether two sentences have the same truth-value, and granted that we can determine whether two proper names refer to the same object, how then can we find out whether two expressions have the same sense? If the principle of substitutivity is to have any application to certain contexts, then we must be able to decide whether two expressions have the same sense. Frege was well aware of this question, but he never arrived at a satisfactory answer.

What possible answers are there? We can give short shrift to the suggestion that two expressions have the same sense if they refer to the same referent. But two expressions may have the same sense if they are "analytically" identical or equivalent. If so, then we could explain why the two sentences 'The earth is round' and 'The earth is a planet' are not interchangeable *salva veritate* in every context, for even though these two sentences are as a matter of fact equivalent, they are not "analytically" equivalent. On the other hand, consider a true logical equivalence statement like

$$(\text{A}p)\ (\text{A}q)\ ((p \lor q) \equiv\ \sim (\sim\text{p} \cdot \sim q)).$$

Many philosophers would say that the expressions '*P* v *Q*' and '$\sim(\sim P \cdot \sim Q)$' are *analytically equivalent*. If so, then these expressions may have the same sense. And if they have the same sense, then it would be possible to substitute these expressions for each other *salva veritate* in all contexts. Now, in certain contexts, so-called modal contexts, we can indeed interchange "analytically" equivalent expressions without change of truth-value. But the same does not hold for sentences which mention mental acts. To see this, think of two logically equivalent expressions *A* and *B*, *A* being a much "simpler" expression than *B*. It may then happen that someone believes *A* but does not believe *B*, even though *A* and *B* are supposed to express the same Thought. It seems that Frege was aware of the fact that "analytic" equivalence (or identity) will not do as a criterion for sameness of sense. He held that the two arithmetical expressions '2⁴' and '4²' do not have the same sense; and he also said that the two sentences '$2^4 = 4^2$' and '$4 \cdot 4 = 4^2$' do not express the same Thought.[83] But arithmetical sentences are commonly thought to be "analytically" equivalent, if equivalent at all.

There is a further possibility.[84] Two expressions, one may propose, express the same sense if and only if they are tokens of the same type. This means, roughly, that two English sentences express the same Thought if and only if they consist of the same letters of the alphabet in the same order and with the same number of spaces between them. For example, even the two sentences 'Peter is a bachelor' and 'Peter is an unmarried male' would have different senses. If we accept this proposal, then the principle of substitutivity becomes rather empty, for it amounts now to the rule that one can substitute tokens of the same type for each other *salva veritate*. But Frege rejected this third criterion for sameness of sense, on other grounds. He held quite explicitly that different expressions may share the same sense or express the same Thought.[85]

A condition for sameness of sense, it appears, must be somewhat stronger than "analytic" identity or equivalence and somewhat weaker than sameness of expressions. What this criterion must be is quite clear, even though Frege never mentions it, if we consider only simple expressions with simple senses. Two labels, which are not abbreviations, express the same sense if and only if they are labels with the same simple sense. Assume now that complex expressions express the same sense if their simple constituents have the same sense. Assume, in other words, that the question of sameness of sense for complex expressions reduces to that of sameness of sense for simple expressions.[86] Then there are two possibilities. It may be the

---

83. *FB*, p. 14; *T*, p. 29.

84. There exists a whole literature about the problem of substitutivity. The third possibility, for example, is discussed in P. D. Wienpahl, "More about Denial of Sameness of Meaning," *Analysis*, XII (1951), 19–23; R. Rudner, "On Sinn as a Combination of Physical Properties," *Mind*, LXI (1952), 82–84; and in a review by Thomson in *Journal of Symbolic Logic*, XVIII (1953), 89.

85. *BG*, p. 196n.; *T*, p. 46n.

86. Most recent attempts to specify conditions for substitutivity rest on this assumption. In particular, the notion of intensional isomorphism rests on this idea. Compare, for example, A. Church, "Intensional Isomorphism and Identity of Belief," *Philosophical Studies*, V (1954), 65–73; and Carnap, *Meaning and Necessity*. The basic idea seems to have come from C. I. Lewis; see his *An Analysis of Knowledge and Valuation* (LaSalle, Ill., 1946), and "The Modes of Meaning," *Philosophy and Phenomenological Research*, IV (1943), 236–50.

case that no two labels ever express the same sense. If so, then we must conclude that no two different expressions ever express the same sense, a conclusion which Frege does not accept. Or if it is the case that there are different simple expressions which express the same sense, then some complex expressions will express the same sense. Yet Frege never gives any examples of complex expressions with the same sense.

□

Can we do any better than Frege? How do we propose to solve the problem of substitutivity? Sentences, I have argued, represent states of affairs. Hence the principle of substitutivity takes on the following form: If in a given sentence *S* we substitute for a certain expression another expression with the same referent, then the new sentence *T* represents the same state of affairs as *S*. Are there any exceptions to this principle? I do not think so, but I shall need a few pages to explain why. The issue is clouded by a whole cluster of further philosophical problems, not all of which are relevant. We shall have to sift the wheat from the chaff.

First. If we consider a context like 'John believes that *P*,' it stands to reason that we cannot hope to preserve its truth-value by substituting for *P* any other sentence with the same truth-value as *P*. The intentional nexus between a mental act and its intention is not a truth-functional connective. If you see this, you will not be surprised at all by the fact that substitution in 'John thinks that *P*' does not follow the same rules as substitution in, say, '*P* or *Q*.' On the other hand, if two sentences *P* and *Q* represent the same state of affairs, whatever that state of affairs may be, then they automatically have the same truth-value. Thus, if we can establish the principle of substitutivity in the form mentioned in the last paragraph, then we also have a rule for truth-values: Two sentences can be interchanged in every context *salva veritate* if and only if they represent the same state of affairs.

Second. We cannot talk in a purely truth-functional language about mental acts and their intentions. Such a language, like the system of *Principia Mathematica*, contains logical connectives but no expression for the intentional nexus between mental acts and states of affairs. Insofar as we cannot talk in such a language about mental acts, the problem of substitutivity for sentences about mental acts cannot arise. If we restrict the discussion to a language in which only logical connectives occur between sentences, then we confine ourselves to truth-functional contexts. Furthermore, if we are interested only in the truth-values of complex sentences rather than in what these sentences represent, then we need not even consider what the simple sentences represent. Even for such a language we may still ask under what conditions we can substitute in a complex sentence, preserving not only its truth-value but also what it represents. If we are interested in sentences about mental acts, however, it is not only possible but necessary to raise this question, for it is obvious that to think of a certain state of affairs is not to think of quite a different state of affairs.

Third. Someone who refuses to consider languages that are not truth-functional cannot be forced to consider under what conditions complex sentences represent the same states of affairs. But we may try to confront him with this problem by calling his attention to sentences about mental acts. We may point out, first, that there are such statements as 'John thinks that *P.*' Then we show that these statements are not truth-functional. Finally, we argue that any language, if it is to be complete, must allow us to speak about mental acts. If he, for some obscure reason or another, cherishes truth-functionality above anything else, our attempt may still be in vain. At this point, our opponent usually proposes to "translate" English sentences about mental acts into his truth-functional language. Depending on his position, he may propose to "define" mental acts either in terms of overt behavior or in terms of physiological changes in the nervous system, or he may think of some other way. Very often these attempts at "reducing" mental acts to behavior are motivated by nothing more than a somewhat vague preference for truth-functional systems.[87] According to our analysis, this preference may be based on the belief that the logical connectives are the only connections between states of affairs. Thus it has its roots in ontology, namely, in the view that there is no connection between mental acts and their intentions.[88]

I shall have to treat all so-called "definitions" of mental acts rather cavalierly.[89] Let us look at the issue in one of its many forms by assuming that mental acts are to be "defined" in terms of physiological states of the nervous system. Now, I do indeed believe that there is a *parallelism* be-

87. Compare, for example, W. V. Quine, *Word and Object* (New York, 1960).

88. Of course, there are other reasons for attempts to "reduce" mind to matter. Also, the "reduction" does not have to occur so openly in the form of "definitions." Two cases in point are G. Ryle, *The Concept of Mind* (New York, 1949), and W. Sellars, *Science, Perception, and Reality* (London, 1963).

89. For more details, see *SM*.

tween mental states and physiological states.[90] But this merely means that a certain sentence about a mental state is *equivalent* to another sentence about a physiological state. A "definition" of a mental state in terms of a physiological state can be based on nothing more than such an equivalence. Neither one of the two sentences is an abbreviation of the other. Nor do the two sentences in any other way represent the very same state of affairs. Hence, even if we assume that we could "coordinate" to every mental state a physiological state, and that physiological states can be represented in a truth-functional language, we still could not talk about mental states in that truth-functional language.[91] The sentences of the truth-functional language could only represent physiological states of affairs; but a part of this language would be isomorphic to a part of another language in which we could talk about mental acts and their intentions. The situation is similar to that of arithmetic and logic. Arithmetic, as we saw, is isomorphic to logic, but to talk about numbers is not the same as to talk about entities and their properties in general. Psychology might turn out to be isomorphic to physiology, but to talk about mental acts is not the same as to talk about physiological states of the nervous system.

Fourth. It would be a mistake to assume that Frege's sense-reference distinction takes the place of an intentional connection in his ontology. Frege does not try to "reduce" intentional contexts to truth-functional contexts; he acknowledges the existence of intentional contexts and then explains in what form substitution *salva veritate* is possible in such contexts. His approach to the problem must not be confused with the quite different and ill-conceived idea of solving the problem of substitutivity by "reducing" intentional to truth-functional contexts.

Since I have rejected Frege's solution in terms of senses, I must now explain what alternative I find satisfactory. Let us first consider so-called modal contexts, for which the principle of substitutivity does not seem to hold. For example, if we use the principle, we can start with the two premises (1) '9 is necessarily greater than 7,' and (2) '9 is the number of

90. That there is such a parallelism is a very general empirical hypothesis. Compare on this point L. Addis, *Ryle's Ontology of Mind* in *Moore and Ryle: Two Ontologists* (The Hague, 1965).

91. I assume that the mental states involve the intentional nexus.

planets,' and derive the false conclusion (3) 'The number of planets is necessarily greater than 7.' Do we therefore have to abandon the principle?

Quite a number of answers have been given since Frege's time.[92] We saw that he saves the principle by claiming that expressions do not refer to their ordinary referents in certain contexts, but instead refer to their ordinary senses. Applied to our example, this means that the expressions '9' and 'the number of planets' do not refer to their ordinary referents when they occur in (1) and (3), but instead refer to their ordinary senses. Since these two expressions do not ordinarily express the same sense, although they have the same referent, the inference does not violate the principle of substitutivity.[93]

Other philosophers have tried to save the principle by restricting it to truth-functional contexts. It must be noted, however, that such a restriction amounts, properly speaking, to a rejection of the principle, for, as it was formulated, the principle governs all contexts, not just truth-functional ones. Moreover, it is not clear that the principle could possibly be false and admit of exceptions. After all, the principle seems to be saying nothing more than that the referent of a sentence does not change if we describe it or represent it by means of different expressions. It seems to grow out of the truism that we do not change the world by talking about it in different ways. If the two expressions '9' and 'the number of planets' really represent the same entity, then it is impossible that (1) and (3) represent different states of affairs and, hence, impossible that they have different truth-values. There can be no exception to the principle.[94] However, if there can be no exception, then we have to explain the mistaken belief that there are contexts which violate the principle. Frege offers such an explanation, albeit a faulty one, when he tells us that we wrongly assume that expressions always represent their ordinary referents.[95] Russell's

---

92. Compare, for example, Carnap, *Meaning and Necessity*.

93. I would object that the numeral in (1) must refer to the number 9 rather than the sense of '9', for it is this number that is necessarily greater than 7. This objection calls to our attention an important difference between the case for sentences and the case for terms. Frege's solution may appear plausible in the case of sentences, because it is more reasonable to assume that mental acts intend Fregean Thoughts than that they intend truth-values. But it is not plausible at all when we turn to terms; when I think of the number 9, I think of that number, not of a certain sense.

94. Insofar as Carnap's method of extension and intension presupposes that there are exceptions, it, too, is unsatisfactory. But this is not the only reason.

95. For an extension and formalization of Frege's idea, see A. Church, "A Formulation of the Logic of Sense and Denotation," in *Structure, Method, and Meaning* (New York, 1951); and also his *Introduction to Mathematical Logic* (Princeton, 1956), vol. I.

explanation is quite different, and very similar to the one I shall give.[96] Let us digress for a moment and look at Russell's view.

Russell considers the following inference: (1) George IV wished to know whether Scott was the author of *Waverley*; (2) Scott is the author of *Waverley*; therefore: (3) George IV wished to know whether Scott was Scott. (1) and (2) are true, while (3) is supposed to be false. Yet we seem to be able to derive (3) from (1) and (2) by means of the principle of substitutivity. Russell's analysis rests on two main ideas.[97] First, he treats the expression 'the author of *Waverley*' as a description, in accordance with his theory of descriptions. Second, he distinguishes between the primary and the secondary scope of a definite description. According to the scope distinction, (1) could mean either (a) In regard to the one person who wrote *Waverley*, George IV wished to know whether that man was Scott; or it could mean (b) George IV wished to know whether precisely one person wrote *Waverley* and Scott was that man. Russell claims that from (a) and (2) we can infer the following sentence: (4) 'In regard to Scott, George IV wished to know whether he was Scott.' But (4), according to Russell, is not false, as (3) is; it is true. Hence there is no problem. On the other hand, from (b) and (2) we cannot derive the false (3).[98] Hence there is again no problem.

Treating 'the author of *Waverley*' as a description, Russell transforms the sentence (2) 'Scott is the author of *Waverley*' into a sentence which no longer contains the expression 'the author of *Waverley*.'[99] Thus the principle of substitutivity can no longer be applied to (1). Even if (3) can be derived from (1) and (2), it cannot be done through a straightforward application of the principle of substitutivity. Next, Russell points out that (1) has two possible interpretations, corresponding to the primary and the secondary scope of the description. Finally, he shows that a certain sentence does indeed follow from (a) and (2), but that this sentence is true rather than false. This sentence follows from (a) and (2), not through any application of the principle of substitutivity but because of a certain logical truth.

With only minor modifications, Russell's analysis can be incorporated

---

96. So is the solution proposed by T. Myhill in "An Alternative to the Method of Extension and Intension," in *The Philosophy of Rudolf Carnap*, (LaSalle, Ill., 1963).

97. See his paper "On Denoting," reprinted in *Logic and Knowledge* (London, 1956).

98. It must be remembered that theorem 14.15 of *PM* can only be proven if the context *g* is either truth-functional or indicates the scope of the description.

99. Of course, neither (a) nor (b) contains the expression 'the author of *Waverley*' either.

into my view of descriptions. According to this view, (2) is more adequately rendered as (2′): 'The individual x wrote *Waverley* and x is the same as Scott.'[100] Now this sentence can no longer be used for the principle of substitutivity; it is not a straightforward identity statement of the form '$a = b$.' Thus we cannot derive (3) from (1) and (2) by means of the principle. However, we should be able to derive from (2′) and some such context as 'G(Scott)' the sentence: (4′) 'The individual x wrote *Waverley* and $G(x)$.' And, indeed, (4′) follows from (2′) and 'G(Scott),' though not by the principle of substitutivity. But (4′) is of course true if the premises are true. It is further obvious that (4′) does not represent the same state of affairs as either (2′) or 'G(Scott).'

Consider now the modal argument: (1) '9 is necessarily greater than 7,' (2) '9 is the number of planets,' therefore, (3) 'The number of planets is necessarily greater than 7.' I argued earlier that different kinds of possibilities are created by different kinds of laws. What holds for possibilities holds for necessities too. I shall therefore change the example, but this does not affect our present interest. Consider, then, the following argument: (5) 'It is an arithmetical truth that 9 is greater than 7,' (6) '9 is the number of planets,' therefore: (7) 'It is an arithmetical truth that the number of planets is greater than 7.' (5) and (6) are true, but (7) is false; it is not an arithmetical but rather an astronomical truth that the number of planets is greater than 7.[101] This result is not at all surprising. Whenever we have a context like 'It is an arithmetical truth that P' or 'It is a logical truth that P,' what we substitute for P must be an arithmetical or a logical truth, respectively, if the context is to remain true. The question is this: Why should an arithmetical truth turn into an astronomical one if we merely replace an expression for something by another expression for the same thing?

'9' is a label rather than a description. 'The number of planets' is clearly a description, and hence, according to my view, really represents a state of affairs. If this is so, then we must also change our conception of (6). (6) is not to be treated as a straightforward identity statement of the form '9 = the number of planets.' Rather, (6) is an identity statement of the form (6′) 'The entity which is a number of planets is the same as 9.'

---

100. According to Russell's view, (2) is expanded into a sentence that contains the so-called existential quantifier and the so-called uniqueness clause.

101. That is to say, it is an astronomical *state of affairs* that there are more than 7 planets. I speak here of arithmetical *truths*, but this way of speaking is obviously derivative.

Since it is an arithmetical truth that 9 is greater than 7, it follows that the entity which is the same as 9 is, as a matter of arithmetic, greater than 7. Hence we may conclude that the entity which is a number of planets is, as a matter of arithmetic, greater than 7. But this conclusion is true, not false, as (7) is.[102]

If we do not realize that (6) is really of the form (6'), we may mistakenly believe that (6) and (5) yield (7). Hence we may mistakenly believe that the principle of substitutivity has been violated. As soon as we recognize that what (6) represents is better expressed by (6'), we see that the principle of substitutivity is not even involved. This does not mean, though, that there is nothing we can derive from (5) and (6'). (5) and (6') do yield a conclusion. But this conclusion is not derived by means of the principle of substitutivity, nor is it false, as (7) is.

To sum up, there are no exceptions to the principle of substitutivity. Apparent exceptions disappear as soon as we realize that descriptions are abbreviated sentences. As it turns out, the principle of substitutivity can only be applied when the relevant identity statement contains labels rather than definite descriptions.[103] If we assume that the language under discussion contains not more than one label for a given entity, the principle cannot be applied at all. On the other hand, if the language does contain more than one label for a given entity, the principle is applicable, but it does not lead to paradoxical results.

It may be objected that one can construct paradoxical arguments with labels alone, that is, without using identity statements containing descriptions. For example, assume that 'Scott' and 'Walter' are two labels for the same person. We can then construct the following argument: (8) 'George IV wished to know whether Scott was Walter,' (9) 'Scott is Walter,' therefore (10) 'George IV wished to know whether Scott was Scott.' The objector claims that (8) and (9) may both be true, while (10) may be false. I think that this is possible, however only if (8) is a rather misleading expression for the intended meaning. Instead of (8), a sentence like the following should really occur: (8') 'George IV wished to know whether the man who had been introduced to him as Scott was the same as the

102. Russell's solution is applied to modal contexts by F. B. Fitch, "The Problem of the Morning Star and the Evening Star," *Philosophy of Science*, XVI (1949), 137–41; and by A. F. Smullyan, "Modality and Description," *Journal of Symbolic Logic*, XIII (1948), 31–37, and "φ–Symbols," *Analysis*, XI (1951), 69–72.

103. These considerations apply, of course, to labels and descriptions of properties of individuals, relations among individuals, and properties of properties of individuals, and so on.

man who is called Walter by other people.' Of course, (8') is just one of many possibilities, but I trust that the idea is clear; only if the correct formulation of the thought behind (8) contains at least one description can that thought be true and the conclusion false.

◻

So much about the principle of substitutivity. Returning to Frege's view on truth, I hope to have shown that Frege's ontology of Thoughts and truth-values is unsatisfactory. My arguments, one might say, amount to a defense of states of affairs.

—— IV ——

Later Papers:
Second Thoughts

FREGE'S PHILOSOPHICAL DEVELOPMENT reaches a peak with the sense-reference distinction. This distinction seems to solve a whole cluster of philosophical problems. It not only yields an answer to the problem of identity but also is used to explicate the nature of "fruitful definitions" and hence the nature of analysis in general. This explication, in turn, adds the finishing touch to one of Frege's greatest achievements, his proof that arithmetic is analytic. Nor is this all. A new theory of truth, the first systematic analysis of intentional contexts, and a solution to the problem of nonexistent objects are all corollaries of Frege's theory of sense and reference.

If the power and scope of that distinction is truly amazing, so is the tension which it creates within Frege's system. A little probing here and there reveals how unstable that system is. Frege, I believe, discovered this fact almost immediately after he had published the three crucial papers at the beginning of the 1890's. Several unpublished manuscripts show his uneasiness about certain parts of his view; they also contain new ideas and further explorations of old consequences. In this chapter I shall discuss some of the second thoughts which Frege had about his system, thoughts that might be shared by a student of Frege's as soon as the initial awe of the power and scope of the sense-reference theory has been replaced by a more critical attitude.

The general direction of the next inquiries is determined by our previous topic. Our guide is the fact that Frege's ontology does not contain states of affairs. Most of the shortcomings of the sense-reference theory can be traced back to that fact. And it is not at all difficult to reconstruct the lines of Frege's thought after his adoption of the sense-reference distinction.

If the saturated part of a sentence has both a reference and a sense, why should the unsaturated part be an exception? Why should only proper names have both a reference and a sense? May not concept words, too, refer to one thing and express something else? These are such obvious questions that we need not be surprised to find that Frege raised them soon after "Über Sinn und Bedeutung" had appeared. Furthermore, assuming that concept words have both a reference and a sense, what kinds of entities do they refer to and express? It will not do to identify the sense-reference distinction for concept words with the traditional and widely accepted distinction between extensions and intensions of concepts. If concept words refer to unsaturated entities, do these entities then yield saturated complexes when complemented by the saturated referents of proper names? If so, then they must yield complex entities which are quite different from either Thoughts or truth-values. But this would mean, first, that Frege's ontology would have to be expanded, and, second, that his ontology would have to contain entities quite similar to states of affairs. However, if we assume that there are such states of affairs, do we not dispense with the need for complex Thoughts? Could one not hold, for example, that two sentences with the same truth-value may nevertheless represent different states of affairs, rather than express different Thoughts? And if we assume that concept words refer to unsaturated entities, we may ask how these entities behave in regard to substitutivity. Is it not true that we can substitute concept words *salva veritate* in logical contexts if the respective concepts are extensionally equivalent? If this is true, are we not forced to hold that concept words could not possibly refer to unsaturated concepts, but must instead refer to saturated extensions (of concepts)? Presumably, the kind of entity that determines the possibility of substitution in ordinary contexts must be the entity referred to.

Frege's notion of truth, too, must be reviewed as soon as we begin to contemplate an extension of the sense-reference distinction to concept words. In particular, what remains of Frege's argument that truth-values cannot be properties of Thoughts? If concept words have a reference, then we can no longer claim, as Frege did earlier, that predication does not transcend the realm of Thoughts. On the contrary, predication must yield something other than a Thought, namely, an entity which does not contain the sense of a concept word but instead contains its referent. Assuming, then, that predication yields something very much like a state of affairs, we may ask why the predication of a truth-value does not also yield a state of affairs — a state of affairs which consists, roughly, of a Thought and either the concept true or the concept false. Why, in other words, do we then have to hold that the relation between a Thought and a truth-value is that between sense and reference rather than that between subject and predicate?

Last, but not least, if analysis, definition, and identity depend ultimately on the recognition of the same sense in different linguistic disguises, how could we disagree so often about such matters? Why do we not recognize senses just as we do colors? Why should it take considerable time and investigation to find out that we are confronted with two senses but one object, if senses themselves are directly presented to us?

No doubt these and other questions occurred to Frege in the wake of the sense-reference distinction for proper names. Let us look at some of his answers.

ABOUT SENSE AND REFERENCE

THE EXTENSION OF THE SENSE-REFERENCE DISTINCTION to concept words, though rather obvious, runs into a great number of obstacles. We are in an excellent position to predict what these obstacles are; from our analysis of the nature of the sense-reference distinction, it is fairly clear that they are quite different from those that arise for objects. Frege, at any rate, considered an extension to concept words but never really carried it out.

Recall our analysis of the sense-reference distinction for names of objects. The reference of a proper name is always an object. Its sense, according to our analysis, is a property, namely, the essential property of the relevant description. Senses of proper names, from our point of view, are nothing but concepts. If this analysis is correct, then it immediately follows that the sense-reference distinction cannot be made for concept words within Frege's system. To see this clearly, you merely have to ask what kinds of entities would qualify as senses and referents of concept words. Of course, there are concepts; hence, concepts could be either referents or senses of concept words. Assume that concepts are the referents of concept words. This, as we shall see, is the only viable alternative, and it is also the possibility which Frege seriously considers. We shall assume, for example, that the concept word 'green' refers to the concept *green*. Now what could the word 'green' express? What could be its sense? To see the full force of these questions, remember how Frege treats such labels of objects as 'Aristotle.' The senses expressed by these labels are always the senses expressed by certain associated descriptions. In effect, then, the sense-reference distinction applies only to descriptions of objects and not to labels of objects at all. This agrees, of course, with our diagnosis that the senses of proper names are nothing else but the concepts mentioned in the descriptions of objects.

The concept word 'green' is certainly not a description; it is a label for a certain color.[1] If it is a label, then it may have a reference but cannot have a sense; for only descriptions, as I just emphasized, have a sense. We must conclude that concept words like 'green' cannot have a sense in addition to having a reference.[2]

It will not do to say that concept words refer to concepts and express (as their senses) different concepts. Of course, one may propose this view.[3] But the important question is whether this interpretation is at all plausible. I do not think so. I would want to know what those concepts are which are supposed to be senses of concept words. And there is no plausible answer to this query. Assuming that the concept (color) green is

1. To be more precise, it is a label for a whole range of colors. To make the example perfect, I would have to speak of a particular shade of green. I hope that the reader will excuse this slight inaccuracy for the sake of brevity.

2. M. Dummett argues as if it were obvious that concept words have (at least) a sense. Two questions must be distinguished. First, is this obvious as far as the rest of Frege's system is concerned, regardless of whether he explicitly says that concept words have a sense? Second, does Frege actually say that they do? My answer to the first question is that it is not obvious at all. Quite to the contrary, labels of concepts cannot possibly express senses. But it is true, in answer to the second question, that Frege sometimes claims that concept words express senses. We must also note in this connection that Frege's talk about the senses of concept words is quite different from his pronouncements about the senses of names, as Marshall points out. Compare M. Dummett, "Frege on Functions, A Reply," *Philosophical Review*, LXIV (1955), 96–107; and W. Marshall, "Sense and Reference, A Reply," *ibid.*, LXV (1956), 352–61.

3. Compare, for example, Jackson's interpretation: Where F is a name of the function ϕ, there exists a function f determined by the rule that the value of f for an argument n is the sense of $F(a)$, where the sense of a is n (H. Jackson, "Frege on Sense-Functions," *Analysis*, XXIII [1963], 84–87). Of course, nothing prevents us from formulating this description of the function ϕ. But there remains the important question of whether there is such a function. I am trying to argue that there is no such function.

the referent of 'green,' what other concept could be said to be expressed by 'green'? When we consider a description of an object, there is a clear intuitive difference between the object described and the manner in which it is described. There is, in other words, a clear difference between the object on the one hand and the property by means of which it is described on the other. For a concept word like 'green,' there is no similar distinction.[4]

Perhaps there is another way out; perhaps we can still save the view that concept words have both a sense and a reference. We may hold, for example, that some concept words, namely, labels of concepts, merely have a referent, while others, namely, descriptions of concepts, have a sense as well. Probing for a way out along this line, one may even wish to grant that objects can be labeled as well as described and that such labels do not express a sense. We may fall back, in other words, on the fundamental distinction between labels and descriptions, regardless of whether they are of objects or concepts, and introduce the sense-reference distinction for descriptions only.

Or else one might try a different gambit and claim that there really are no labels for concepts, just as there really are no labels for objects. One may hold, that is, that the sense of 'green' is the sense of some description of that color, where the description may change from person to person or even for one person from occasion to occasion. According to this view, 'green' refers to the concept *green* and expresses the sense of a certain description.

These two roads lead nowhere. Frege cannot take the first way out, because he does not hold that definite descriptions of concepts refer to concepts. He claims, remember, that 'the concept horse' refers not to a concept but to an object. This means, in our terminology, that in Frege's system concepts are always labeled, never described. This further means that the sense-reference distinction for concept words could be a sense-reference distinction only for labels of concepts. The situation for concepts is therefore quite different from what it is for objects. In the case of objects, only their descriptions have sense and reference; labels derive their sense

---

4. Compare Russell's remark: "This theory of indication [Frege's] is more sweeping and general than mine, as appears from the fact that *every* proper name is supposed to have the two sides. It seems to me that only such proper names as are derived from concepts by means of *the* can be said to have meaning, and that such words as *John* merely indicate without meaning. If one allows, as I do, that concepts can be objects and have proper names, it seems fairly evident that their proper names, as a rule, will indicate them without having any distinct meaning; but the opposite view, though it leads to an endless regress, does not appear to be logically impossible" (B. Russell, *Principles of Mathematics* [London, 1903], Appendix A, "The Logical and Arithmetical Doctrines of Frege," p. 502).

and reference from certain descriptions. In the case of concepts, on the other hand, only their labels can have a sense and a reference, because there are no descriptions of concepts, according to Frege. Since the assumption that there are senses derives its intuitive justification from the fact that there are descriptions of entities, no such justification exists in the case of concepts. We can put it even more strongly: it follows from the very nature of concept words, as conceived of by Frege, that they cannot have a sense in addition to a reference.

There is still another reason why Frege's view precludes his taking the first way out. Consider the sentence 'The book on my desk is green.' This sentence is said to express a Thought. The Thought contains the sense of the description 'the book on my desk,' but it is not identical with that sense. It must, therefore, contain something else, namely, the sense of the concept word 'green.' [5] If labels like 'green' have no sense, then it is hard to see how sentences like 'The book on my desk is green' could express a Thought rather than merely a sense of a description. Even labels like 'green' must have a sense if we are to accept the Fregean contention that sentences express Thoughts. This conclusion points up another tension in Frege's system. One part of that system — the idea that there are no descriptions of concepts — stands in the way of an extension of the sense-reference distinction to concept words, while another part — the view that sentences express complex Thoughts — demands such an extension.

It is even more obvious that the second road is not open to Frege. According to this alternative, labels of concepts like 'green' receive a sense from descriptions of concepts like 'the color of the book on my desk.' This clashes with Frege's insistence that all definite descriptions refer to objects rather than to concepts. Even if we disregard Frege's idiosyncratic view about the referents of descriptions, there is little that recommends the second way out. It seems clear that not every expression for a concept can be a description; otherwise no concept whatsoever could be described. More accurately, the view that there are only descriptions of concepts leads to an endless regress. In order to describe a concept F, we obviously need a second concept G. But this second concept, we assume for the moment, can only be described, not labeled. Hence we need a third concept H, in terms of which G is described. And so on. The description of any given concept would involve an infinite number of further descriptions. This endless series of descriptions can only be avoided if we assume that there are expres-

5. I am still assuming that the concept *green* is the referent of 'green.'

sions for concepts which are not descriptions but labels. Concluding, then, that there are labels of concepts, we cannot hold that all expressions that look like labels are really abbreviations of descriptions and hence express the senses of these descriptions.

There are thus a number of weighty reasons against an extension of the sense-reference distinction to concept words, yet, in the *Grundgesetze*, Frege distinguishes quite explicitly between the sense and the reference of concept words. He holds that concept words refer to concepts, and that they must have a sense. It is likely, therefore, that Frege thought he had some equally serious reasons for extending the distinction. Leaving aside the obvious reason of symmetry, elegance, or whatever one may wish to call it, is there any clue to what these reasons are? In some unpublished papers Frege mentions three considerations.

First. Starting with the view that sentences express Thoughts, Frege distinguishes between a saturated and an unsaturated part of Thoughts.[6] The unsaturated part is conceived of as the sense of that part of the sentence which is left after we remove the proper name. Next, Frege raises the question of whether there corresponds to the unsaturated part of the Thought something which must be regarded as the reference of the unsaturated part of the sentence. In other words, assuming that concept words express a sense, he asks whether they also refer to something. His answer is that it is improbable that only proper names should have a reference; rather, we must assume that concept words also have a reference if the whole Thought is to be located in the realm of truth.[7] I take Frege to mean that it stands to reason that the truth-value of a sentence cannot be a function merely of the referent of the proper name in the sentence. Whether a sentence is true, Frege is saying, cannot depend just on the object mentioned in the sentence but must also depend on what it is we say about that object.[8]

6. Compare "Einleitung in die Logik in Form von Tagebuchaufzeichnungen," *FN*, no. 16. (1906?).

7. "Nun ist es doch unwahrscheinlich, dass der Eigenname sich so verschieden von dem übrigen Teile eines singulären Satzes verhalten sollte, dass nur bei ihm das Bestehen einer Bedeutung von Wichtigkeit wäre. Vielmehr müssen wir annehmen, dass auch dem übrigen Teile des Satzes, der als Sinn den ungesättigten Teil des Gedankens hat, etwas im Bereiche der Bedeutung entsprechen müsse, wenn der ganze Gedanke sich im Gebiet der Wahrheit befinden sollte" (*ibid.*).

8. Notice, first, that here as elsewhere Frege takes for granted that concept words have a sense, so that the question is whether they also have a reference. This agrees with my

However, Frege's remark is far too brief to allow for more than speculation about his real reasons. Precisely how do truth-values require referents for concept words? He gives no answer to this question, nor is it easy to make one up. The view that proper names and concept words refer clashes with the Fregean doctrine that sentences refer to truth-values. The more we lean toward the view that concept words refer, the less plausible does it appear that sentences refer to truth-values. Now, insofar as Frege suggests in this unpublished paper that the truth of a Thought depends upon what object is said to fall under what concept, he implicitly repudiates this doctrine, because he is saying, in effect, that a sentence refers to a state of affairs, circumstance, or whatever you wish to call it, such that a certain object falls under a certain concept. At the very least he is admitting that there are such states of affairs in addition to truth-values, so that it becomes an open question whether sentences refer to states of affairs or to truth-values. I am not pulling this assessment out of thin air, as can be seen from the following passage which occurs a little later in the same paper:

If we conceive of a singular sentence as being composed of a proper name and the rest, then the proper name has as reference an object, the rest has as reference a concept, and object and concept appear here as in a special connection or relation which we call subsumption. The object is subsumed under the concept.

What else could an object and a concept form but a state of affairs when they are so connected?

Second. Frege's second reason for extending the distinction to concept words relates to the fact that the unsaturated part of a sentence may contain a proper name whose referent is important. Consider, for example, the sentence 'Jupiter is bigger than Mars.' The Thought expressed by this sentence can be divided in different ways into a saturated and an unsaturated part. We may either divide it into *Jupiter* and *is-bigger-than-Mars* or into *Jupiter-is-bigger-than* and *Mars*.[9] Considering the first way, we have

---

earlier claim that Frege first introduced the sense-reference distinction only for proper names and sentences. Notice, second, that as late as 1906 he still tries to find arguments for an extension of the distinction to concept words. We may perhaps infer that he felt somewhat uneasy about his uncritical attitude toward the extension in the *Grundgesetze*.

9. "Dazu kommt, dass auch in diesem übrigen Teile des Satzes Eigennamen vorkommen können, deren Bedeutung wichtig ist. Wenn in einem Satze mehrere Eigennamen vorkommen, so kann der zugehörige Gedanke in verschiedener Weise in einen abgeschlossenen und einen ungesättigten Teil zerlegt werden. Der Sinn jedes dieser Eigennamen kann als abgeschlossener Teil dem übrigen Teile des Gedankens als dem ungesättigten gegenübergestellt werden" (*FN*, no. 16).

to admit that (at least) 'Jupiter' has a referent, since it is a saturated expression. Similarly, considering the second division, we have to say that (at least) 'Mars' has a referent. Then the question arises of how 'Mars' can have a referent if we assume that the expression 'is bigger than Mars' does not have a referent. If a part of an unsaturated expression can be shown to have a referent, is it possible that the unsaturated expression as a whole does not have a referent? Frege, it seems, believes that this is impossible, or at least unlikely, and that, therefore, we must conclude that unsaturated expressions refer just as proper names do. But notice that Frege's argument does not rest on the assumption that the referent of 'Mars' is part of the referent of 'is bigger than Mars.' If we assume that the referent of a complex expression *consists* of the referents of its linguistic parts, in other words, that a complex referent is built up from simpler referents, then we have a much stronger case for the conclusion that 'bigger than Mars' must have a referent. We could then argue that since a part of this expression has a referent, the whole expression must at least have this referent. Further, since it is obvious that 'Mars' and 'is bigger than Mars' do not have the same referent, if they have any, we may even conclude that the expression 'is bigger than Mars' must have a referent which consists of the referent of 'Mars' and some further referent(s). As it is, however, we cannot use that assumption. Frege did at first assume that the referent of a complex expression consists of the referents of its constituents, but in a later unpublished paper he repudiates this assumption. He points out that even though 'Sweden' is part of the expression 'the capital of Sweden,' Sweden is not part of the capital of Sweden, that is, of Stockholm.[10] Since we cannot make the general assumption that the referent of a complex expression consists of the referents of its linguistic parts, Frege's argument is not as compelling as it may at first appear.

I would like to linger for a moment and add a few words about Frege's comment on the description 'the capital of Sweden.' We can confine ourselves to definite descriptions as the only relevant complex expressions. It

10. Compare "Wie ich zum Logiker geworden bin," *FN*, no. 19: "Der Satz kann als Abbildung des Gedankens betrachtet werden in der Weise, dass dem Verhältnisse vom Teil zum Ganzen bei den Gedanken und Gedankenteilen im Grossen und Ganzen dasselbe Verhältnis bei den Sätzen und Satzteilen entspricht. Anders ist es im Reiche der Bedeutung. Man kann nicht sagen, dass Schweden ein Teil der Hauptstadt von Schweden sei. Derselbe Gegenstand kann Bedeutung verschiedener Ausdrücke sein, und einer dieser Ausdrücke kann einen Sinn haben, der verschieden ist von dem eines andern dieser Ausdrücke. Dem Zusammenfallen im Reiche der Bedeutung kann ein Auseinanderfallen im Reiche des Sinnes zu Seite stehen."

is clear that two different descriptions of the same object contain quite different expressions. According to Frege, this difference mirrors a difference in sense but not a difference in object. Therefore it is possible for different descriptions to describe the same object; in fact, Fregean objects do not even have any parts that could be mirrored by the different constituents of different descriptions. According to my view, on the other hand, definite descriptions are disguised sentences; their parts represent constituents of states of affairs. Hence, even though I agree with Frege that individual things are simple (ontologically speaking), I am not forced to hold that what descriptions of individuals represent is simple. For example, although Stockholm is a simple individual thing, the expression 'the capital of Sweden' *represents* not an individual but a complex state of affairs. Of course, this fact does not prevent us from saying that the expression 'the capital of Sweden' *describes* the individual thing labeled 'Stockholm.' Sentences, though they cannot be said to represent individuals, can obviously be said to describe them. At any rate, this consideration points up once more that Thoughts correspond, structurally speaking, to states of affairs.

Third. Frege's third reason is, I think, the most profound one. Take again the sentence 'Jupiter is bigger than Mars.' What is this sentence about? Obviously, it is about two planets; we are talking about the referents of 'Jupiter' and 'Mars.' What we are saying is that the two planets Jupiter and Mars stand in a certain relation to each other, namely, in the relation called being bigger than. This relation holds between the two referents of 'Jupiter' and 'Mars.' Hence the relation itself must belong to the realm of referents.[11]

Frege's reasoning here is straightforward and completely sound. Unless relation words have referents, objects cannot be related. But objects are related. Hence relation words must refer. Relations cannot be senses of relation words, for then they could only connect senses. If the relation of being bigger than were a sense, then it would have to hold between the senses of 'Jupiter' and 'Mars,' not between the two planets Jupiter and Mars.

---

11. See *FN*, no. 16: "Es ist undenkbar, dass es nur bei den Eigennamen auf eine Bedeutung ankommen könne, nicht bei den sie verbindenen übrigen Satzteilen. Wenn wir sagen 'Jupiter ist grösser als Mars,' wovon sprechen wir da? Von den Himmelskörpern selbst, von den Bedeutungen der Eigennamen 'Jupiter' und 'Mars.' Wir sagen, dass sie in einer gewissen Beziehung zueinander stehen, und das tun wir mit den Worten 'ist grösser als.' Diese Beziehung findet statt zwischen den Bedeutungen der Eigennamen, muss also selbst dem Reiche der Bedeutungen angehören."

The true nature of things now makes itself felt; Frege is no longer able to suppress states of affairs. When we say that Jupiter is bigger than Mars, what we say certainly is not a truth-value, nor is it a Thought. That it is not a truth-value is obvious; that it is not a Thought follows from the fact that we are talking about two planets and their relationship, not about senses and their connection. What we say, then, is that a certain state of affairs obtains. Yet Frege's ontology does not acknowledge states of affairs.

Be that as it may, Frege concludes that concept words not only express unsaturated senses but also refer to concepts. He does not tell us what the senses of concept words are, except that they must belong to the category of concepts, since they are unsaturated. His silence on this point is not surprising. We saw earlier that there are no plausible candidates for the role of sense of concept words. But this is not the only difficulty with Frege's conclusion, decisive as it is. He himself calls attention to another problem and discusses it at great length.[12] This problem arises from the assumption that concept words refer to concepts. Once again Frege is caught between the devil and the deep blue sea, as it were. Some considerations speak for the contention that concept words refer to concepts; others, of equal importance, speak against it.

Frege begins the discussion by calling attention to the traditional distinction between concepts and their extensions. This distinction comes naturally to mind in connection with the sense-reference distinction for concept words. Hence one may be led to believe that concept words express concepts as their senses and refer to extensions. But Frege warns us that this would be a mistake. Extensions of concepts, he reminds us, are objects and hence cannot be the referents of concept words. The sentence '*a* is *F*' states that the object *a* falls under the concept *F*. It does not say that *a* belongs to a certain extension. Concept words must refer to concepts, and not to extensions of concepts.

No sooner has Frege stressed this point than he notices that "just as proper names of the same object can be substituted for each other *salva veritate*, so the same holds also for concept words, if the extension is the same." But this seems to pose a real problem for his view. Recall his first

12. "Ausführungen über Sinn und Bedeutung," *FN*, no. 7.

reason for the assumption that concept words have referents. Frege argued then that the truth of a Thought is a function not only of the relevant object but also of the referent of the unsaturated part of the sentence. He argued that the truth-value of a Thought is a function of both the referent of the proper name and the referent of the concept word. He seemed to assume, moreover, that the referent of either expression must be the kind of entity that influences the truth-value. Recall, in this connection, Frege's approach in "Über Sinn und Bedeutung," where he said: "We have seen that the reference of a sentence may always be sought, whenever the reference of its components is involved; and that this is the case when and only when we are inquiring after the truth-value."[13] What poses the problem is this notion that the referents of words must be the kinds of entities that influence the truth-values of sentences. Just as objects must be the referents of proper names because they, rather than senses of proper names, affect truth-values, so extensions, it seems, must be the referents of concept words because they, rather than concepts, affect truth-values.

Frege's contention that concept words refer to concepts clashes with his notion that their referents must influence truth-values. What happens therefore if we reject one of these two views? If we deny that concept words refer to concepts, then we must argue that the reasons given earlier for this view are not compelling after all. On the other hand, if we deny the second view, then we jeopardize the sense-reference distinction for proper names, for then one may argue that proper names refer to senses rather than to objects. As it turns out, neither alternative is very appealing. Small wonder that Frege searched for another. Unfortunately, it is rather difficult to explain his eventual solution, because an entirely different matter continually threatens to intrude into the presentation. I shall therefore proceed slowly and step by step, as it were, in order to sort out the different issues as we go along.

Frege argues, first, that concepts cannot be identical because they are unsaturated entities. He insists that the relation of identity can only hold between objects. Since concepts are unsaturated, concept words must contain empty spaces, that is, they too must be unsaturated. For this reason, we cannot simply write '$F = G$,' nor can we be satisfied with an expression of the form '$F(\ ) = G(\ )$.' According to Frege, the argument places in

13. *SB*, p. 33; *T*, p. 63.

this schema have to be filled. But if we fill the argument places with the names of objects, then we no longer state that two concepts are identical; instead we identify two objects. Frege concludes from these considerations that identity cannot obtain between concepts. We are familiar with his general line of reasoning from earlier chapters; I shall therefore not analyze it again. For the sake of exposition we shall temporarily agree with Frege's conclusion.

Frege claims, second, that even though concepts cannot be identical, a somewhat similar relation holds between them. While two objects are identical if and only if they fall under the same concepts, the analogous relation obtains between two concepts if and only if the same objects fall under them, that is, if and only if their extensions are the same. This claim raises at least two questions.

How, we may ask, can there be any relation between two concepts if the earlier argument against the identity of concepts is sound? Assume, as I contend, that '$a = b$' is not an abbreviation of '(f) $(f(a) \equiv f(b))$.' Introduce a sign, say, 'R,' for Frege's new relation between concepts. Lastly, assume that 'FRG' is not an abbreviation of '(x) $(F(x) \equiv G(x))$.' [14] Now, is the expression 'FRG' admissible, provided Frege's reason for rejecting '$F = G$' is sound? I do not think so. No matter how we turn it, we cannot really say that two concepts stand in that relation. [15] If we assume, on the other hand, that 'R' is merely an abbreviation of some longer expression, then there is no reason why we should be impressed with Frege's argument against the identity of concepts. To put the matter differently, Frege's argument against the identity of concepts works only if we assume that identity statements are not abbreviations of longer expressions in which the unsaturatedness of concepts is clearly indicated. But if we assume this, then we may also assume that contexts in which the sign 'R' occurs are not abbreviations. If such contexts are not abbreviations, then

14. Frege's view on this point is not too clear. Compare the following passage in which the italics are mine and in which I have made some notational changes: "We would express this *Thought* in the way indicated earlier as follows: $(x^2 = 1)R((x + 1)^2 = 2(x + 1))$. Here we have in reality that relation of the second level which corresponds to identity between objects, but must not be confused with it. If we write (x) $((x^2 = 1)=((x + 1)^2 = 2(x + 1)))$, then *we express essentially the same Thought*, conceived of as the generality of an equation between values of functions. We have here the same relation of the second level; we also have the sign of identity; however, the latter does not suffice by itself to represent this relation, but only in connection with the expression for generality: *we have primarily a generality, not an equation*" (FN, no. 7).

15. And hence Frege's expression '$(x^2 = 1)R((x + 1)^2 = 2(x + 1))$' from the passage quoted in the last footnote is really not admissible.

we can bring Frege's argument against the identity of concepts to bear on the new relation R. On the other hand, if we assume that expressions of the form 'FRG' are short for expressions like '$(x)\ (F(x) \equiv G(x))$,' then we may make a similar assumption for identity statements of the form '$F = G$.'[16] If we make the similar assumption, then there is no longer any reason why identity should not obtain between concepts as well as objects.

At any rate, the most interesting point of Frege's deliberation is that he proposes the condition expressed by '$(x)\ (F(x) \equiv G(x))$,' rather than the condition expressed by '$(h)\ (h(F) \equiv h(G))$,' for the relation R between concepts. His reason, we saw, has nothing to do with the unsaturatedness of concepts; rather, it derives from the principle that the referents of concept words must behave like extensions in regard to substitutivity. Hence for the time being I shall neglect the complications arising from the unsaturatedness of concepts. This leads us to the second question.

Does Frege claim that the relation of identity never obtains between concepts, but that there is quite a different relation, represented by 'R,' which does? Or is he merely saying that concepts can be the same but the condition for their identity is different from the condition that holds for objects?[17] Neither view, I think, fits comfortably into Frege's system.

Consider the first alternative. Assume that there is a certain relation between two concepts if and only if their extensions are the same. What does this relation have in common with the relation of identity? In what respect is this relation *similar*, as Frege claims, to the relation of identity? Obviously, when we say that two concepts have the same extension, we do not mean that the two concepts are in some sense identical. If concepts have identical extensions, then they may or may not be the same. The relation R is quite mysterious. It is supposed to be like identity, without being identity. I simply do not know of any such relation.

Of course, the mystery disappears if we take the relation R to be none other than the "relation" of having identical extensions, if to say that the concepts F and G stand in the relation R is to say nothing more than that

---

16. Since Frege's ontology does not contain states of affairs, he does not use the equivalence sign. However, I shall continue to represent certain circumstances in the traditional way, rather than by means of the identity sign as Frege does.

17. It is not clear from Frege's remarks what he has in mind. Witness the following ambiguous sentence: "If we keep all this in mind, then we are able to assert 'What two concept words refer to is the same, if and only if the relevant extensions coincide [*zusammenfallen*],' without being misled by the deviant [*uneigentlichen*] use of the word 'same' " (*FN*, no. 7).

they have the same extension. But in this case, there is only one "relation" involved, not two, as in the case of identity, where we have the relation of identity and the quite different "relation" of sharing all properties. If we take it that R is the "relation" of having identical extensions, then Frege's view amounts to the perfectly harmless contention that different concepts can have the same extension. Surely, no one can quarrel with this claim. By the same token, however, this view does not support Frege's further notion that the referents of concept words, even though they are concepts rather than extensions, nevertheless behave like extensions.

According to the second view, concepts are supposed to be identical if and only if their extensions are the same. In this respect, they allegedly differ from objects, for objects are identical if and only if they share all their properties. Now, we know what it means to say that different expressions represent the same extension. We also know that different expressions may represent the same concept. Finally, we know that two different concepts may determine the same extension; that is, we know that the same class of things may be determined by two different properties. But this knowledge is simply irreconcilable with the second view. It may be objected that this disagreement merely shows that Frege and I must be talking about different things when we speak of concepts (or properties). It may be said, in the same vein, that Frege's concepts simply *are* extensional entities. But this kind of reply only substitutes obscurity for a clear, albeit mistaken, position; Frege's notion of a concept then becomes shrouded in mystery. What could it possibly mean to say that concepts are extensional entities? It may mean that they are extensions, but this contradicts Frege's doctrine that extensions are objects. Or it may mean that concepts behave like extensions when it comes to substitutivity, but this is simply false, because they do not. Given two properties which determine the same class of individuals, we cannot automatically substitute the property expressions for each other *salva veritate* whenever we can substitute the corresponding class expressions for each other without change of truth-value. To insist that concepts behave like extensions when they so clearly do not, contributes nothing to our understanding of Frege's view.[18]

18. M. Furth seems to be of a different opinion. Compare the introduction to his translation of parts of *GG*, *The Basic Laws of Arithmetic* (Berkeley and Los Angeles, 1964). Some philosophers and many logicians have the bad habit of speaking of *concepts in extension*. Compare, for example, the following passage from W. V. Quine's *Mathematical Logic*, rev. ed. (Cambridge, Mass., 1955), p. 120: "But classes may be thought of as properties if the latter notion is so qualified that properties become identical when their

Of course, I am not denying that it is possible to substitute concept words for each other *salva veritate* in *certain contexts*. But this does not mean that for such contexts different concepts become identical. Whether concepts are identical does not depend on any context; it is not the case that they are identical in some contexts and different in others. Like all other entities, either concepts are identical or they are not. If they are identical, then they share all their properties. Hence their expressions can be substituted for each other *salva veritate* in *all* contexts. What holds for concepts holds for all entities; two expressions either represent the same entity or they do not. If they do, then they are interchangeable *salva veritate* in *all* contexts.

We have seen that Frege's attempt to extend the sense-reference distinction to concept words runs into still another difficulty. Frege wants to hold that concepts, rather then extensions, are the referents of concept words. At the same time, however, he also wants to maintain that the referents of concept words behave like extensions with regard to substitutivity. Since this latter view amounts to saying that concept words refer to extensions, Frege is left with the impossible task of having to reconcile two irreconcilable positions.

An old nemesis reappears as soon as Frege tries to discuss the referents of concept words, namely, the problem of *the concept horse*. So far, I have talked freely about *the* referents of concept words and about the identity between *the* concept F and *the* concept G; I could not really have avoided these locutions. But we must remember that according to Frege the definite article indicates a name for an object and not a concept word; the expression 'the referent of the concept word "F"' refers not to a concept but to an object. Yet Frege wants to say, as we saw, that concept words refer to concepts. He discusses this difficulty in some detail.[19] He proposes to

instances are identical. Classes may be thought of as properties in abstraction from any differences which are not reflected in differences in instances."

P. Geach's criticism of Quine reflects my attitude: "Quine here uses the strange notion of abstraction so often criticized by Frege. How do things or properties *become* identical merely because somebody chooses to *abstract from*, i.e., ignore, the differences between them?" ("Quine on Classes and Properties," *Philosophical Review*, LXII [1953], 409–12).

19. *FN*, no. 7: "We have now recognized that the relation of identity between objects cannot also be thought between concepts, but that there is a corresponding relation for concepts. The expression 'the same' which is used for that relation between objects, can therefore not really also be used for the latter relation. But we can hardly help but say 'the concept *f* is the same as the concept *g*,' whereby we, however, name a relation between objects, when we mean a relation between concepts. We have the same case when we

use the phrase 'what the concept word A refers to' rather than the expression 'the reference of the concept word A,' because the former can be used predicatively and hence reflects the predicative nature of concepts.

We are all too familiar with the problems arising from Frege's dogma that all definite descriptions refer to objects. A suggestion by M. Furth is therefore of great interest, because it seems to provide Frege with a way out of these problems.[20] Frege, as we know, holds (a) that concept words, if they refer at all, refer to concepts rather than objects, and (b) that concept words indeed have referents. Furth, if I understand him correctly, interprets these assertions as follows. He takes (a) to mean *not* that the relation of referring must obtain between concept words and concepts rather than between concept words and objects, but that there is quite a different relation between concept words and their referents. He interprets Frege to hold that there are two different ways in which expressions may refer, rather than that there is just one way in which expressions may refer to two kinds of entities.[21] But Furth also thinks that these two ways are sufficiently similar to justify our speaking of reference in both cases; this is his explanation of (b).

The heart of the matter, it seems to me, is that Frege holds that concept words cannot refer to objects. I take him to mean that a concept word cannot stand in the relation of referring to a saturated object but can only stand in that relation to an unsaturated concept. He is not denying that this relation, which also obtains between proper names and objects, can hold between concept words and concepts. Rather, he is denying that this very relation can obtain between concept words and saturated objects. Furth, on the other hand, believes that Frege rejects the idea that the same relation of referring obtains both between proper names and objects and between concept words and concepts. Furth's interpretation seems to be a little farfetched. However, in fairness it must be pointed out that Frege does say things which may suggest that there are two relations of

---

say 'the reference of the concept word A is the same as that of the concept word B.' The expression 'the reference of the concept word A' is really to be rejected, because the definite article in front of 'reference' indicates an object and denies the predicative nature of the concept. It would be better to say 'what the concept word A refers to,' because this expression may be used predicatively."

20. Compare Furth, *Basic Laws of Arithmetic*, pp. xxvii–xxx.

21. I am not quite sure about Furth's view on this point. Is he saying that the saturated-unsaturated distinction is the same as the distinction between his two ways of having reference? Or is he merely saying that saturated and unsaturated entities, distinguishable in some other fashion, are also referred to in different ways?

referring. Furth fastens on these remarks in order to make a case for his interpretaion.

Frege specifies at one point in the *Grundgesetze* the conditions under which a concept word has a *reference*: "A name of a first-level function of one argument has a *reference* (*refers* to something, succeeds in *referring*), if the proper name that results from this function-name by its argument-places' being filled by a proper name always has a reference if the name substituted refers to something."[22] Let us call the part after the first 'if' condition *C*. Now, Furth, after calling attention to *C*, draws an analogy between *C* and the condition of *referring to an object* which proper names must fulfill if we are to say that they have a reference, refer to something, or succeed in referring. Thus he claims that we have two quite different conditions, namely, *C* and the condition of referring to an object. However, he also maintains that these conditions are sufficiently similar to allow us to speak of having reference in both cases. Since the conditions, though similar, are not the same, Furth seems to reason, the relations for which they are conditions cannot be the same either. Hence there are two ways in which words can refer.

First, a minor point. I think that the circumstance that a proper name refers to an object is not a *condition* for its having a reference *in the same sense* in which *C* may be said to be a condition for a concept word's having a reference. In the first case, the so-called condition seems to be the very same state of affairs as the one for which it is supposed to be a condition, while in the second case, the two states of affairs are quite different. But we can make the two cases more nearly alike if we accept the following condition for proper names:

A proper name has a reference if (a) the proper name that results from that proper name's filling the argument-places of a referring name of a first-level function of one argument always has a reference, and if (b) the name of a first-level function of one argument that results from the proper name in question's filling the ξ-argument-places of a referring name of a first-level function of two arguments always has a reference, and if (c) the same also holds for the ζ-argument-places.[23]

What here appears after the first 'if' I shall call condition *D*.

Conditions *C* and *D* are admittedly different. But from this fact alone

22. *GG*, pp. 45–46.
23. *Ibid.*, p. 46.

we cannot conclude, as Furth seems to do, that the referring relations under discussion must be different. I take Frege to be saying that the referring relation holds between a proper name and a certain kind of entity if and only if condition D is fulfilled, while that very same relation holds between a concept word and a different kind of entity if and only if condition C is fulfilled. There is only one referring relation.[24] But since it can hold between different kinds of pairs of entities, there exist different conditions for its obtaining between these different kinds of pairs.

Someone who thinks of C and D not as *conditions* but rather as parts of "definitions" may reach a very different conclusion. If we think of the phrase 'A proper name refers to something' as an abbreviation of D, and of the expression 'A concept word refers to something' as an abbreviation of C, then we may come to the conclusion that there are two relations of referring because there are the two different circumstances C and D. We may then reason as follows. To say that a proper name *refers* to something is to say nothing else but that D obtains; similarly, to say that a concept word *refers* to something is to say nothing else but that C obtains. However, C and D are clearly different. Hence, the meaning of the word 'refer' cannot be the same in both cases. Hence, there are really two quite different relations of referring. Furth, I submit, may have arrived at his interpretation along these lines.[25] Be that as it may, I cannot accept Furth's interpretation, because I believe that Frege thought of C and D as different *conditions* for the same referring relation; that he did not treat 'a proper name has a reference' as an abbreviation of D and 'a concept word has a reference' as an abbreviation of C; and that he did not hold that there are two different — though similar — referring relations.[26]

To sum up, the sense-reference distinction cannot really be extended to

24. I do not hold that expressions by themselves refer to entities, but for the sake of brevity I shall discuss the matter under consideration in these somewhat misleading terms.

25. Compare, for example, the following two sentences: "In these terms, the question whether 'ξ^2,' for example, has denotation, should be viewed not as asking whether there exists an unsaturated entity ξ^2 that 'ξ^2' names, but rather as asking whether every completion of 'ξ^2' by a denoting complete name of the language is a denoting complete name of the language." And a moment later, Furth adds: "Nor need there be any confusion as to what in concrete cases the ascription of denotation to an incomplete name was supposed to assert; that has just been cited" (*Basic Laws of Arithmetic*, p. xxviii).

26. Compare the following comment by Frege: "These sentences are not to be regarded as explanations of the expressions 'to have a reference' or 'to refer to something,' because their application always presupposes that one has already recognized some names as having a reference; but they may serve to extend the circle of such names step by step" (*GG*, p. 46).

concept words within Frege's system. Nevertheless, Frege does at one point hold that concept words express a sense and refer to concepts. The most important reason why concept words cannot express a sense is that concepts have no definite descriptions in Frege's philosophy. The most important reason that concept words cannot refer to concepts is that according to Frege's reasoning their referents must behave like extensions. Finally, there is the difficulty that Frege's attitude toward the definite article does not even allow him to say that the referent of a concept word is a concept. In view of all these difficulties, one might expect that Frege would abandon his attempts to extend the sense-reference distinction to concept words. Indeed, I believe that his last three published papers on the Thought were written in a new spirit; he no longer tries to maintain that concept words must express a sense and have a referent.

Before I outline Frege's later view, a word of caution is in order. My interpretation, I must confess, is built not so much on what Frege explicitly says, but on what he fails to say, even though he has ample opportunity. If it is contended, therefore, that Frege's later view does not differ from his earlier one but that he simply does not discuss many of the relevant topics in his later papers, then I have no counter-argument. Perhaps I ought to be cautious and merely claim that Frege may have abandoned his earlier view or that he might have held a different view in his later works. But I would then fail to convey my honest impression that we are dealing with more than a mere possibility. The whole structure of the three papers on the Thought, Frege's terminology at crucial points, his manner of avoiding certain issues which he discusses at great length in his earlier publications — all these factors have convinced me that he had at this stage consolidated his views and arrived at a somewhat simpler and less problematic system without abandoning his most cherished discoveries.

The essential feature of this new view is that it does not contain a sense-reference distinction for either concept words or sentences; the distinction is only made for proper names. As a consequence, Thoughts acquire a central position in Frege's ontology, for they become the most important *complex* entities of his ontology. Truth-values are no longer conceived of as referents of sentences; their place is not altogether clear, except that they somehow attach to Thoughts. Concepts, it seems, occur only as the unsaturated parts of Thoughts. Thus, Thoughts consist of the senses of proper names and of concepts (or relations). This later view obviously resembles the one outlined in "Über Sinn und Bedeutung," with the difference that truth-values are no longer conceived of as referents of sentences.

Three kinds of entities move into the limelight: Frege takes great pains to distinguish between (a) perceptual objects, (b) ideas, and (c) Thoughts. In his brilliant refutation of idealism, he defends the distinction between ideas and Thoughts.[27] He insists at the same time, however, that Thoughts are not perceptual objects, even though both are objective rather than subjective entities.[28] Concepts, on the other hand, do not play a dominant role in these three papers; they are more or less taken for granted as constituents of Thoughts. Although there is a lengthy discussion of the nature of truth, Frege never claims that truth-values are referents of sentences. In the main, he seems to be intent on making two points about truth, namely, that truth attaches to Thoughts and that the correspondence theory of truth is false. As I said, his interest centers around perceptual objects, Thoughts, and ideas. The main topic, as the title of the papers indicates, is the structure of Thoughts.

Even though this later view is simpler than the one described in the *Grundgesetze*, it retains all of what Frege probably considered to be his main ideas — the distinctions between subjective and objective entities, between saturated and unsaturated entities, and between the sense and the reference of a proper name.

Aside from the matter of ideas, how does Frege's later view compare with ours? Are there essential differences between the two ontologies? The most important difference arises from a different treatment of descriptions. Frege's system contains the earlier distinction between the sense and the reference of a proper name. Thus two entities are connected with every proper name. According to my view, on the other hand, there is only one such entity; labels represent individuals, while descriptions represent states of affairs.[29] Otherwise, the two ontologies are rather similar. To see this, we must realize that Fregean Thoughts later bear a great struc-

27. *G*, trans. in *Mind*, pp. 301–3.
28. *Ibid*, p. 292.
29. In the case of descriptions of individuals, there remains the following parallel between Frege's and my accounts. According to Frege, the description *refers* to a certain individual and *expresses* a certain sense; according to my view, the description *describes* a certain individual and *represents* a certain state of affairs.

tural similarity to states of affairs, as the following remark immediately shows: "What is a fact? A fact is a Thought that is true." [30] While for Frege some Thoughts are facts, namely, all true Thoughts, I hold that some states of affairs are facts, namely, all the actual ones. Even so, Thoughts still differ from states of affairs in at least three significant respects.

First. Thoughts do not contain individual objects. They do not contain the referents of proper names but rather their senses. States of affairs, by contrast, may contain individual things. Senses cannot be constituents of states of affairs because there are no senses, according to our ontological assay. This difference is, of course, a consequence of our rejection of Frege's sense-reference distinction. According to Frege's later view, the fact that Jupiter is bigger than Mars does not concern the planets Jupiter and Mars but involves the senses of the expressions 'Jupiter' and 'Mars.' To be more precise, Frege is forced to hold at this stage that the relation of being bigger than holds not between the two planets but between two senses. Surely, this is an unacceptable feature of Frege's later system.

Second. Thoughts exist even when they are false, while states of affairs exist only if they are actual. Frege argues in "Die Verneinung" that (1) even false Thoughts exist, and (2) even false Thoughts can be grasped by several people, and hence even false Thoughts are objective.[31] He presents three reasons for (1): false Thoughts must exist, because (a) they are the senses of interrogative sentences, (b) they are part of hypothetical Thought complexes, and (c) they can be negated.

A critical evaluation of Frege's arguments is impeded by the fact that some of his considerations appear much more plausible than they really are, because he appropriates the word 'thought' for entities that bear little resemblance to what we ordinarily regard as thoughts. Whatever else may be true of thoughts, it is clear that they would not exist in a world in which there are no minds. When there were no living beings there were no thoughts either. Fregean Thoughts are not mind-dependent in this sense; they are objective rather than subjective entities, to use Frege's favorite terms. Now, even though it is perfectly proper to speak of true and false thoughts, I do not think that it makes any sense to speak of true and false Thoughts. When we turn to the objective counterparts of

30. *G*, trans. in *Mind*, p. 307.
31. "Die Verneinung," in *Beiträge zur Philosophie des deutschen Idealismus* I (1919), 143–57, trans. P. T. Geach in *T*, pp. 117–35.

245

thoughts — to those entities which we call states of affairs, or to Frege's Thoughts — the contrast between truth and falsehood is supplanted by the difference between actuality and possibility, between fact and fiction.

With these terminological deviations in mind, let us look at Frege's argument for the existence of false Thoughts. Frege's main point is that we must understand the sense of a question before we can answer it, and hence that there must be such a sense, no matter what the answer to the question may be. It may be recalled that I used a somewhat similar argument for my view that even false thoughts intend states of affairs. From the fact that we understand false sentences, Frege concludes in the traditional fashion that there must therefore be false Thoughts. I rejected this conclusion earlier. What I conclude instead is that we can think of states of affairs which do not exist, that is, that thoughts can intend states of affairs which do not exist.

Frege's second reason for the contention that false Thoughts exist is that complex Thoughts may contain false Thoughts, and hence that there must be such false Thoughts which enter into complex Thoughts. Take the Thought expressed by the sentence 'If P, then Q.' Assume that P happens to be false. Since the whole Thought is true, it exists. But this Thought couldn't exist, according to Frege's line of reasoning, unless 'P' expressed a Thought, even though it is false. Again, there is nothing wrong with Frege's premises, yet his conclusion is false. His argument contains a hidden premise which is false. In this particular case, it is the assumption that the logical connection represented by 'if . . . then . . .' must obtain between existents. I claimed earlier that this connection may obtain between actual and merely possible states of affairs.

Frege's third and last argument concerns the nature of negation. He claims that a false Thought can be negated. Hence, there must be false Thoughts, since one cannot possibly negate what is not there. From this formulation one may get the mistaken impression that Frege thinks of negation as a kind of mental act, but he takes great pains to refute this conception of negation. He argues for the view that negation is an unsaturated part of a Thought; it is an objective constituent of Thoughts. Since I basically agree with this assessment, conceiving of negation as a constituent of states of affairs, I can immediately proceed to reformulate Frege's argument: Never mind what one can or cannot do with Thoughts, an unsaturated entity like negation cannot be saturated by something that does not exist; hence there must be false Thoughts because the negations of false Thoughts exist. My answer is once again that negation simply is a kind of entity that can "connect with" or "attach to" something that is not there, namely, a possible state of affairs.

In regard to Frege's conclusion that even false Thoughts can be grasped by several people and that they are therefore objective, it is obvious that my conception of states of affairs is compatible with this general idea.

Third. Fregean Thoughts cannot be perceived; they are not entities of the outer world.[32] States of affairs, on the other hand, can be perceived whenever they concern perceptual objects. For example, we *see* that the sun has risen or we *hear* that the car's engine is operating. Frege objects to this. "That the sun has risen is not an object which emits rays that reach my eye, it is not a visible thing like the sun itself." [33] This reply does not touch the heart of the matter. We do not have to deny, as Frege seems to think, that there is a difference between individual things like the sun and states of affairs like that the sun has risen. We not only admit that the state of affairs that the sun has risen is not an individual thing like the sun, but we insist on their difference. Since the state of affairs is not an individual thing, it does not have the kind of properties which individual things have — it is not round, it does not emit rays, and so on. But is it true, and this is the crucial point, that only individual things can be perceived? I do not think so, but I cannot argue for my position in this context.[34] It is clear, at any rate, that Frege's contention requires a further argument; the fact that Thoughts or states of affairs are not visible individual *things* does not suffice to establish that Thoughts or states of affairs cannot be perceived.

These are some of the differences between Thoughts and states of affairs. Frege's later philosophy contains a sense-reference distinction for proper names but not for concept words or sentences. As a consequence, Thoughts move into the center of Frege's ontology and come to resemble states of affairs, yet, the differences between the two remain profound. One difference can be traced to Frege's sense-reference distinction for proper names, which leads him to hold that senses of proper names, rather than their referents, enter into Thoughts. A second difference arises because Frege does not realize that there may be "connections" between ac-

32. Compare *G*, trans. in *Mind*, pp. 292–93, 302, 308–9.
33. *Ibid.*, p. 292.
34. Compare *SM*.

tual and merely possible entities. As a result, he is led to maintain that false Thoughts exist. Finally, a third difference follows from Frege's philosophy of mind, which, in a traditional manner, considers Thoughts to be a matter of judgment, not of perception.

ABOUT DEFINITIONS

IN EARLIER CHAPTERS, I repeatedly called attention to Frege's confused analysis of the nature of definitions. But there exists a remarkable unpublished paper, apparently written in 1914, which deals with the nature of definitions.[35] I call it remarkable because it contains a number of penetrating insights.

A *genuine definition* (*eigentliche Definition*), according to Frege, has the following characteristics: (1) It introduces a simple expression for a group of expressions. (2) The simple expression receives the same sense as the complex expression. (3) Genuine definitions are not really necessary for a system, since the new simple sign does not add anything new but merely yields more manageable expressions. (4) After the simple expression has received its meaning, the definition turns into an identity statement. (5) But this identity statement is tautological and does not extend our knowledge.

What Frege so accurately describes here are precisely what I have called *abbreviations*. But such abbreviations, as I pointed out, are not involved in Frege's "definitions" of the basic arithmetical notions. Frege seems to realize this now, for he says:

Indeed, no truth must become provable by means of a definition, if it would otherwise be unprovable. Wherever something that purports to be a definition makes the proof of a truth possible, we have no pure definition. Rather, the definition must contain something which either must be proven as a theorem or must be acknowledged as an axiom.

Applying this insight to Frege's "reduction" of arithmetic to logic, it is clear that most of his so-called definitions of arithmetical notions contain something which must be either proved as a theorem or accepted as an axiom. Our earlier characterization of these so-called definitions as true equivalence (or identity) statements was justified and still stands. By

35. "Über Logik in der Mathematik," *FN*, no. 17.

distinguishing between genuine definitions on the one hand and true identity statements on the other, Frege is only one small step away from a re-evaluation of his proof that arithmetical statements are analytic.

From this description of genuine definitions, Frege concludes that they are rather unimportant, but, in the same breath, he also announces some strong objections against this conclusion. These objections arise if one moves to a different point of view, thinking of definitions now as containing a logical analysis (*logische Zerlegung*):

> As little as it is indifferent whether I analyze a body chemically, in order to see of what elements it consists, can it be unimportant whether I undertake a logical analysis of a logical configuration in order to learn of its components, or whether I leave it unanalyzed, as if it were simple, when it is in fact complex.

From this new point of view, definitions appear not as unimportant abbreviations but as essential tools of analysis. Surely they cannot be both.[36]

It may happen during the development of science, Frege explains, that people use a certain expression for a long time, believing that the sense of this expression is simple, until they succeed in analyzing the sense into its logical components. Such an analysis may make it possible to reduce the number of axioms needed for a certain purpose, for a truth which contains a complex constituent can perhaps not be proved as long as the constituent remains unanalyzed. However, it may be provable with the help of other truths which contain parts of that constituent, parts which an analysis of the constituent would reveal. This means that a definition, since it amounts to an analysis, may make a proof possible that otherwise would have been impossible. Hence it appears now that definitions may extend our knowledge, which contradicts Frege's previous assessment of the usefulness of definitions.

Before Frege tries to resolve this contradiction, he raises a further question: "On what basis does one judge that a logical analysis is correct? A proof of it is impossible." If we believe we have analyzed the sense of an expression which has been in common use, Frege reasons, then we have obtained a complex expression, the parts of which have known senses. The sense of the complex expression is determined by these partial senses. Does the sense of the complex expression coincide with the sense of the original unanalyzed expression? An affirmative answer, Frege

---

36. In the following paragraphs, I paraphrase Frege's remarks almost verbatim.

believes, is only possible if it is immediately obvious. Hence one has an axiom to the effect that the sense of a certain expression is the same as that of another expression. However, it is just this coincidence between the senses which the definition was supposed to determine. This consideration seems to show, although Frege does not state it explicitly, that definitions as tools of analysis are nothing but axioms, that is, true identity or equivalence statements.

Next, Frege distinguishes between two different cases. First, we may build up a sense from other senses and introduce a completely new and simple sign for the complex sense: "One could call this constructive definition (*aufbauende Definition*); but we shall rather simply call it definition." Second, a sign may have been in use for some time. We believe that we can so analyze its sense that we get a complex expression with the same sense as the original unanalyzed sign. In this case, too, one speaks of definition. But Frege thinks that it would be better to avoid this term, since what is here called a definition is in reality an axiom. He concludes: "In this second case, there remains no room for an arbitrary decision, because the simple sign has already a sense. One can only arbitrarily assign a sense to a sign which does not already have a sense."

The contradiction is thus resolved. However one may wish to use the term 'definition,' one must distinguish between two quite different cases. One can introduce abbreviations for longer expressions and one can assert that a shorter and a longer expression have the same sense. Obviously, if one calls the first a case of definition, one must not also use this term for the second, and vice versa. Frege chooses to speak of definitions only in the case of abbreviations. If I used the word at all, I too would want to use it in this way. As for logical analysis, we shall have to look into its nature presently.

■

Frege returns to the question of how we can determine that a logical analysis is correct. Assume that *A* is a simple sign which is in common use with a certain sense. Assume further that *B* is a complex expression which, we hope, has the same sense as *A*. Since we are not as yet sure that *B* has the same sense as *A*, Frege proposes that we introduce a new sign *C* as an abbreviation for *B*. This raises the question of whether *A* and *C* have the same sense. Frege claims that we can avoid this question if we rebuild our system, not using the sign *A* but using the sign *C* instead. *C*, we know, has a sense, because it is an abbreviation of *B*, and *B* is supposed to have a sense.

Frege then continues:

If we now succeed in this fashion to build the system of mathematics, without needing the sign *A*, then we can leave it at that and do not need to answer at all the question with what sense the sign *A* has been used previously. This is the unobjectionable way to do it. However, it may be convenient to use the sign *A* instead of the sign *C*. But then we have to treat it as a newly introduced sign which had no sense before it was defined.

A little later Frege adds: "Our analyzing activity, too, must be conceived of as a mere preparation, a preparation which does not appear in the new formulation of the system."

To take an actual case, let us assume that we propose to analyze the sense of the commonly used sign '2,' and that we are inclined to believe that this simple expression has the same sense as the complex expression 'the next integer after 1.' In order to avoid any final decision on this matter we follow Frege's method. First, we introduce a new sign, say, 'ii,' as an abbreviation of 'the next integer after 1.' Then we build a new system using the sign 'ii' instead of the usual '2.'

Our example seems to show that we can avoid the question of whether '2' and 'the next integer after 1' have the same sense. But this appearance is deceptive, if we avoid the question, we cannot decide whether our new system is a system of arithmetic, that is, whether it deals with, among other things, the number 2. The most we can say about our new system is that, although it may or may not be about the number 2, it is at least isomorphic to what we traditionally call arithmetic. However, this objection presupposes that a difference in sense determines a different system, if I may so put it. But this is not necessarily so. Since '2' and 'the next integer after 1' refer to the same number, and since 'ii' is just an abbreviation of the latter expression, it makes no difference whether our system contains the sign '2' or the sign 'ii.' Hence there can really be no doubt that the new system is a system of arithmetic as long as we know that '2' and 'the next integer after 1' have the same referent, regardless of what senses they express.

But if our example is completely irrelevant, what would an analysis of a sense look like? Frege provides no examples. The crucial "definitions" of his "reduction" of arithmetic to logic are identity statements, and therefore, they maintain that *different* senses belong to the *same* referents. They do not assert that the senses of different expressions are the same. Aside from abbreviations, all the crucial "definitions" of Frege's "reduction" are informative identity statements. Perhaps there is no such thing as a logical analysis of a sense.

□

Earlier, in the discussion of definite descriptions, I claimed, among other things, that the expression 'the pen on my desk' is merely short for the expression 'the individual thing which is a pen on my desk.' I did not mean, of course, that somewhere there is a written rule to this effect; I meant to say that the thought usually expressed by the former expression could equally well be expressed by the latter. In my opinion, it is merely a matter of linguistic convenience, a matter of brevity, that we commonly use the former rather than the latter expression. In making this claim, I neither introduced a new sign nor did I state an identity in the ordinary sense of this term. One might be tempted to say that I analyzed the meaning of an expression. However, I do not particularly care what one calls this enterprise. It is more important to note that it may well be what Frege calls the logical analysis of a sense.

If so, then there are many examples of logical analysis in Frege's writings. For example, Frege's reformulation of sentences of the form 'All F are G' by means of the universal quantifier qualifies as a logical analysis. Frege could claim that his reformulation expresses the same Thought as the more familiar sentence. It should be obvious by now that I have no quarrel with this notion of analysis, nor, of course, do I disagree with Frege's particular analysis of the form 'All F are G.' Naturally, I would not say that two sentences express the same *Thought*; rather, I would claim that they represent the same state of affairs. But this difference does not detract from the principle of the matter, namely, that in addition to proposals for abbreviations, and in addition to identity statements which contain descriptions, there are also statements to the effect that certain labels happen to be used for the same entity and that certain sentences happen to be used for the same state of affairs. The case of labels is relatively uninteresting; but this is not so for sentences. In contrast to labels, sentences have a structure, and it may happen that a given sentence structure is a poor guide to the structure of the state of affairs which is depicted by the sentence. In that case, it may be advantageous to represent the same state of affairs by a more adequate sentence.

This leaves one final question. How can there ever be any doubt that a certain sentence represents the same state of affairs as another sentence if the states of affairs represented by both sentences are known? How, in other words, can there be any disagreement about the result of a "logical analysis"? Taking into consideration that Frege talks about senses where I think of states of affairs, and keeping in mind that the expressions involved may both be complex, Frege's answer to the question appears to me basically correct:

Indeed, if the sense of the simple sign is clearly grasped, then there can be no doubt whether or not it agrees with the sense of the other expression. If the question arises, even though the sense of this latter expression can be clearly discerned from its composition, then the reason must be that the sense of the simple sign is not clearly grasped, but appears only in hazy outline as through a fog.

Frege's notion of definition has at long last become clear and unobjectionable. He finally realizes that neither informative identity statements nor statements of analysis ought to be called definitions. These two kinds of statements are not as harmless as proposals for abbreviations.

If, in conclusion, we look back at Frege's system, we see that another of its main flaws has been eliminated. What remains as before is Frege's conviction that there are senses — both senses of proper names and Thoughts. I have argued that a correct ontology contains states of affairs instead of Fregean senses. What descriptions represent — as distinguished from what they describe — are states of affairs, not senses. What sentences represent are states of affairs, not Thoughts. The sense-reference distinction, Frege's most original and most famous metaphysical innovation, must be rejected. Some metaphysical mistakes are so profound that generations of philosophers continue to discuss and learn from them. This is such a mistake.

Index

Abbreviations: compared with definitions, 116–18, 122–23, 136–37, 139–40, 248; compared with logical truths, 139–40; and definite descriptions, 168–69; and definition of mental acts, 218; and identity of concepts, 236–37; and true statements, 151

Accidents: as dependent entities, 74; and substances, 99

Acquaintance: and description, 19; with individual things, 106–7; and labels, 158–59; with numbers, 148–50; with quantifiers, 150

Addis, L., 91n, 218n

Addition, defined, 118–19

Affirmation: compared with assumption, 5–6; contrasted with fact, 27; and presentation, 12; of states of affairs, 188; and truth, 4; and truth-values, 184–85

Allaire, E. B., 75n, 76n, 96n, 104n, 106n; on constituents of individual things, 104–6

Analysis: and complex senses, 249–52; and definitions, 249–50; different kinds of, 97–98, 105; logical and ontological, 115; ontological and spatial, 93–98, 107; rejected by Wittgenstein, 97–98; and sense-reference distinction, 224–26; and simple objects, 94–98; of spatial things and classes, 91–93; and structure of state of affairs, 252–53

Analytic statements: according to Kant, 140; according to Wittgenstein, 96–97; and arithmetic, 115, 136; and color comparison, 150–51; and definitions, 116–18, 123; and empirical observation, 144–46; explicated, 115; and identity statements, 154; as matter of linguistic convention, 145–46; about natures, 100–101; and other kinds of truths, 140; and synthetic statements, 144–46

Angelelli, I., ix

Anscombe, G. E. M., 94n

Aquinas, Thomas, 104

Aristotle, 104

Arithmetic: and analytic statements, 108–9; compared with ontology, logic, and set-theory, 142; and experience, 145–52; and identity, 108; and induction, 148–50; and logical truths, 136–38; and Peano's axioms, 136–37; and perception, 148

Berg, J., 29n

Bergmann, G., 8n, 61n, 74n, 104n, 106n, 141n, 196n; on Frege's content stroke, 7–9, 13

Berkeley, 10

Bernays, P., 166n

Birjukov, R. V., ix

Black, M., 61n

Bochenski, I. M., 102n

Bolzano, B., 10n, 29n; as critic of Kant, 10, 31

Bradley, F. H., 81, 209n

Brentano, F., 8, 194n, 208n

Brodbeck, M., 144n

Carnap, R., 164n, 198n, 215n, 219n, 220n; on propositions, 198–200

Categorial laws: and ontological truths, 141–42; and possibility, 210–12; and spatial analysis, 93; and type-theory, 76–78

Categories: and acquaintance, 106–7; and Bradley regress, 81; of classes and individual things, 85; colors as, 98; and numbers, 108–14; and objects, 107; and ontological truths, 141–42; and properties, 146; and theory of types, 76–77; Wittgenstein's search for, 97–98

Certainty, about communication, 36

Church, A., 164n, 215n, 219n

Circumstance: and complex ideas, 9; as conceptual content, 16; as intention, 9; as judgmental content, 12. *See also* States of affairs

Classes: definition of, 89–90; existence of, 86–89; as objects, 83–85; and properties, 85; and spatial wholes, 91–93; and value-ranges, 83–85

Clatterbaugh, K., 104n, 106n

Colors: analysis of, 98; existence of, 44; as objective concepts, 31–33; as properties to reflect light, 44; as sense-impressions, 31–33, 44–45

Common names, Frege on, 51–52

Communication: about ideas, 33–38; and skepticism, 38, 41–43; about spatial entities, 39–41, and subject-predicate distinction, 15

Complex concepts, and states of affairs, 12–13. *See also* Complex ideas

Complex ideas: according to Bergman, 7; as conceptual contents, 5–6, 16; and identity, 20; as judgmental contents, 12

Concept words: as labels, 53–54; plural of, 51–52; and proper names, 50–51; referents of, 239–42; and relations, 233–34; and sense-reference distinction, 189–91, 225–43; as unsaturated, 61. *See also* Unsaturatedness

Conceptual content: as circumstances, 16; and complex ideas, 27; as determinations, 23; distinguished from content, 13, 15,

20–21; explicated, 13–14; and function-argument distinction, 24; identity of, 21; and logical equivalence, 13–14; and senses, 14; and subject-predicate distinction, 14–17

Connections: between concepts, 236–39; kinds of, 93, 96, 98–100, 209; logical, 209; between numbers, 149; between numbers and concepts, 120–21; between quantifiers, 149; of referring, 240–42; between sense and reference, 156–57; between Thought and truth-value, 185–89

Content stroke: in Frege's earlier and later philosophy, 7, 8; three functions of, 11–12

Conventionalism, rejected, 145–46

Copleston, F., 102n

Correspondence theory, of truth, 191–94

Criterion: for identity of numbers, 124–25; for sameness, 124–25

Definite descriptions: according to Russell, 167–74; and acquaintance, 19–20, 158–59; and complex concepts, 22; as complex expressions, 232–33; of concepts, 190; contain predication, 171–74; describe and represent, 180; as disguised sentences, 170–74; distinguished from labels, 19–20, 157–60, 165; and existence, 166–67; and false sentences, 195; and identity statements, 163–64, 179–80; as incomplete symbols, 167–70; meaning of, 22–23, 177–78; and names, 19; as names of concepts, 24; in ordinary discourse, 174–77; and postulated referents, 166–67; and presuppositions, 175–77; scope of, 220; and sense, 160–62, 178, 180–81; and sense-reference distinction, 227–29; and states of affairs, 171–74, 244, 253; and substitution, 182–83, 220–23; and truth-values, 183–84

Definitions: and abbreviations, 116–17, 127–28; adding to meanings, 128; of addition, 118–19; and analytic statements, 116–18, 123; of being a number, 133; contrasted with conditions, 242; as convention, 122–23; and descriptions, 88; as equivalence statements, 142–43; of existence, 70–71; and existence of classes, 86–88; and identity statements, 123–27, 138; by intension and by extension, 89–90; justification for, 125–26; and meaning, 121–23; of mental acts, 217–18; of numbers, 113–14, 132; and reduction of arithmetic, 136–37; of sameness, 126–27;

as true statements, 122–23; of truth, 192–94. *See also* Abbreviations

Dependent entities: compared with independent entities, 25–26; and judgmental contents, 25

Determinations: as conceptual contents, 23; and descriptions, 19–20; and informative identity statements, 155; as senses, 23, 155

Domain calculus, Frege's criticism of, 91–93

Dummett, M., 47n, 227n

Egidi, R., 8n

Empty predicates, 198–200

Equivalence statements: and definitions, 133–34, 248–49; distinguished from identity statements, 20; between logic and arithmetic, 137–39, 142–43; for properties and classes, 132; and Russell's definition of definite descriptions, 170; and sameness, 125

Erdmann, B., 10n

Exemplification, compared with other connections, 209

Existence: according to Moore, 68; according to Russell, 173; attempts at definition of, 70–71; of classes, 86–89; as concept of second level, 69–70; and definite descriptions, 166–67; and existential quantifier, 70–71; of falling under relation, 80–81; of false propositions, 198–200; of individual things, 65–68; as irreducible entity, 70–71; and labels, 165–66; modes of, 200–201; not a property, 206; and predicative entities, 65–71; of states of affairs, 206–9; of Thoughts, 245–47

Experience: and analytic statements, 144–46; and arithmetical truths, 145–52; and synthetic *a priori* truths, 150–51

Extensions: and identity of concepts, 236–39; as numbers, 113; as objects, 83–85; and referents of concept words, 234–39; and sense-reference distinction, 234–39; as value-ranges, 83–84. *See also* Classes

Fact, and affirmation, 11

Findlay, J. N., 200n, 203n

Fisk, M., 52n

Fitch, F. B., 222n

Formalists, Frege's criticism of, 54–56

Furth, M., 84n, 238n, 240n; on referring, 240–42

Geach, P., 25n, 84n, 239n

General ideas, and concepts, 30

Goodman, N., 92n

Gram, M. S., 100n

Hermes, H., xiii

Hilbert, D., 166n

Hintikka, J., 70n; on existence, 70–71

Hochberg, H., 74n, 105n, 106n, 139n

Husserl, E., 7, 51n, 116n

Idealism: in *Begriffsschrift*, 9; Frege's refutation of, 32–34, 38; in Kant, 10; and mental acts, 194–95

Ideas: distinguished from perceptual objects and Thoughts, 244; and senses, 157, 162–63

Identity statements: and concepts, 190, 235–39; with definite descriptions, 179–80; and definitions, 248–49; as informative statements, 101, 154–55; with labels and descriptions, 163–64; and reduction, 4; and sense-reference distinction, 155. *See also* Definitions

Images, ideas as, 29

Incomplete symbols, and definite descriptions, 167–70, 172–73. *See also* Definite descriptions

Individual concepts, and sense-reference distinction, 164

Individual things: acquaintance with, 106–7; and classes, 84–85, 87, 89; compared with bare particulars, 75, 104–7; compared with properties, 4; compared with substances, 103–4; and definite descriptions, 180; existence of, 65–68; and function-argument distinction, 24; and identity of conceptual content, 21–22; and labels and descriptions, 157–60; and spatial wholes, 92–93; and states of affairs, 17–18, 104–7, 247; and subject-predicate distinction, 15–16; and Thoughts, 245

Induction: and arithmetical statements, 148–50; and relations among colors, 149–50

Intention: as complex ideas, 9; and different mental acts, 8; of false thoughts, 207–9; intented by content of act, 7; of judgments, 8; and mental act, 5

Intentional equivalence, compared with logical equivalence, 14. *See also* Substitution

Intentional nexus: compared with truth-functional connectives, 216; and nonex-

istent objects, 208–9; and sense-reference distinction, 218; and substitution, 216
Interpretation, of axiom forms, 40–41
Intuition: and complex ideas, 29; and concepts, 30–31; and description, 29; in Kantian system, 31; and numbers, 49–50; and senses, 156–57; and sensibility, 30; and singular ideas, 30; and space and time, 30

Jackson, H., 227n
Judgment: as analytic, 140; confused with fact, 11; expressed by sentence, 48; as mental act, 5–6; and objective entities, 48–50; and states of affairs, 188, 205; and truth, 181, 186, 188–89
Judgment stroke: function of, 11, 17–18, 188–89; not a name, 18–19; as substitute for state of affairs, 18
Judgmental content: as circumstance, 12; as complex idea, 11–12; and concepts and objects, 82; and identity, 20–22; and independent entities, 25; structure of, 17, 26

Kant, I., 10n, 12n; on analyticity, 140; and idealistic terminology, 10; on intuitions and concepts, 30–31, 49–50; on presentation and judgment, 12; and the term "idea," 29
Kerry, B., 57n, 58n, 81; on object and concept, 57–58, 78
Khatchadourian, H., 61n
Kneale, W. and M., 3n

Labels: and acquaintance, 158–59; compared with descriptions, 19–20, 52–54, 157–60, 165; of concepts, 227–29; of concepts and objects, 53–54; existence, 65–66, 165–66; and identity sign, 179–80; and identity statements, 163–64; and logical proper names, 158–59; names as, 51; and sense, 157, 161–63; and sense-reference distinction, 227; and substitution, 222–23. *See also* Definite descriptions
Leibniz, 126n, 180n; and definition of identity, 126–27; on definition of numbers, 118
Level of concepts, 25–27, 61, 71–74
Lewis, C. I., 215n
Lewis, D., 91n
Logic: and arithmetic, 4, 115; explicated, 141–42; and geometry, 96; and mathematical induction, 134–35; nature of, 3; and object-concept distinction, 83; and

objective ideas, 29; and psychology, 10; and subject-predicate distinction, 15
Logical atomism, according to Russell, 75
Logical equivalence: and conceptual content, 13–14; and intentional equivalence, 14; and sameness of sense, 214–15
Logical truth: and abbreviations, 139–40; and arithmetic, 119; and conventions, 145–46; and definition of definite descriptions, 168; and ontological reduction, 143; and Peano's axioms, 135–36

McGuiness, B. F., 96n
Marsh, R., 65n
Marshall, W., 60n, 61n, 227n
Mathematical induction, 134–35
Meaning: and analysis, 252; of color words, 31–33; and communication, 42; of concept words, 55; of definite descriptions, 22–23, 55, 177–78; determined by context, 28, 46–50; of empty predicates, 196; and incomplete symbols, 169–70; and rules, 43; of sameness, 124–25; and sense-reference distinction, 164; and substitution, 126; and use, 41, 43
Meinong, A., 48n, 170n, 200n, 208n, 209n: and act-object distinction, 7; about the golden mountain, 195; his theory of objectives, 200–205; and possible states of affairs, 211–12
Mental acts: attempts to define, 217–18; kinds of, 5–7; of meaning and understanding, 42–43; and objects, 10; privacy of, 42; as propositional, 196–97; as relational, 194–95; and sense, 157; and substitution, 212–13; their contents, 5–9, 17; and truth, 185; and truth-functional language, 216–17
Mental entities: and communication, 33–35; and ideas, 9; in Kant, 30; and non-mental entities, 4, 10–11; and object-concept distinction, 44–46
Mental picture: confused with act, 10; as idea, 10; and meaning of words, 49; and number, 50
Modal contexts, and substitution, 214, 218–23
Moore, G. E., 68n, 91n, 218n; on existence, 68; on sense-impressions, 46

Names: distinguished from proper names, 51; and existence, 66; and identity, 19; and judgment stroke, 18–19; senses of, 160–62; and states of affairs, 18–19; understanding of, 75–78. *See also* Labels

Index

Natures: identical with substances, 100–101; individuated, 101–2; and objects, 99, 107

Negation, of false Thoughts, 246–47

Nerlich, G., 177n

Nonexistent objects: and false sentences, 195–96; and intentional nexus, 208–9; problem of, 194–212

Numbers: according to Leibniz, 118–19; and colors, 151; compared with properties, 110; defined as concepts, 113–14; defined as extensions, 113–14; defined in terms of similarity, 128–32; defined through identity statements, 123–27; and identity statements, 112–13; indifferent to type, 110; and logical entities, 144; nature of, 108–14; as nonmental entities, 108–9; not sensible, 47; as objects, 49, 109–14; presented through judgment, 47–50; as properties, 131–32; as quantifiers, 109–12, 120, 149

Objective ideas, two kinds of, 29

Objectives: according to Meinong, 200–206; compared with states of affairs, 205–6; compared with Thoughts, 201, 205; and existence of objects, 204; factual and unfactual, 202–3

Ontological truths, explicated, 141–42

Ontology: and complex entities, 80; and determinations, 155; and function-argument distinction, 24; and grammar, 16–17, 53, 59, 61; and ideal language, 87; and judgment stroke, 18; and reduction of arithmetic to logic, 115; and spatial analysis, 93–98; and structure of judgmental content, 17; and subject-predicate distinction, 15–17

Pabst, W., 23n

Particulars: compared with individual things, 104–7; as individuators, 104–5; in Kantian system, 31

Part-whole relation, 91–93

Peano, G., 135, 136n, 137, 143

Pears, D. F., 96n

Perception, and Thoughts, 247

Pitcher, G., 97n

Possibility: and conceivability, 211; and contradiction, 210–11; explicated,210–12; kinds of, 211–12

Predicate, understanding of, 75–78

Predication, and judgment stroke, 17–18

Predicative entity: and concepts, 52, 58–64, 82; and descriptions, 59–60; and

existence, 65–71; and identity statements, 113; and nexus of falling under, 59–60; and nonpredicative entity, 25–27; and quantifiers, 112; and saturated-unsaturated distinction, 26, 61, 71–74; and unity of Thought, 78–81. See also Unsaturatedness

Presentation: according to Brentano, 8; as foundation of judgment, 8; as mental act, 5–6

Presupposition, and definite descriptions, 175–77

Privacy: of ideas, 35–37; of mental acts, 42–43

Proper names: and concept words, 50–51; and definite article, 50–52, 58–59; and definite descriptions, 52–57; distinguished from names, 51; as labels, 53–54; of numbers, 111–12; and predicative expression, 64; and sense-reference distinction, 226; senses of, 160–63. See also Labels; Names

Properties: compared with individual things, 105–6; compared with numbers, 110; and definite descriptions, 180–81; distinguished from classes, 85, 131; and function-argument distinction, 24; and individual things, 4; labels and descriptions of, 157–60; logic as theory of, 141; numerical, 131–32; of properties, 74; relations among, 149–51; and states of affairs, 17–18; and subject-predicate distinction, 15–16; and substance-accident distinction, 99–100

Propositions: according to Carnap, 198–200; and complex properties, 198–99; as intentions, 9; and truth, 4

Psychology, and logic, 10

Quantifiers: compared with properties, 72–74; and existence, 70–71; indifferent to type, 112; numbers as, 109–12, 149; and predicative entities, 112

Quine, W. V., 40n, 84n, 217n, 238n, 239n

Rank, of concepts, 24–27

Realism, in Frege, 9, 12

Reason: eye of, 31, 45; presents objective entities, 47–50

Representation, of concept by object, 58

Rudner, R., 215n

Russell, B., 65n, 75n, 84n, 86n, 93n, 96n, 104, 109n, 121n, 156n, 159n, 165, 168n, 169n, 170n, 179n, 180n, 201n, 221n, 228n; in defense of states of affairs, 18–

259

19; defines classes, 89–90; on definite descriptions, 72, 167–74, 177; on existence, 166, 173; on existence of classes, 86–88; on existence of individual things, 65–66; on incomplete symbols, 167–70; on logical proper names, 158–59; on substitution, 220; on understanding predicates and proper names, 75–78

Ryle, G., 91n, 217n, 218n

Saturated entities: compared with unsaturated entities, 26; and predicative entities, 26. *See also* Proper names; Unsaturatedness

Schröder, E., 89n, 91n, 93n

Schröter, K., 166n, 172n

Sellars, W., 99n, 217n

Sensations, in Kant's system, 31

Sense-impressions: and colors, 31, 44–45; and communication, 33–35; comparison of, 35–36; in hallucinations, 196; and ideas, 29; and numbers, 47. *See also* Ideas

Sensibility: as characteristic of intuitions, 30; contrasted with judgment, 48

Sentences, as names, 18

Set-theory, compared with ontology and logic, 142

Singular ideas, and intuitions, 30

Skepticism: about communication, 38, 41–43; and meaning of words, 41

Smullyan, A. F., 222n

Sobocinski, B., 84n

Space: as form of intuition, 30; objective constituents of, 39–41

Spatial whole, compared with individual thing, 92–93. *See also* Analysis

States of affairs: actual and possible, 207, 209–12; and analysis, 115, 252–53; and categorial laws, 210–12; compared with individual things, 104–7; compared with objectives, 205–6; compared with Thoughts, 182–83, 197, 244–47; and complex ideas, 12; and definite descriptions, 171–74, 180; existence of, 231; and false sentences, 206–9; and individual things and properties, 17–18; kinds of, 146–47; and names, 18–19; and perception, 247; rejected by Frege, 17; and relations, 233–34; and role of judgment, 205; and sense-reference distinction, 225–26; and substances, 103; and Thoughts, 186–87, 191–94; and unsaturatedness, 75

Stenius, E., 144n

Sternfeld, R., ix, 52n

Stoothoff, R. H., 4n

Substances: compared with individual things, 103–4; compared with objects, 99–104; as complex entities, 75, 102–3; consist of form and matter, 102–3; identical with natures, 100–101; as independent entities, 74–75; and states of affairs, 103. *See also* Natures

Substitution: based on equivalence statements, 143; and definite descriptions, 182–83, 220–23; and definitions, 126–27; and extensions, 234–39; and identity of concepts, 239; and intentional equivalence, 215–16; and intentional nexus, 216; and labels, 222–23; in modal and intentional contexts, 218–23; Russell on, 220; and sameness of sense, 214–16; and sense-reference distinction, 212–18; of terms, 213–14; in truth-functional language, 216–17; and truth-values, 212–13

Synthetic statements: and identity statements, 20–21, 154, 162–64; and the problems of identity, 179. *See also* Analytic statements

Thiel, Christian, ix

Thought: analysis of, 63–64; compared with objectives, 201, 205; compared with states of affairs, 182–83, 197, 225, 244–47; and concept, 62–63; and definite descriptions, 174–77; and false sentences, 197, 245–47; in Frege's later philosophy, 243–48; and perception, 247; and relation to truth-values, 185–89; as sense of a sentence, 182–83; and subject-predicate distinction, 64; unity of, 78–81

Time, as form of intuition, 30

Truth-value: and affirmation, 184–85; attempts to define, 192–94; and definite descriptions, 183–84; as function of extension, 235; and judgment stroke, 18; and reference of concept words, 230; as referent of sentence, 183–85; relation to Thought, 184–89, 191–92; and sense-reference distinction, 231–32; and sense-reference distinction for concept words, 190–91; and substitutions, 212–13

Twardowski, K., 200n, 208n

Types: and numbers, 110; and quantifiers, 112; theory of, 75–78

Universal quantifier, as second level concept, 27

Universals: in Kantian system, 31; and natures, 192. *See also* Properties

Index

Unsaturatedness: and Bradley regress, 81–82; of concepts, 71–74; explication, 61, 74–78; and falling under relation, 79–81; and identity, 235–38; and predicative entities, 61; and states of affairs, 75; and substances, 75; and unity of thought, 78–81; and value-ranges, 84–85. *See also* Predicative entities

Value-ranges, and classes, 83–85

Veatch, H., 100n

Walker, J. D. B., ix
Wells, R., 84n, 114n
Wienpahl, P. D., 164n, 215n
Wilson, F., 40n
Wittgenstein, L., 33n, 47n, 76n, 93n, 94n, 96n, 200n; on ontological analysis, 94–98; and states of affairs, 18–19
Wright, G. H., 94n